Values in Education
and
Education in Values

D0473910

Values in Education
and
Education in Values

Edited by

J. Mark Halstead and Monica J. Taylor

 The Falmer Press

(A member of the Taylor & Francis Group)
London • Washington, D.C.

UK   The Falmer Press, 4 John Street, London WC1N 2ET
USA   The Falmer Press, Taylor & Francis Inc., 1900 Frost Road, Suite 101, Bristol, PA 19007

© J.M. Halstead and M.J. Taylor, 1996

First published in 1996

A catalogue record for this book is available from the British Library

Library of Congress Cataloging-in-Publication Data are available on request

ISBN 0 7507 0509 4 cased
ISBN 0 7507 0510 8 paper

Jacket design by Caroline Archer

Typeset in 10/12 pt Garamond by
Graphicraft Typesetters Ltd., Hong Kong

*Printed in Great Britain by Biddles Ltd Guildford and King's Lynn
on paper which has a specified pH value on final paper
manufacture of not less than 7.5 and is therefore 'acid free'.*

Contents

Preface   vii

Introduction   1

1   Values and Values Education in Schools   3
    J. Mark Halstead

Part I: Values in Education   15

2   Liberal Values and Liberal Education   17
    J. Mark Halstead

3   The Ambiguity of Spiritual Values   33
    John M. Hull

4   Moral Values   45
    Mary Warnock

5   Environmental Values and Education   54
    John C. Smyth

6   Democratic Values and the Foundations of Political Education   68
    Francis Dunlop

7   Values in the Arts   79
    David Best

8   Food, Smoking and Sex: Values in Health Education   92
    Michael J. Reiss

9   Values and Education Policy   104
    Richard Pring

Part II: Education in Values   119

10   Voicing their Values: Pupils' Moral and Cultural Experience   121
    Monica J. Taylor

11   Vision, Values and Virtues   143
    Jasper Ungoed-Thomas

Contents

12 School Mission Statements and Parental Perceptions   155
    Andrew Marfleet

13 Planning for Values Education in the School Curriculum   167
    Janet Edwards

14 An Inner-city Perspective on Values Education   180
    Elaine Foster-Allen

15 Assessing Children's Personal Development: The Ethical
    Implications   191
    Ruth Merttens

Notes on Contributors   203

Index   207

Preface

The major purpose of this volume is to set out some of the key issues and debates relating to the importance of values in education and of education in values, and to stimulate discussion and reflection among teachers, administrators, researchers and educational policymakers.

The volume has a twofold structure, one formal the other informal. At a formal level, the structure falls in two parts. After an introductory chapter about the concept of values and values education, Part I provides a variety of perspectives on the values that underpin contemporary education: in theory and practice, from the point of view of the government and the school, and from the perspective of the growing diversity of modern society. Chapter 2 argues that education in western democratic societies is invariably grounded on the fundamental liberal values of freedom, equality and rationality. In Chapters 3 to 8, six groups of values are identified – spiritual, moral, environmental, democratic, and those of the arts and of health education – and the meaning and importance of these values for education is discussed. Chapter 9 examines the values behind government education policy and compares these to the goal of educating the whole person. These chapters are by no means based on a common ideology (nor are they necessarily a reflection of the editors' own views), but their very diversity is designed to challenge taken-for-granted views, to offer new insights and to encourage further discussion.

Part II focuses on school practice. The chapters examine a variety of ways in which values may be incorporated into the activities of schools, and aim to encourage further reflection on the processes of values education. Chapter 10 examines pupils' values in the light of their experiences at school. Chapter 11 suggests ways in which schools can develop a clear vision of their goals. Chapter 12 examines school mission statements and the influence of these on parents' choice of schools. Chapter 13 considers whole school issues and ways of approaching values education within the school curriculum. Chapter 14 draws on the author's own experience as a recent headteacher of a multiethnic inner-city school and describes the link between values education and the school's ethos and structures. Finally, Chapter 15 examines the ethical implications of assessing children's personal development.

Alongside this formal structure is an undercurrent of debates about values and education which surface from time to time throughout the book. These include the meaning and nature of values; the concept of education; the impact of social change and cultural diversity; the relationship between religion and values; children's developing understanding of values; the role of the teacher; and the inspection of values education.

The book has its origins in a conference on Spiritual and Moral Education held at the University of Plymouth in September 1993. Four of the chapters – those by John Hull, Andrew Marfleet, Ruth Merttens and Jasper Ungoed-Thomas – are revised versions of the papers they presented at that conference. The remaining chapters have been written especially for this volume.

In addition to the authors of individual chapters, there are many others who have contributed indirectly to this volume, both through conversations and discussions and through practical and moral encouragement during the pressures of writing. Our thanks are due to them all.

J. Mark Halstead
Monica J. Taylor

Introduction

Chapter 1

Values and Values Education in Schools

J. Mark Halstead

ABSTRACT: *The first half of this chapter examines the concept of values in an educational context, and the difficulty in a pluralist society of finding a framework of shared values to underpin the work of the school. The second half focuses on the concept of values education and by reference to practice in both Europe and North America explores current debates and dilemmas. The chapter concludes with a brief discussion of the inspection of values education.*

Values are central to both the theory of education and the practical activities of schools in two ways. First, schools and individual teachers within schools are a major influence, alongside the family, the media and the peer group, on the developing values of children and young people, and thus of society at large. Secondly, schools reflect and embody the values of society; indeed, they owe their existence to the fact that society values education and seeks to exert influence on the pattern of its own future development through education. However, the values of society are not as uniform or unchanging as this suggests. Many groups within society have a legitimate claim to a stake in the educational process – parents, employers, politicians, local communities, leaders of industry and taxpayers, as well as teachers and children themselves – and within each of these groups there is a wide diversity of political, social, economic, religious, ideological and cultural values. The expectations of interested parties are thus often in conflict, and schools sometimes become the battleground where groups with different value priorities vie for influence and domination.

The part schools play in the teaching of values and the part values play in the organization of schools are closely connected. The values of schools are apparent in their organization, curriculum and discipline procedures, as well as in the relationships between teachers and pupils. Values are reflected in what teachers choose to permit or encourage in the classroom and in the way they respond to children's contributions to learning, and children learn values from such responses. Even the seating arrangements in a classroom convey certain values. When teachers insist on precision and accuracy in children's work, or praise their use of imagination, or censure racist or sexist language, or encourage them to show initiative, or respond with interest, patience or frustration to their ideas, children are being introduced to values and value-laden issues (cf. Jackson, Boostrom and Hansen, 1993).

Frequently the values of the school are not fully explored or articulated. This may be simply because the values are hard to analyze, since they are deeply embedded in teachers' taken-for-granted world view; or because teachers are often not well prepared in their initial training for reflection on values; or else because teachers have to make so many day-to-day decisions at a classroom level that they tend to rely on what may be termed a moral instinct. Even where a school has produced a values statement, this is not the end of the matter. For example, if a policy statement says 'all pupils are entitled to be treated with respect by staff' (see Chapter 14), there needs to be a shared understanding of what is meant by 'being treated with respect'. In addition, there is likely to be a considerable difference between the values a school proclaims and those which in fact underpin its practice (see Taylor, 1994a, 29). Many values, however, are left within the domain of the hidden curriculum. Where there is no systematic discussion of values and value issues in the classroom, children may be more likely to develop values haphazardly, and indeed it is not uncommon for the values which pupils develop in school to be different from those the school intends. Partly this may be a reflection of the critical perspective the school seeks to develop through the curriculum, and partly it may result from a lack of congruence and coherence in value implementation.

These factors suggest a need for schools to reflect on and voice their values with greater precision (McLaughlin, 1995). This need is made the more pressing by four further considerations:

- growing cultural diversity (and therefore diversity of values) within all western societies;
- a growing gulf between the values of government and teachers (see Chapters 2 and 9 in this volume), which has led to a breakdown of trust and to stronger demands for accountability (Halstead, 1994);
- the perceived 'moral decline' not only among young people but also in public life;
- the determination of government to uphold certain values, for example, by subjecting the contribution of schools to the spiritual and moral development of children to regular inspection.

Any examination of the links between values and education brings to light a number of the key questions. Several of these are touched on in this chapter and others surface from time to time throughout the book.

- Is there a distinction to be made between private and public values?

- Do particular values (whether political, aesthetic, moral or religious) have validity only within particular cultures or traditions?
- Are there overarching principles by which conflicts between values may be resolved?
- Is there a sufficient basis of shared values in our society to support a common framework of education for all children, or should parents be free to choose between schools with different sets of values?
- Do the values which are currently taught in schools necessarily reinforce (intentionally or otherwise) the privileged position of certain social classes or religious or cultural groups?
- Are there any absolute values, or merely changing and relative ones?
- Should schools reflect *traditional* values or seek to transform these?
- Should schools instil values in pupils or teach them to explore and develop their own values?
- Should teachers aim for a neutral (or value-free) approach to their subject matter?

Before any of these questions can be considered, however, the first step is to examine more closely what is meant by the term *values*.

What are Values?

Although several surveys of moral and social values in Britain and Europe have been carried out over the last fifteen years (Abrams *et al.*, 1985; Barker *et al.*, 1992), there is still much disagreement about the term 'values'. Values have been variously defined as things which are considered 'good' in themselves (such as beauty, truth, love, honesty and loyalty) and as personal or social preferences. Raths, Harmin and Simon (1966, 28) describe values as 'beliefs, attitudes or feelings that an individual is proud of, is willing to publicly affirm, has [sic] been chosen thoughtfully from alternatives without persuasion, and is [sic] acted on repeatedly'. Fraenkel (1977, 11) considers values as being 'both emotional commitments and ideas about worth'. Beck (1990, 2) defines values as 'those things (objects, activities, experiences, etc.) which on balance promote human wellbeing'. Further definitions are suggested by several of the contributors to the present volume (see in particular Chapters 4 and 6). In the present chapter, however, the term *values* is used to refer to *principles, fundamental convictions, ideals, standards or life stances which act as general guides to behaviour or as points of reference in decision-making or the evaluation of beliefs or action and which are closely connected to personal integrity and personal identity.*

This definition is open to criticism on the grounds that it fails to differentiate quite distinct things like virtues, convictions and commitments and that it treats values as a kind of possession, something which people have. It is true that to talk of the *value* of something (as in the phrase *value-added*) has always been to talk of its worth, and that when we *value* something we are making a high estimate of its worth. However, the term *values* (in the plural) now seems to be used to refer to the criteria by which we make such value judgments, to the principles on which the value judgments are based. Thus Shaver and Strong say

> Values are our standards and principles for judging worth. They are the criteria by which we judge 'things' (people, objects, ideas, actions and situations) to be good, worthwhile, desirable; or, on the other hand, bad, worthless, despicable (1976, 15).

This raises the question of whether the values by which we judge worth are subjective or objective, relative or absolute. An initial distinction must be made between merely personal value judgments or preferences (for example, 'I prefer heavy metal to country-and-western') and 'true' judgments of value, which purport to have a more rational character (for example, 'that was a kind act'). But this is not enough. For even within the latter group, it is possible to distinguish a number of different points on a continuum:

- At one extreme is the view of values as a set of subjective criteria for making judgments. This may be linked to a relativist view that no set of values can be shown to be better than another. The roots of this view may lie in the strong sense of individualism in western societies, or more specifically if unconsciously in the logical positivist position that value judgments are merely expressions of personal opinion since they are not open to verification through observation and experiment. This view has sometimes been claimed to provide a useful way of resolving disputes over values in culturally plural societies: 'you have your values and I have mine.'
- At the other end of the continuum is the view of values as absolute, that is, as applying everywhere and at all times. On this view, certain human actions are always right or always wrong, irrespective of circumstance.
- Somewhere in between is the view that certain values, such as animal rights, patriotism, equal opportunities or bravery, have some kind of objective quality, insofar as 'some social arrangements and patterns of behaviour promote well being more than others' (Beck, 1990, 3). These values may therefore be explored in a systematic and objective fashion, though it is also recognized that they are socially constructed and may vary over time and from one group or society to another.

Values in a Pluralist Society

In a monocultural society, the middle view as set out in the last paragraph offers a clear basis for values education. Children will be introduced to the values and practices of their own society as objective reality. In a pluralist society, however, such an approach is not possible, since not everyone shares the same values (or even shares the same understanding of what values are; cf. Haydon, 1995, 56). Yet without shared values it is impossible to find a basis for the establishment of common institutions in society. Clearly there could be no society at all without a minimum set of common values and standards of behaviour. These are likely to include, first, a basic social morality (in particular, a respect for justice and a recognition that other groups have as much right as one's own to avoid physical pain and death among their members); second, the acceptance of a common system of law and government by all groups within the broader society (though the systems need not be the same for all 'broader societies') and a commitment to seek to change these only through democratic means; and third, a commitment to values presupposed by the pluralist ideal (in particular, the toleration of groups with different ideals to one's own and the rejection of violence as a means of persuasion). Haydon expands this third category by arguing that citizenship within a plural society requires that everyone should be taught not only about morality but also 'about the plurality, not merely of values, but of the kinds of significance attached to values' (1995, 54).

However, the minimum framework of common values remains a very *thin* one (cf. White, 1987, 16), certainly not sufficient to support a common system of education as extensive as we have today. If the common school is to be retained, it is widely assumed that some way must be found of making this minimum framework of values more substantial. But how? There is no shortage of possible answers. In the past it has tended to be the values of the dominant group that have filled the vacuum, and it has frequently been claimed that schools have promoted middle-class values (Rich, 1993:164f). In conservative circles, the traditional values of religion, the family and the national heritage have found favour; the ill-fated slogan 'back to basics' also represented an emphasis on *standards*, whether moral, social or academic. Liberals may look to those values which can be rationally justified as universally appropriate (see Chapter 2), or may suggest that an expansion of the minimum framework of common values may be negotiated democratically (cf. Haydon, 1987). However, in a pluralist society, there will be suspicion of all these approaches among some minority groups. Even democratic negotiation presupposes certain shared values and shared goals (such as valuing a democratic form of life), which may not, in fact, be shared by all and may even be perceived as a threat to the traditional way of life of some groups (cf. Halstead, 1988: Ch. 8).

The introduction of market forces into educational provision, as Elliott (1994:415ff) points out, 'enables a pragmatic solution to the problem of value pluralism to be effected'. The market, he suggests, provides the context for the negotiation of values between providers and customers. In order to thrive, the school cannot uphold values which diverge significantly from those of the community it serves. If this approach is accepted, it implies that in a plural society there will be a diversity of provision, with different schools reflecting not only different curricular emphases but also different cultural or ideological values (cf. Hargreaves, 1994). This is a view which some minority goups, including Muslims, Jews, evangelical Christians and others, have been putting forward for some time (Halstead, 1995). However, it undermines the principle of the common school, which among other things seeks to show equal respect to a diversity of cultural values and promote mutual tolerance and understanding.

The task, which schools and other educational institutions are now facing, of discussing and clarifying their values and making them public is thus enormously complex. It would be a serious mistake to view it as a matter of dreaming up a list of values or opting for a prepackaged set (for example, those suggested by the National Curriculum Council, 1993). Schools must pay attention to the diversity of values in the communities they serve (which are themselves in flux) as well as in society at large, and to the legitimate expectations of interested parties. They must examine their aims and their curriculum provision and practices to see what values lie embedded there and must reflect on the justifiability, appropriateness and coherence of these values. In the end, the statements of value that emerge may be ambiguous, provisional and less than totally clear (cf. McLaughlin, 1994:459). But unless schools make the effort to articulate their values and develop some clarity of vision, they will not be in a strong position to pursue their task of developing pupils' understanding of values and helping pupils to develop their own commitments. It is to this latter task that we must now turn.

Values Education: Principles and Practice

The term *values education* has a much shorter history in England and Wales than it has it North America, or even in Scotland. Nevertheless, a recent directory of research and resources in values education in the UK lists 113 entries, made up of research projects, organizations, publications and other initiatives (Taylor, 1994b). The establishment of the Values Education Council in the UK in 1995 may prove an important turning point; it aims to bring together organizations with a shared interest in values education, its purpose being 'the promotion and development of values in the context of education as a lifelong process, to help individuals develop as responsible and caring persons and live as participating members of a pluralist society'. (Taylor, 1995:24)

The emphasis here on personal and social values, moral values and democratic citizenship is not intended to exclude other values. Indeed, recent official publications tend to link moral with spiritual values (National Curriculum Council, 1993; Office for Standards in Education, 1994a), and strong claims are commonly made about links between moral and aesthetic values (cf. Jarrett, 1991) and between spiritual and aesthetic (Starkings, 1993). Other values frequently mentioned in the context of the school include values relating to cultural diversity, cultural identity and national consciousness; intellectual and academic values; peace, international understanding, human rights and environmental values; gender equality and antiracism; work and economic values; health; and common human values such as tolerance, solidarity and cooperation (cf. Taylor, 1994a). Many of these are discussed more fully in Chapters 2 to 9.

One of the main differences between the American and the British approach to values education is that the former, in the absence of organized traditions of religious or social authority in public institutions, places a stronger emphasis on democratic education, both in terms of teaching the child about how society works and in terms of preparation for citizenship through active participation in school life. Values education in British schools, on the other hand, as in much of Europe, is affected by closer involvement with religion: a third of British schools are denominational institutions, religious education is still a compulsory part of the basic curriculum in all schools, collective worship is part of the statutory school day, and there is a strong official view that religious education and collective worship are central to children's moral and spiritual development (National Curriculum Council, 1993). There is an assumption among those who do not share this official view that a gradual decline among religiously based values will occur (White, 1987:22), leading to the slow disappearance of specialized religious and moral instruction and the emergence of citizenship courses as the main focus for children's moral development in school (Cha, Wong and Meyer, 1988:12). Whether this asumption is justified, however, is very much open to question.

Whatever form values education takes, there is a major debate about whether schools should instil values in pupils or teach them to explore and develop their own values. On the former view, which is sometimes called character education (Lickona, 1991), values education involves two tasks:

1   the identification of appropriate values, which is the responsibility of schools, educationalists, or society at large through its elected representatives (see Chapters 11 and 12);

2   the transmission of these approved values to children. This may be carried out in many different areas of the school's provision: in curriculum subjects and cross-curricular themes (see Chapter 13), and in sport, community links, fundraising for charity, extra-curricular activities generally, teacher–pupil relationships, the structures and management of the school, school discipline, the pastoral system, the processes of teaching and learning, the hidden curriculum and the ethos of the school (see Chapter 14).

There are two main problems with the character education approach. The first is the difficulty of identifying appropriate values and ensuring a consistent approach within the school; there is no shortage of lists, but often little agreement between them (cf. Goggin, 1994; Lickona, 1988:8; Beck, 1990:148). The second problem is that the approach pays too little attention to, and may be in direct conflict with, the values that children learn outside the school, from the home, the media and their peers. Thus it takes no account of how young people make sense of these different sources of values (see Chapters 10 and 15).

The second view of values education, that it is centrally concerned with teaching children to explore and develop their own feelings and values, has been linked in North America particularly to the approach known as values clarification. This approach, developed particularly by Raths, *et al.* (1966) and Simon, Howe and Kirshenbaum (1972), is based on two assumptions: that children will care more about values which they have thought through and made their own than about values simply passed down by adults; and that it is wrong, particularly in a pluralist society, to seek to impose values. According to Raths, *et al.* (1966), legitimate valuing involves seven criteria: values must be 1) chosen freely 2) from alternatives 3) after consideration of the consequences, and an individual must 4) cherish, 5) publicly affirm, and 6) act on, the value, and 7) do so repeatedly. Undoubtedly, values clarification can develop confidence and self-esteem, but it has been criticized widely for being rooted in a spurious relativism and for failing to recognize that it is possible to make mistakes in matters of value (cf. Kilpatrick, 1992: Ch. 4). Values clarification has rarely been advocated openly in the UK, though the influence of its philosophy can be seen in the Humanities Curriculum Project (Schools Council/Nuffield Humanities Project, 1970), and it may in fact underlie the approaches of many texts and materials in use in schools.

Alternative approaches to teaching children to explore and develop their own values include the *moral reasoning* approach and the *just community* approach, both associated with Kohlberg (1981–1984). In *moral reasoning,* children are presented with moral dilemmas and are encouraged to discuss them in a way which it is intended will help them to see the inadequacies of their current moral thinking and move to a higher level (Blatt and Kohlberg, 1975). The *just community* approach is designed to help students to develop responsible moral behaviour by coming to share group norms and a sense of community. A community cluster within a school is made up of about 100 students and five teachers who meet on a weekly basis to make rules and discipline and to plan community activities and policies. The aim is to introduce students to participatory democracy and to give them greater opportunities for self regulation and moral awareness (Kohlberg and Higgins, 1987).

These approaches, too, have been subject to strong criticism, as playing down the social and cultural influences on people's values, underestimating the need to learn basic values before tackling controversies and failing to take adequate account of a more feminine ethic of care, responsibility and love (Gilligan, 1992; Noddings, 1984).

Current thinking about values education tends to favour eclecticism. In the USA, former proponents of values clarification tend now to support an approach which combines the best of moral guidance *and* values clarification

(Harmin, 1988; Kirschenbaum, 1992). Similarly in the UK, Carr and Landon (1993) suggest that there are three main forms or processes of values education: modelling and imitation; training and habituation; and enquiry and clarification.

There is a diversity of methods used by teachers in values education even at nursery level (Holligan, 1995). Discussion-based approaches and other student-centred active learning strategies are most common, though Taylor (1994a:52) points out that more experiential and less didactic teaching and learning approaches may be associated in pupils' eyes with low-status studies. Other methods for values education include drama, project work, practical activities, cooperative learning and group work, pupil-directed research, educational games and theme-days. Explicit teaching and learning methods make up only part of a school's provision, however, and the implicit values education which derives from the teacher as exemplar or from other aspects of the hidden curriculum must not be underestimated.

The Inspection of Values Education

The resurgence of interest in values education in the UK owes much to the statutory requirement that the spiritual, moral, social and cultural development of pupils should be subject to official inspection. The Education (Schools) Act 1992 requires Her Majesty's Chief Inspector to keep the Secretary of State informed about the quality of education and specifically about the spiritual, moral, social and cultural development of pupils, and also requires registered inspectors to report on these aspects as part of the regular inspection of all schools (Great Britain, Statutes, 1992). The *Handbook for the Inspection of Schools* (Office for Standards in Education, 1994b) sets out the evaluation criteria and evidence by which the teams of inspectors are to appraise these and other aspects of the life and work of schools, including behaviour and discipline and pupils' welfare and guidance. A school is said to be exhibiting high standards in the area of pupils' personal development and behaviour 'if its work is based upon clear principles and values expressed through its aims and evident in its practice' (Part 4:15), and inspectors are expected to assess, *inter alia*, 'whether pupils are developing their own personal values and are learning to appreciate the beliefs and practices of others' (Part 4:16). The final report is expected to include an 'evaluation of how the school promotes pupils' spiritual, moral, cultural and social development and how the pupils respond to that provision' (Part 2:22).

Some insight into how inspectors approach these tasks in practice is provided by Ungoed-Thomas (1994). Yet it is clear that inspectors also face several challenges. First, there is the problem of defining terms so that schools have a shared understanding of precisely what is being inspected; at the same time, the temptation must be avoided of defining the spiritual, moral, social and cultural in measurable terms simply for the convenience of inspection.

Second, there is the problem of ensuring that schools are treated fairly; not all schools start from the same base line, and it is possible that a school may not always get credit for what it achieves against the odds. Third, it is difficult to establish links between the educational provision of a school and changes in attitudes, values, beliefs and behaviour on the part of the student. This is because students will inevitably be subject to other social influences in addition to those of the school. Fourth, it seems ethically questionable to make formal judgments about the personal development of students at all, let alone in order to evaluate a school's educational provision (see Chapter 15). This last point in particular has led to a recent shift in the criteria for inspection, with a greater emphasis on the provision made by schools and less on the outcomes observable in individual pupils.

Many teachers have understandably been less than enthusiastic about the extension of inspection to cover spiritual and moral development; they may be suspicious of the government's motives and may worry about overloading the curriculum and about compromising the autonomy of the subject by making it instrumental to goals not intrinsic to it. Above all, they may be confused by the lack of clarity in the expectations that are now being placed upon them. What is needed most is an attempt to address the issues more clearly and systematically, perhaps through an informed national debate. It is this need which the present volume is designed to address.

References

ABRAMS, M., GERARD, D. and TIMMS, N. (1985) *Values and Social Change in Britain*, London, Macmillan.

BARKER, D., HALMAN, L. and VLOET, A. (1992) *The European Values Study, 1981–1990*, Aberdeen, Gordon Cook Foundation for European Values Group.

BECK, C. (1990) *Better Schools: A Values Perspective*, London, Falmer Press.

BLATT, M.M. and KOHLBERG, L. (1975) 'The effects of classroom moral discussion upon children's level of moral judgment', *Journal of Moral Education*, **4**, 2, pp. 129–61.

CARR, D. and LANDON, J. (1993) *Values in and for Education at 14+*, Edinburgh, Moray House Institute of Education, Heriot-Watt University.

CHA, Y-K., WONG, S-Y. and MEYER, J.W. (1988) 'Values education in the curriculum: Some comparative empirical data', in CUMMINGS, W.K., GOPINATHAN, S. and TOMODA, Y. (Eds) *The Revival of Values Education in Asia and the West*, Oxford, Pergamon Press.

ELLIOTT, J. (1994) 'Clarifying values in schools', *Cambridge Journal of Education*, **24**, 3, pp. 413–22.

FRAENKEL, J.R. (1977) *How to Teach about Values: An Analytical Approach*, Englewood Cliffs, NJ, Prentice-Hall.

GILLIGAN, C. (1982) *In Another Voice*, Cambridge, MA, Harvard University Press.

GOGGIN, P. (1994) '"Basic values" and education', *Pastoral Care*, December, pp. 16–20.

GREAT BRITAIN, STATUTES (1992) *Education (Schools) Act 1992*, Chapter 38, London, HMSO.

HALSTEAD, J.M. (1988) *Education, Justice and Cultural Diversity: An Examination of the Honeyford Affair, 1984–85*, Basingstoke, Falmer Press.

HALSTEAD, J.M. (1994) 'Accountability and values', in SCOTT, D. (Ed) *Accountability and Control in Educational Settings*, London, Cassell.

HALSTEAD, J.M. (1995) 'Voluntary Apartheid? Problems of schooling for religious and other minorities in democratic states', *Journal of Philosophy of Education*, **29**, 2, pp. 257–72.

HARGREAVES, D. (1994) *The Mosaic of Learning: Schools and Teachers for the Next Century*, London, Demos.

HARMIN, M. (1988) 'Value clarity, high morality: let's go for both', *Educational Leadership*, **45**, 8, pp. 24–30.

HAYDON, G. (1987) 'Towards a framework of commonly accepted values', in HAYDON, G. (Ed) *Education for a Pluralist Society: Philosophical Perspectives on the Swann Report* (Bedford Way Paper 30), London, University of London Institute of Education.

HAYDON, G. (1995) 'Thick or Thin? the cognitive content of moral education in a plural democracy', *Journal of Moral Education*, **24**, 1, pp. 53–64.

HOLLIGAN, C. (1995) *Values in the Nursery*, Paisley, University of Paisley, Faculty of Education.

JACKSON, P.W., BOOSTROM, R.E. and HANSEN, D.T. (1993) *The Moral Life of Schools*, San Francisco, CA, Jossey-Bass.

JARRETT, J.L. (1991) *The Teaching of Values: Caring and Appreciation*, London, Routledge.

KILPATRICK, W. (1992) *Why Johnny Can't Tell Right from Wrong: and What We can Do About It*, New York, Touchstone/Simon and Schuster.

KIRSCHENBAUM, H. (1992) 'A comprehensive model for values education and moral education', *Phi Delta Kappan*, **73**, 10, pp. 771–6.

KOHLBERG, L. (1981–84) *Essays on Moral Development*, **1; 2**, San Francisco, CA, Harper and Row.

KOHLBERG, L. and HIGGINS, A. (1987) 'School democracy and social interaction', in KURTINES, W.M. and GEWIRTZ, J.L. (Eds) *Moral Development through Social Interaction*, New York, John Wiley and Sons.

LICKONA, T. (1988) 'Educating the moral child', *Principal*, **68**, 2, pp. 6–10.

LICKONA, T. (1991) *Educating for Character: How our Schools can Teach Respect and Responsibility*, New York, Bantam Books.

McLAUGHLIN, T.H. (1994) 'Values, coherence and the school', *Cambridge Journal of Education*, **24**, 3, pp. 253–70.

McLAUGHLIN, T.H. (1995) 'Public values, private values and educational responsibility', in HALDANE, J. (Ed) *Values, Education and Responsibility*, St Andrews, Centre for Philosophy and Public Affairs, University of St Andrews.

NATIONAL CURRICULUM COUNCIL (1993) *Spiritual and Moral Development – A Discussion Paper*, York, NCC.

NODDINGS, N. (1984) *Caring: A Feminine Approach to Ethics and Moral Education*, Berkeley, CA, University of California Press.

OFFICE FOR STANDARDS IN EDUCATION (1994a) *Spiritual, Moral, Social and Cultural Development: An OFSTED Discussion Paper*, London, OFSTED.

OFFICE FOR STANDARDS IN EDUCATION (1994b) *Handbook for the Inspection of Schools* (Consolidated Edition), London, OFSTED.

RATHS, L.E., HARMIN, M. and SIMON, S.B. (1966) *Values and Teaching: Working with Values in the Classroom*, Columbus, OH, Charles E. Merrill.

RICH, J.M. (1993) 'Education and family values', *The Educational Forum*, **57**, 2, pp. 162–7.

SCHOOLS COUNCIL/NUFFIELD HUMANITIES PROJECT (1970) *The Humanities Project – An Introduction*, London, Heinemann.

SHAVER, J.P. and STRONG, W. (1976) *Facing Value Decisions: Rationale-building for Teachers*, Belmont, CA, Wadsworth.

SIMON, S.B., HOWE, L.W. and KIRSCHENBAUM, H. (1972) *Values Clarification: A Handbook of Practical Strategies for Teachers and Students*, New York, Hart.

STARKINGS, D. (Ed) (1993) *Religion and the Arts in Education: Dimensions of Spirituality*, Sevenoaks, Hodder and Stoughton.

TAYLOR, M.J. (1994a) *Values Education in Europe: A Comparative Overview of a Survey of 26 Countries in 1993*, Dundee, Scottish Consultative Council on the Curriculum for CIDREE/UNESCO.

TAYLOR, M.J. (1994b) *Values Education in the UK: A Directory of Research and Resources*, Slough, National Foundation for Educational Research for Gordon Cook Foundation.

TAYLOR, M. (1995) 'An umbrella and a strong support', *The Times Educational Supplement*, June 9, p. 24.

UNGOED-THOMAS, J. (1994) 'Inspecting spiritual, moral, social and cultural development', *Pastoral Care*, December, pp. 21–5.

WHITE, J. (1987) 'The quest for common values', in HAYDON, G. (Ed) *Education for a Pluralist Society: Philosophical Perspectives on the Swann Report* (Bedford Way Paper 30), London, University of London Institute of Education.

Part I

Values in Education

Chapter 2

Liberal Values and Liberal Education

J. Mark Halstead

ABSTRACT: *This chapter argues that the values of liberal education can best be understood in terms of the fundamental values of
liberal societies. The values of freedom, equality and rationality
underpin all liberal institutions, including schools, and provide a
justification for contemporary approaches to multicultural education and education for democracy. The chapter concludes with a
brief discussion of the challenges posed to liberal education by the
values of the marketplace and by non-liberal communities within
the West.*

For most of the last thirty years, theoretical approaches to educational values
have typically begun with an analysis of the concept of education. However,
I shall argue in this chapter that the best way to come to understand the
educational values of any society is to examine the broader framework of
values in that society. This chapter therefore begins with an account of liberalism, which, it is argued, provides the theoretical framework of values that
comes closest to the actual political and economic circumstances that prevail
in western societies generally. In the second section, the influence of fundamental liberal values on the dominant concept of education in the West will
be explored. The chapter concludes with a brief discussion of some of the
challenges to this dominant form of liberal education that have arisen both
from within and from outside the fundamental framework of liberal values.

Fundamental Liberal Values

Although it is, of course, acknowledged that many different versions of liberalism exist, it is not relevant to the purposes of the present chapter to discuss
the arguments between these different versions in any detail, or to discuss
their historical origins. The understanding of liberalism which I shall adopt will
be as broad as possible, though it will be necessary to establish the boundaries
of liberalism by contrasting it with non-liberal world views such as totalitarianism. The chapter is written in the belief that liberal values are to be found
in a wide range of political perspectives from conservatism (in spite of attempts

by Dworkin, 1978:136ff, Scruton, 1984:192ff; and others to treat liberalism and conservatism as totally different world views) to certain forms of socialism (cf. Freeden, 1978:25ff; Siedentop, 1979:153). Where it is necessary to concentrate on one typical form of liberalism, I shall focus on the particular strand which can be traced from Kant to contemporary philosophers like Rawls, Dworkin, Hart, Ackerman and Raz, and in the area of education to liberal philosophers such as Peters, Hirst, Dearden and Bailey, because this strand seems to me to be the most influential one in contemporary liberal thought.

Core Values: Freedom, Equality, Rationality

Liberalism is generally considered to have its origin in conflict, but this conflict is variously depicted. Gaus (1983:2f) depicts it as being between individuality and sociability, while Ackerman (1980:3) sees it as a conflict between one individual's control over resources and another individual's challenge to that claim. In the present chapter I shall argue that there are three fundamental liberal values:

1 individual liberty (i.e. freedom of action and freedom from constraint in the pursuit of one's own needs and interests);
2 equality of respect for all individuals within the structures and practices of society (i.e. non-discrimination on irrelevant grounds);
3 consistent rationality (i.e. basing decisions and actions on logically consistent rational justifications);

and that the primary conflict exists between 1) and 2) (cf. Ackerman, 1980:374ff; Norman, 1982). In fact, some liberals have argued strongly that the first value is the more fundamental (Berlin, 1969; Hayek, 1960) and others have made out an equal strong case for the second (Dworkin, 1978; Gutmann, 1980; Hart, 1984:77f). However, I want to argue that it is precisely the tension between the first two values which gives rise to the need for the third. It is with these three fundamental liberal values and their inter-relationships that I shall be mainly concerned in this section.

Though they may be understood in a variety of ways (see below), there seems to be fairly widespread agreement among liberals that these are the most fundamental values, and that liberal ethical theory is based on them. Thus the principles of impartiality and tolerance are linked to the second and third values, and the principle of personal autonomy (Raz, 1986: Chs. 14–15) to the first and third. The interaction between all three values provides the basis for the just resolution of conflict and the rule of law.

It is when we proceed beyond the three fundamental values that the different versions of liberalism part company. The first parting of the ways comes between those who believe that *good* is of prior importance and therefore justify actions and decisions in terms of their consequences, and those who believe that *right* is of prior importance and therefore justify actions and decisions in terms of a set of moral duties. The dominant view in the former category is utilitarianism, which maintains that the justice of institutions may be measured by their capacity to promote the greatest happiness of the greatest number; classical exponents of utilitarianism include Bentham (1948) and Mill (1972a), and it has found a modern upholder in J.C.C. Smart (Smart and Williams, 1973). The latter category has produced a range of different views, depending on how the moral duties are conceived. An initial distinction may be made between *intuitionism* (which involves the attempt to fit a set of unrelated low-level maxims of conduct together into a consistent whole, and thus may be considered the nearest philosophically respectable approximation to 'common sense'; Bendiff, 1982:81ff; cf, Raphael, 1981:44f.) and *distributive justice* (which involves the claim that the plurality of moral duties must be conceived hierarchically). There are two main approaches to distributive justice: that of libertarians such as Hayek, Friedman and Nozick who emphasize equality of opportunity within the market place and the individual's right to a fair reward for his talents and labour; and that of egalitarians such as Rawls, Dworkin and Gutmann, who emphasize (among other things) civil and moral rights, social welfare and meeting the needs of the least advantaged. To pursue the differences between these conceptions of liberalism, however, would take me beyond the very limited brief of this chapter, and I want now to return to a consideration of the three fundamental liberal values.

The framework of values can be classified initially by considering what is *excluded* by the three fundamental values. The first value, that of individual liberty, clearly excludes a totalitarian emphasis on communal unity to the extent that it endangers individuality; thus liberalism is broadly incompatible with Marxism. (This does not mean, of course, that everyone opposed to totalitarianism must be a liberal, as Solzhenitsyn's criticisms of liberalism make clear: see Walsh, 1990:228ff). The second value, that of the equality of respect, excludes the hierarchical ranking of individuals according to which some have a greater claim to freedom than others. Thus liberalism rejects slavery, for example, or Nazi claims to superiority over Jews (cf. Ackerman, 1980:6). The third value, that of consistent rationality, excludes arbitrariness, inconsistency and the failure to take account of relevant factors (cf. Taylor, 1982). It rules out the uncritical acceptance of dogma, whether based on authority or revelation, and equally it refuses to drift into the sort of relativism which insists that cultures, for example, can only be understood from within and on their own terms (cf. Hollis and Lukes, 1982).

There is considerable scope, however, for different understandings of the three fundamental liberal values:

- Individual *liberty*, for example, may involve freedom to satisfy one's desires (as in Benthamite utilitarianism: cf. Bentham, 1948) or to realize one's rationally determined interests (as in Kant, 1948), or simply to be oneself by being free from constraint. It may, but need not, involve the construction of a life-plan (cf. Gaus, 1983:32ff; Rawls, 1972:407ff).

- *Equality* of respect focuses on one's dealings with others (Peters, 1966: Ch. 8). It is understood in a fairly minimal way by some libertarians to imply formal equality of opportunity, but is sometimes expanded (especially by modern liberals) into a stronger form of equality, such as attempts to equalize life prospects or to distribute wealth and power more equitably (cf. J. White, 1994).

- Consistent *rationality* may, on a utilitarian view, involve no more than the rational appraisal of utility (i.e. what will promote happiness and reduce happiness), which is taken to provide the basis for the just resolution of conflict. A Kantian view of consistent rationality, on the other hand, is much richer, as it not only provides the basis for the just resolution of conflict, but also is an end in itself (the 'search for truth') *and* enriches our understanding of the first two liberal values: thus the freedom of the individual is understood in terms of rational autonomy and the will (which itself may provide the basis for certain supererogatory virtues such as generosity and humility), and the equal right of all other individuals to similar freedom provides the basis for an ethical system which includes respect for persons, promise keeping, refraining from deceit, tolerance, openness, fairness and freedom from envy. Even those who argue that liberalism is grounded in agnosticism about moral issues (eg. P. White, 1983) are committed to the principle of consistent rationality, in that they insist on remaining sceptical only because no good reasons have as yet been provided to justify a change of view.

Rights

Rights are central to liberalism, particularly in its distributive justice mode. They may be analyzed in terms of content, status, origin, context, or the grounds on which they are justified. They are usually prefixed by some sort of defining adjective: moral, political, legal, social, natural, human, constitutional, civil, individual, religious, women's, children's, and so on. In this section, however, I shall distinguish only two types of rights, which I shall call moral rights and social rights.

By *moral rights* I mean those rights without which the three fundamental liberal values cannot be achieved. Examples of these are the right to life itself, the right not to be enslaved, the right not to be brainwashed. These come closest to the status of absolute rights, though there has always been a debate among liberals as to whether there really are any absolute rights (Gewirth, 1984), for it is not difficult to imagine situations where one set of *prima facie* rights may be in direct conflict with another (McCloskey, 1985:133ff).

By *social rights* I mean those rights which are established by rational debate as the most appropriate means of ensuring the just resolution of conflict and general human well-being. These rights are open to negotiation even among liberals, and may have to be fought for, even though they involve claims based on liberal ethics. They are often defined by law; examples include the right to education, the right to low cost housing, the right to free medical care or to a minimum income. Often these rights are to do with the definition of roles and relationships and the distribution of power (for example, women's rights, parents' rights). Sometimes the rights are little more than a rhetorical expression of desires and needs, or a preference for particular social goals, such as students' rights and animal rights (cf. Jenkins, 1980:241f). A right is only a claim or a demand unless it is built into the social structure and there is an apparatus for implementing it. As Jenkins points out, rights are not usually invoked except to redress injustice *(ibid.*:243).

Typically, no one conception of the good life is favoured in liberalism, and a vast range of life-styles, commitments, priorities, occupational roles and life-plans form a marketplace of ideas within the liberal framework (cf. Popper, 1966). Liberalism makes an important distinction between the private and public domains (Hampshire, 1978), though Devlin (1965) and others have disputed the validity of this distinction. Thus, for example, religion is seen as a private and voluntary matter for the individual (though the practice of religion is a moral right based on the fundamental liberal value of respect for the freedom of the individual). Certain forms of human behaviour, however, are ruled out in principle by reference to freedom, equality and rationality; these include prejudice, intolerance, injustice and repression. Other forms of human behaviour are necessary in principle on a liberal view in certain contexts (such as impartiality), though ways of putting them into practice or even conceptualizing them are still hotly debated. In contexts where certain forms of behaviour are considered essential to a liberal perspective, a liberal theory can be developed. The liberal framework of values has produced in particular a political theory and an economic theory.

Democracy

The political domain has always been the central arena for liberal debate. Democracy is seen by liberals as the most rational safeguard against tyranny and a way of guaranteeing the equal right of citizens to determine for themselves what is in their own best interests. It provides a clarification of the role of the state and the law (Benn and Peters, 1959; Duncan, 1983). The state is not an end in itself but 'exists to regulate the competition among individuals for their private ends' (Strike, 1982b:5). It provides the means of protecting the public interest and ensuring social justice (Miller, 1976). The law exists to maintain order in society, by protecting persons and property (Jenkins, 1980) and to prevent harm (Mill, 1972b). Key liberal causes include human rights, free speech, opposition to censorship, racial equality, and opposition to the enforcement of morality through the criminal law (Hart, 1963). The liberal state is expected to show official neutrality on religious matters, together with a respect for individual freedom of conscience. As Fishkin points out,

> The state could not enshrine the religious convictions of any particular groups by public commitments and avoid the charge that it was bias-ing the marketplace of ideas by giving certain metaphysical and reli-gious claims, certain ultimate convictions, the stamp of state authority and legitimacy (1984:154).

Some major debates within liberal political theory include the extent to which democracy should entail representation, which may satisfy the protection of interests, or participation, which may contribute also to human development (cf. Lucas, 1976; Pateman, 1970, 1979); the extent to which political liberalism is part of a comprehensive liberal world view as opposed to an 'overlapping consensus' among different comprehensive views (Rawls, 1993); the extent to which nationalism is compatible with the liberal state (Miller, 1993; Tamir, 1993) the balancing of state power with civil liberties (cf. Dworkin, 1977:206ff; Strike, 1982a); and the conflict between the right-wing emphasis on stability, non-interference, free enterprise, initiative and merit, and the left-wing empha-sis on egalitarianism and the combating of social injustice.

Economic Values

Liberal economic theory accepts the holding of private property as legitimate and supports the notion of the free market economy in which free markets provide the goods and services which consumers choose to buy, though the state may intervene to regulate the economy if necessary, to ensure free and fair competition and to prevent harm to others (Ackerman, 1992:9–10; Dworkin, 1978:119; Gaus, 1983: Ch. 7; Koerner, 1985:315f). Liberalism does not, how-ever, require a particular stance with regard to any of the following debates: the debate between those like Hayek (1960) who continue to support the old liberal principle of *laissez-faire* and more modern liberals who emphasize the need for tighter government control, for example, in monetary policy or wel-fare distribution (Freeden, 1978: Ch. 6); the debate between the supporters of capitalist free enterprise like Friedman (1962) and those who wish to see a significant redistribution of wealth and income, for example, by providing a minimum wage or by progressive taxes (Dworkin, 1978:122); and the debate between those who emphasize the need for free enterprise and efficiency, and those who argue for an increase in industrial democracy (Gaus, 1983:257–61). The relevance of economic liberalism to educational issues will be considered later.

The Values of Liberal Education

Like liberalism, liberal education has a long history and a range of different meanings (Kimball, 1986; Peters, 1977: Chs. 3 and 4). Its roots are often traced to ancient Greece, where liberal education involved the development of mind and the pursuit of knowledge for its own sake (Hirst, 1974a:30–2), and to nineteenth-century thinkers like Mill, Newman and Arnold, with their emphasis on all-round development, the pursuit of excellence and high culture and their continuing belief in the humanizing effect of the liberal arts (R. White, 1986). It is the argument of this chapter, however, that the central strands of liberal education may be best understood in terms of the liberal framework of values outlined above. The vision of education which these values encompass has come to dominate western educational thinking. All the values typically associated with liberal education – including personal autonomy, critical openness, the autonomy of academic disciplines, equality of opportunity, rational morality, the celebration of diversity, the avoidance of indoctrination, and the refusal to side with any definitive conception of the good – are clearly based on the three fundamental liberal values of freedom, equality and rationality, as, indeed, is the more recent emphasis in liberal educational thought on democratic values, citizenship and children's rights. Supporters of liberal education have gone so far as to suggest that it is the only justifiable form of education (Hirst, 1974b, 1985). For them, education *is* liberal education (Peters, 1966: 43).

Rationality

The development of the rational mind is at the very core of liberal education (Dearden, 1972; Strike, 1982b:12); Hirst, for example, tells us that education 'involves a commitment to reason on the part of the educator, no more and no less' (1974b:83f). The nature of rationality is much debated, but it is generally taken to involve having good reasons for doing or believing things (though what counts as a good reason is itself problematic; cf. MacIntyre, 1988). To make rationality a fundamental educational ideal, as Scheffler (1973:60) points out, is 'to make as pervasive as possible the free and critical quest for reasons, in all realms of study'. The fostering of rationality in children requires that they be taught critical thinking (Hirst, 1993; Siegel, 1988) and open-mindedness (Hare, 1985). Together, these values involve teaching beliefs to children in a way that leaves the beliefs open to critical, rational evaluation, and they rule out any taking for granted of the truth of ideas that cannot be shown objectively to be true. Thus indoctrination is considered unacceptable in principle in liberal education (Snook, 1972; Thiessen, 1993). Critical openness involves impartiality and objectivity in assessing the validity of one's own beliefs and a willingness to revise these beliefs as new evidence, circumstances and experience comes to light (Hare and McLaughlin, 1994). Free critical debate and the critical examination of alternative beliefs are considered the best ways of advancing the search for truth. Open-mindedness is sometimes associated with neutrality, and implies that children should not be influenced towards any definitive conception of the good life. As Gutmann points out,

> If public schools predisposed citizens towards a particular way of life by educating them as children, the professed neutrality of the liberal state would be a cover for the bias of its educational system (1987:55).

The principle of neutrality has led some liberals to argue that moral education should develop the capacity for moral reasoning and choice without predisposing children towards specific virtues (see Chapter 1). Others, however, argue that there are certain moral values such as justice and equality about which liberalism can never be neutral (Dworkin, 1986:441) and that moral education should be based on initiation into a rational morality built on these fundamental values (Hirst, 1974b; 1993:187). The emphasis in liberal education on rationality has sometimes been criticized as emotionally empty and lacking a balanced sense of personhood (cf. O'Hear, 1982:127f), but many liberals are careful to avoid construing a commitment to reason too narrowly. The dispositions and emotions are not ignored, and, as Hirst points out, there is 'much more to a person than the activities of reason' (1974b:83).

Personal Autonomy

Linked to the fundamental liberal values of freedom and rationality is the development of personal autonomy. Bailey (1984) describes a liberal education as one which liberates individuals from the restrictions of the present and the particular, so that they can become free choosers of what is to be believed and what is to be done. This is in line with Dearden's classic definition of autonomy:

> A person is autonomous, then, to the degree that what he thinks and does in important areas of his life cannot be explained without reference to his own activity of mind. That is to say . . . to his own choices, deliberations, decisions, reflections, judgements, plannings or reasonings (1972:453).

Kleinig points out that, in addition to choice, autonomy involves 'personal control' and 'initiating agency' (1982:70).Thiessen identifies autonomy in terms of freedom, independence, authenticity, self-control, rational reflection and competence (1993:118–9). J. White argues that autonomy is closely linked to personal well-being (1990). There are many things that are likely to contribute to the development of personal autonomy in children: a breadth of knowledge and understanding; an awareness of alternative beliefs and lifestyles; rational decision-making; the ability to think for oneself and rely on reason rather than authority; other desirable dispositions and social competences; self-knowledge and imagination. Personal autonomy as a fundamental educational ideal has been criticized as paying inadequate attention to human emotions and desires (Stone, 1990), as elitist (Halstead, 1986:38; cf. Pring in this volume), as too 'masculine' a concept (Stone, 1990), and as conflicting with the goal of promoting morally desirable conduct (Lee and Wringe, 1993). However, I have argued elsewhere that we should not construe personal autonomy too narrowly as involving lonely agents 'in an emotionally empty state of rational reflection who have no feeling of what it is to be a person among other persons' (Halstead, 1986:53). An enriched understanding of autonomy must take account of emotions, needs, attitudes, preferences, feelings and desires, as well as community structures and social interdependence (Kleinig, 1982:71, 76).

Equality of Respect

Reference to community structures and social interdependence leads directly to a consideration of the remaining fundamental liberal value – equality of respect. This is a key value in liberal education, not least because abuse and disrespect generate friction in society (Beck, 1990:10) and are impediments to the autonomous flourishing of individuals (J. White, 1994:179). This value provides the foundation for educational policies opposing discrimination on irrelevant grounds such as the race, gender, ethnicity, nationality, religion, social class or sexuality of the individual. Equality of respect, of course, does not imply complete uniformity or identity of treatment or of achievement in every respect (J. White, 1994); on the contrary, equality implies the welcoming of diversity, as even Scruton acknowledges in his acerbic comment on liberalism, 'In the perfect liberal suburb, the gardens are of equal size, even though decked out with the greatest possible variety of plastic gnomes' (1984:192).

Equality of opportunity, however, is implicit within equality of respect, though it is itself an ambiguous term: it is sometimes applied to genuine attempts to increase opportunities for disadvantaged groups and individuals to gain access to valued goals like higher education, but it is also used to justify a competitive approach in which certain opportunities are *formally* available to all, though the inequality among the competitors makes it much harder for some to succeed. At its simplest level, equality of opportunity in education is about the rights of individuals to have equal access to goods and resources, so that no future citizens are unfairly disadvantaged in terms of life chances.

Multicultural Education and Education for Citizenship

I have argued so far that the three fundamental values of liberalism are central to the liberal vision of education as a political and moral enterprise. This becomes even clearer when we examine the response of liberal educational-ists to the increasing pluralism in the western world. This response includes the development of multicultural education and an increasing emphasis on education for citizenship and democracy.

Insofar as multicultural education is concerned with preparing children for life in a pluralist society by encouraging them to respect those whose beliefs and values differ from their own, to see diversity as a source of enrich-ment and to be open to a variety of ways of looking at the world, it is clearly a liberal approach (cf. Halstead, 1988: Ch. 8). Multicultural education contrib-utes to the development of rationality; encouraging children to go beyond the framework of their own culture and beliefs is an important way of helping them to develop lively, enquiring minds, imagination and a critical faculty. Multicultural education is also liberating and a means to the development of moral awareness. As Parekh points out, it is

> an education in freedom – freedom from inherited biases and narrow feelings and sentiments, as well as freedom to explore other cultures and perspectives and make choices in full awareness of the available and practicable alternatives . . . If education is concerned to develop such basic human capacities as curiosity, self-criticism, capacity for reflection, ability to form an independent judgment, sensitivity, intel-lectual humility and respect for others, and to open the pupil's mind to the great achievements of mankind, then it must be multicultural in orientation (1985:22–3).

Education for citizenship and democracy is based on the assumptions that in a culturally plural society all children equally need to be prepared for life as citizens of the democratic state and that democratic values are an 'indispen-sable bulwark against social coercion and manipulation' (P. White, 1991:207). It is thus potentially a unifying influence in a plural society, though McLaughlin (1992) has rightly drawn attention to the tension that exists between the desire to develop a sufficiently substantial set of civic virtues in children that will satisfy the communal demands of citizenship, and the need to tolerate diver-sity within the liberal state. J. White argues that as a minimum citizens will need some knowledge and understanding of their own political situation and of the principles of democracy and 'a ready disposition to apply all this knowl-edge and understanding in the service of the community' (1982:117). Others have placed more emphasis on the use of education to protect and promote human rights (Starkey, 1991). P. White and others have argued that demo-cratic values should permeate through all the structures of the school, so that pupils have practical opportunities to participate in decision-making and to develop an awareness of the responsibilities of group life (Chamberlin, 1989; P. White, 1983). However, Gutmann (1987:88–94) and Dunlop in this volume have expressed doubts about the wisdom of making schools into democratic institutions.

Criticisms of the liberal democratic vision of education outlined above, as I have already hinted, are not thin on the ground. It has been criticized in particular for neglecting human nature, basic human values like friendship and in particular the emotional dimension of human life (Dunlop, 1991; O'Hear, 1982:127f). However, many of these criticisms, I have suggested, can be taken on board in an enriched understanding of liberal education, particularly if it takes account of the critiques of liberal values offered from a communitarian perspective (MacIntyre, 1981; Mulhall and Swift, 1992; Sandel, 1984; Taylor, 1990). Hirst, for example, now favours an understanding of liberal education as concerned to develop 'capacities for critical reflection across the range of basic practices necessary to any flourishing life within a given context' (1993:198). But there are two particular kinds of criticism that are currently challenging liberal education at a more fundamental level. The first comes from within the liberal framework of values outlined in the first section, but offers a very different emphasis from the one traditionally associated with liberal education. The second comes from groups that reject the whole structure of liberal values. This chapter concludes with a brief examination of these.

Challenges to Liberal Education

Traditionally, liberal education has been thought to be opposed to strictly utilitarian ends. However, as Pring points out in Chapter 9, there has been over the last fifteen years a renewed emphasis on utilitarian goals for education, such as producing skilled manpower, developing work-related skills and competences and facilitating 'effective competition in the international market-place' (McMurtry, 1991). In fact, the enterprise culture and free market approach now play a prominent part in school organization and management, and a not insignificant one in the curriculum. These changes are reflected in the language of school management, where parents are customers, the success of a school is judged in terms of its ability to attract customers, senior management teams devise frameworks of quality control, and performance indicators are used by external auditors to monitor progress and effectiveness. As Pring (1994:18) points out, the new vocationalism 'uses the language of usefulness' and 'cherishes different values'.

What is happening is a clash between a particular version of economic liberalism on the one hand and political liberalism on the other for the control of education. It is a clash between those who want the curriculum to reflect economic relevance and the needs of industry and those who want it to promote personal autonomy and the pursuit of truth, between those who think the performance of a school can best be judged by quantifiable outputs and recorded in league tables and those who would judge a school in terms of the critical understanding, imaginative insight and human relationships it generates. This clash generates very real tensions for teachers who may feel that the interests of the school and the interests of the child are no longer in harmony and that they are trapped between the market values which schools are being forced to adopt and the values which they as educators wish to pass on to their pupils. Undoubtedly it is such tensions which lie behind the strong opposition there has been within the teaching profession to many of the recent educational reforms in the UK.

Although the growth of the enterprise culture and market values in education is thus strongly regretted by many liberals (Bailey, 1992), others express the belief that they are not as incompatible with traditional liberal education as is sometimes claimed. This is because broadly educated students with some knowledge of social problems and moral issues may ultimately be of more use to business and industry than students with specific work-related skills, and also because enterprise education may be seen as an extension of liberal education, in that it develops certain kinds of personal qualities and specific areas of understanding (cf. Bridges, 1992; Pring in this volume).

A more fundamental challenge to liberal education comes from those who do not share its basic values. In particular, the values of liberalism and liberal education are broadly incompatible with Marxism (cf. Harris, 1979; Matthews, 1980), radical feminism (cf. Graham, 1994), postmodernism (cf. Aronowitz and Giroux, 1991; Carr, 1995: Ch. 9) and various religious world views, including the Roman Catholic (see Arthur, 1994; Burns, 1992) and the Islamic (see Halstead, 1995), which claim that liberalism lacks a moral and spiritual foundation. To those committed to such world views, liberal education may appear as just one more challengeable version of what is good for children. The Islamic world view, for example, which is based on values drawn from divine revelation, produces an approach to education which is at odds at several crucial points with liberalism. In Islam, the ultimate goal of education is to nurture children in the faith, to make them good Muslims, and children are not encouraged to question the fundamentals of their faith but are expected to accept them on the authority of their elders. How should liberals respond to such a view? Some consider it intolerable and suggest that the state should intervene to protect the rights of the children to be liberated from the constraints of their cultural environment and to grow up into personally autonomous adults (Raz, 1986:424). The moral justification of such intervention according to liberal principles, however, needs to be tempered by considerations of the social disunity and conflict it would cause. The best hope for a way forward in this situation, in my view, lies with a more tolerant and culturally sensitive approach which combines values drawn from political and moral liberalism (including freedom of conscience, respect for diversity and the search for shared civic values) and values drawn from economic liberalism (including freedom of parental choice and diversity of educational provision; cf. Halstead, 1994), which would allow non-liberal forms of life (i.e. communities, traditions, cultures) to pursue their own vision of the good as they choose, either inside or outside the common school.

References

ACKERMAN, B.A. (1980) *Social Justice in the Liberal State*, New Haven, CT, Yale University Press.

ACKERMAN, B.A. (1992) *The Future of Liberal Revolution*, New Haven, CT, Yale University Press.

ARONOWITZ, S. and GIROUX, H.A. (1991) *Postmodern Education: Politics, Culture and Social Criticism*, Minneapolis, MN, University of Minneapolis Press.

ARTHUR, J. (1994) 'The ambiguities of Catholic schooling', *Westminster Studies in Education*, **17**, pp. 65–77.

BAILEY, C. (1984) *Beyond the Present and the Particular*, London, Routledge and Kegan Paul.

BAILEY, C. (1992) 'Enterprise and liberal education: Some reservations', *Journal of Philosophy of Education*, **26**, 1, pp. 99–106.

BECK, C. (1990) *Better Schools: A Values Perspective*, London, Falmer Press.

BENDITT, T.M. (1982) *Rights*, Totowa, NJ, Rowman and Littlefield.

BENN, S.I. and PETERS, R.S. (1959) *Social Principles and the Democratic State*, London, Allen and Unwin.

BENTHAM, J. (1948) *An Introduction to the Principles of Morals and Legislation*, Oxford, Blackwell.

BERLIN, I. (1969) *Four Essays on Liberty*, London, Oxford University Press.

BRIDGES, D. (1992) 'Enterprise and liberal education', *Journal of Philosophy of Education*, **26**, 1, pp. 91–8.

BURNS, G. (1992) *The Frontiers of Catholicism: The Politics of Ideology in a Liberal World*, Berkeley, University of California Press.

CARR, W. (1995) *For Education: Towards Critical Educational Enquiry*, Buckingham, Open University Press.

CHAMBERLIN, R. (1989) *Free Children and Democratic Schools: A Philosophical Study of Democratic Education*, Basingstoke, Falmer Press.

DEARDEN, R.F. (1972) 'Autonomy and education', in DEARDEN, R.F., HIRST, P.H. and PETERS, R.S. (Eds) *Education and the Development of Reason*, London, Routledge and Kegan Paul.

DEVLIN, P. (1965) *The Enforcement of Morals*, Oxford, Oxford University Press.

DUNCAN, G. (1983) *Democratic Theory and Practice*, Cambridge, Cambridge University Press.

DUNLOP, F. (1991) 'The rational-liberal neglect of human nature', *Journal of Philosophy of Education*, **25**, 1, pp. 109–20.

DWORKIN, R. (1977) *Taking Rights Seriously*, London, Duckworth.

DWORKIN, R. (1978) 'Liberalism', in HAMPSHIRE, S. (Ed) *Public and Private Morality*, Cambridge, Cambridge University Press.

DWORKIN, R. (1986) *Law's Empire*, Cambridge, MA, Belknap/Harvard University Press.

FISHKIN, J.S. (1984) *Beyond Subjective Morality*, New Haven, CT, Yale University Press.

FREEDEN, M. (1978) *The New Liberalism*, Oxford, Clarendon Press.

FRIEDMAN, M. (1962) *Capitalism and Freedom*, Chicago, IL, University Press.

GAUS, G. (1983) *The Modern Liberal Theory of Man*, London, Croom Helm.

GEWIRTH, A. (1984) 'Are there any absolute rights?', in WALDRON, J. (Ed) *Theories of Rights*, Oxford, Oxford University Press.

GRAHAM, G. (1994) 'Liberal vs radical feminism revisited', *Journal of Applied Philosophy*, **11**, 2, pp. 155–70.

GUTMANN, A. (1980) *Liberal Equality*, Cambridge, Cambridge University Press.
GUTMANN, A. (1987) *Democratic Education*, Princeton, NJ, Princeton University Press.
HALSTEAD, J.M. (1986) *The Case for Muslim Voluntary-aided Schools: Some Philosophical Reflections*, Cambridge, Islamic Academy.
HALSTEAD, J.M. (1988) *Education, Justice and Cultural Diversity: An Examination of the Honeyford Affair, 1984–85*, Basingstoke, Falmer Press.
HALSTEAD, J.M. (1994) 'Parental choice: An overview', in HALSTEAD, J.M. (Ed) *Parental Choice and Education: Principles, Policy and Practice*, London, Kogan Page.
HALSTEAD, J.M. (1995) 'Towards a unified view of Islamic education', *Islam and Christian–Muslim Relations*, **6**, 1, pp. 25–43.
HAMPSHIRE, S. (Ed) (1978) *Public and Private Morality*, Cambridge, Cambridge University Press.
HARE, W. (1985) *In Defence of Open-Mindedness*, Kingston and Montreal, Canada, McGill-Queen's University Press.
HARE, W. and McLAUGHLIN, T.H. (1994) 'Open-mindedness, commitment and Peter Gardner', *Journal of Philosophy of Education*, **28**, 2, pp. 239–44.
HARRIS, K. (1979) *Education and Knowledge*, London, Routledge and Kegan Paul.
HART, H.L.A. (1963) *Law, Liberty and Morality*, Oxford, Oxford University Press.
HART, H.L.A. (1984) 'Are there any natural rights?', in WALDRON, J. (Ed) *Theories of Rights*, Oxford, Oxford University Press.
HAYEK, F.A. (1960) *The Constitution of Liberty*, London, Routledge and Kegan Paul.
HIRST, P.H. (1974a) *Knowledge and the Curriculum*, London, Routledge and Kegan Paul.
HIRST, P.H. (1974b) *Moral Education in a Secular Society*, London, Hodder and Stoughton.
HIRST, P.H. (1985) 'Education and diversity of belief', in FELDERHOF, M.C. (Ed) *Religious Education in a Pluralistic Society*, London, Hodder and Stoughton.
HIRST, P.H. (1993) 'Education, knowledge and practices', in BARROW, R. and WHITE, P. (Eds) *Beyond Liberal Education: Essays in Honour of Paul H. Hirst*, London, Routledge.
HOLLIS, M. and LUKES, S. (Eds) (1982) *Rationality and Relativism*, Oxford, Blackwell.
JENKINS, I. (1980) *Social Order and the Limits of Law*, Princeton, NJ, University Press.
KANT, I. (1948) *The Moral Law* (tr. H.J. PATON), London, Hutchinson.
KIMBALL, B.A. (1986) *Orators and Philosophers: A History of the Idea of Liberal Education*, New York, Teachers College Press.
KLEINIG, J. (1982) *Philosophical Issues in Education*, London, Croom Helm.
KOERNER, K.F. (1985) *Liberalism and its Critics*, London, Croom Helm.
LEE, J.-H. and WRINGE, C. (1993) 'Rational autonomy, morality and education' *Journal of Philosophy of Education*, **27**, 1, pp. 69–78.
LUCAS, J.R. (1976) *Democracy and Participation*, Harmondsworth, Penguin.
McCLOSKEY, H.J. (1985) 'Respect for human moral rights versus maximising good', in FREY, R.G. (Ed) *Utility and Rights*, Oxford, Blackwell.
MacINTYRE, A. (1981) *After Virtue*, London, Duckworth.
MacINTYRE, A. (1988) *Whose Justice? Which Rationality?*, Notre Dame, IN, University of Notre Dame Press.
McLAUGHLIN, T.H. (1992) 'Citizenship, diversity and education: A philosophical perspective', *Journal of Moral Education*, **21**, 3, pp. 235–50.
McMURTRY, J. (1991) 'Education and the market model', *Journal of Philosophy of Education*, **25**, 2, pp. 209–17.

MATTHEWS, M. (1980) *The Marxist Theory of Schooling*, London, Routledge and Kegan Paul.

MILL, J.S. (1972a) *Utilitarianism* (first published 1863), London, Dent.

MILL, J.S. (1972b) *On Liberty* (first published 1859), London, Dent.

MILLER, D. (1976) *Social Justice*, Oxford, Clarendon Press.

MILLER, D. (1993) 'In defence of nationality', *Journal of Applied Philosophy*, **10**, 1, pp. 3–16.

MULHALL, S. and SWIFT, A. (1992) *Liberals and Communitarians*, Oxford, Blackwell.

NORMAN, R. (1982) 'Does equality destroy liberty?', in GRAHAM, K. (Ed) *Contemporary Political Philosophy: Radical Studies*, Cambridge, Cambridge University Press.

NOZICK, R. (1974) *Anarchy, State and Utopia*, Oxford, Oxford University Press.

O'HEAR, A. (1982) *Education, Society and Human Nature: An Introduction to the Philosophy of Education*, London, Routledge and Kegan Paul.

PAREKH, B. (1985) 'The gifts of diversity' in *The Times Educational Supplement*, 29 March, pp. 22–3.

PATEMAN, C. (1970) *Participation and Democratic Theory*, Cambridge, Cambridge University Press.

PATEMAN, C. (1979) *The Problem of Political Obligation: A Critical Analysis of Liberal Theory*, Chichester, John Wiley.

PETERS, R.S. (1966) *Ethics and Education*, London, Allen and Unwin.

PETERS, R.S. (1977) *Education and the Education of Teachers*, London, Routledge and Kegan Paul.

POPPER, K.R. (1966) *The Open Society and its Enemies, Vols I and II*, London, Routledge and Kegan Paul.

PRING, R. (1994) 'Liberal and vocational education: A conflict of value', in HALDANE, J. (Ed) *Education, Values and the State: the Victor Cook Memoral Lectures*, St Andrews, Centre for Philosophy and Public Affairs, University of St Andrews.

RAPHAEL, D.D. (1981) *Moral Philosophy*, Oxford, Oxford University Press.

RAWLS, J. (1972) *A Theory of Justice*, Oxford, Oxford University Press.

RAWLS, J. (1993) *Political Liberalism*, New York, Columbia University Press.

RAZ, J. (1986) *The Morality of Freedom*, Oxford, Clarendon.

SANDEL, M. (1984) *Liberalism and its Critics*, Oxford, Blackwell.

SCHEFFLER, I. (1973) *Reason and Teaching*, London, Routledge and Kegan Paul.

SCRUTON, R. (1984) *The Meaning of Conservatism* (2nd edition), London, Macmillan.

SIEDENTOP, L. (1979) 'Two liberal traditions', in RYAN, A. (Ed) *The Idea of Freedom*, Oxford, Oxford University Press.

SIEGEL. H. (1988) *Educating Reason: Rationality, Critical Thinking and Education*, London, Routledge.

SMART, J.J.C. and WILLIAMS, B. (1973) *Utilitarianism: For and Against*, Cambridge, Cambridge University Press.

SNOOK, I. (1972) *Indoctrination and Education*, London, Routledge and Kegan Paul.

STARKEY, H. (Ed) (1991) *The Challenge of Human Rights Education*, London, Cassell.

STONE, C.M. (1990) 'Autonomy, emotions and desires: Some problems concerning R.F. Dearden's account of autonomy', *Journal of Philosophy of Education*, **24**, 2, pp. 271–83.

STRIKE, K.A. (1982a) *Liberty and Learning*, Oxford, Martin Robertson.

STRIKE, K.A. (1982b) *Educational Policy and the Just Society*, Urbana, IL, University of Illinois Press.

TAMIR, Y. (1993) *Liberal Nationalism*, Princeton, NJ, Princeton University Press.

TAYLOR, C. (1982) 'Rationality', In HOLLIS, M. and LUKES, S. (Eds) *Rationality and Relativism*, Oxford, Blackwell.

TAYLOR, C. (1990) *Sources of the Self*, Cambridge, Cambridge University Press.

THIESSEN, E.J. (1993) *Teaching for Commitment: Liberal Education, Indoctrination and Christian Nurture*, Montreal and Kingston, Canada, McGill-Queen's University Press.

WALSH, D. (1990) *After Ideology: Recovering the Spiritual Foundations of Freedom*, New York, Harper Collins.

WHITE, J. (1982) *The Aims of Education Restated*, London, Routledge and Kegan Paul.

WHITE, J. (1990) *Education and the Good Life: Beyond the National Curriculum*, London, Kogan Page.

WHITE, J. (1994) 'The dishwasher's child: Education and the end of egalitarianism', *Journal of Philosophy of Education*, **28**, 2, pp. 173–81.

WHITE, P. (1983) *Beyond Domination: An Essay in the Political Philosophy of Education*, London, Routledge and Kegan Paul.

WHITE, P. (1991) 'Hope, confidence and democracy', *Journal of Philosophy of Education*, **25**, 2, pp. 203–8.

WHITE, R. (1986) 'The anatomy of a Victorian debate: An essay on the history of liberal education', *British Journal of Educational Studies*, **34**, 1, pp. 38–65.

Chapter 3

The Ambiguity of Spiritual Values

John M. Hull

ABSTRACT: *The use of the word spirituality reveals not only
vagueness but contrast and conflict. While it is often suggested
that this feature of spirituality reflects the spontaneous and
undefinable character of the spirit, it will be argued here that a
sociological approach helps us to understand the phenomenon.
Spirituality is generated by the character of society itself, especially
(in the case of modern Britain) by the character of the money-
culture. These elements of self-interest tend to be obscured and
denied, which results in the ambiguity and conflict in the use of
the expression. The educational implications of this crisis in
spiritual values will be discussed, in the light of the general conclusion: spiritual education is that education which inspires young
people to live for others.*

Current British use of the word *spirituality* can be summarized as follows. It
is most frequently found in phrases such as women's spirituality, creation spirituality, Eastern spirituality, Benedictine spirituality and so on. These refer to
movements or points of view or practices which are sufficiently understood to
be used in the media without further comment or explanation.

Other uses of the word reveal a striking ambiguity. Spirituality may be
transcendent and other-worldly or it may be secular and political. It may be
opposed to the scientific outlook; on the other hand, there may be a spirituality of science. There may be a spirituality of pure reason, or alternatively
spirituality may be intuitive, mystical and beyond all reasoning. Spirituality
may be inward, private and more or less inaccessible, or it may be a distinctive
characteristic of the behaviour of an ethnic or national group. Spirituality may
be the essence of religion, on the other hand, religion may become unspiritual
and there may be a non-religious spirituality. Spirituality may be contrasted
with the body. On the other hand, it may be expressed through the body.
There may be a spirituality of sexuality. Nevertheless, sex and spirituality may
be at loggerheads.

How are we to account for this uncertainty, these conflicts in the meaning
of the word? It looks as if we know how to recognize spirituality when we see
it, in more or less well-established expressions such as *Russian spirituality* or

creation spirituality but we do not know what to make of it, where it comes from or where it goes.

Rather than discussing this ambiguity with the claim that the spirit is indeed a bit mysterious and spontaneous, let us regard the tensions and contrasts as symptoms of deeper disturbances. Perhaps in examining popular usage, we were dealing with the froth, the linguistic veil which conceals deeper realities.

We do not know to what it might be related, or what it signifies. It is these qualities of vagueness, of fervent assertion, of puzzling inconsistency or contradiction, combined with a mixture of yearning admiration and a sort of no nonsense dismissal which invites further study. Something seems to be troubling the language. It hesitates, deviates, makes a claim, then cancels itself out. Let us try to trace these disturbances to their source.

Spirituality as Deception

The idea that religious and spiritual beliefs and ideals may be used to serve the interests of powerful groups in society can be traced back at least as far as Machiavelli's *The Prince* in the early sixteenth century, and is a popular theme in Voltaire and other pre-revolutionary French social critics (Larrain, 1979). It was not until the middle decades of the nineteenth century that the structural connections between industry and commerce, on the one hand, and law, religion, art and philosophy, on the other, were explored. The mode of production characteristic of industrialized society, together with the relations of production which the mode requires, is looked upon as the base from which the superstructure is generated. Society not only produces but reproduces the assumptions of its mode of production, and it does this through creating an ideology in which the values and assumptions of the base are reaffirmed. Education, law and art, the state itself, together with religion and spirituality all form part of this ideological superstructure. The mode of production itself requires and thus reproduces a social class distinction in which labour and capital confront each other. This social class distinction is reproduced in the superstructure from the point of view of capital and the distinctions and assumptions which capital requires in order to operate successfully.

The spirituality engendered by such a society will pass through a number of phases, as the character of capitalist society itself evolves, and we may distinguish the spirituality of early capitalism (Daniel Defoe, *Robinson Crusoe*, 1719) from that of liberal capitalism (Charles Dickens, *Hard Times*, 1854) and, finally, from that of organized capitalism (John Steinbeck, Ernest Hemingway and F. Scott Fitzgerald). As the internal divisions within national capitalism give way to the world-wide search for wealth, new forms of religious and spiritual consciousness are created on the frontiers of European commerce and pre-industrial patterns of life in primal societies (Wolf, 1982) and the superstructure becomes the rationale and legitimation of imperial expansion (Porter, 1991).

The characteristics of the religion and spirituality thus generated vary considerably in accordance with these factors but generally emphasize inwardness, individualism, transcendence, asceticism and authority. Inwardness ensures that attention is focused away from the world of real human relations (Gutierrez, 1984; Sobrino, 1988); individuality maintains the privacy of the entrepreneurial spirit essential to the market, at the same time denying wider and more complex social bonds (Hartsock, 1983; Marcuse, 1968: Ch. 2) transcendence ensures that spirituality is not dynamically orientated towards innovation and change but fixated upon the eternal and unchanging nature of the world above (Bloch, 1959; 1968). Asceticism concentrates the sense of taboo upon the orifices of the body encouraging a false purity and discouraging prophetic holiness (Alves, 1985; Douglas, 1966) while authority discourages criticism, promotes passivity and engenders respect for tradition and the powers that be (Cartledge-Hayes, 1990; Taylor, 1990).

If, for the moment, we leave on one side the conservative type of spirituality, then the most typical and influential form of mid-twentieth century European spirituality is that created by the existentialist movement, brilliantly described, attacked and unmasked by Theodore Adorno (1974). There is no doubt that well on into the 1980s and 90s literalistic conservative and existentialist liberal forms of spirituality contributed very significantly to the depoliticization of the church.

In adopting this sociological approach to the character of spirituality, it is necessary to draw upon disciplines in the social sciences such as hermeneutics, ideology critique and discourse analysis (Thompson, 1984; 1990). Of course, the consciousness of the spiritual person is innocent of these complexities. In order to create a bridge from such broad, functional social theories of spirituality to the subjectivity of the spiritual individual we need to invoke the psychological concept of self-deception (McLaughlin and Rorty, 1988; Welschon, 1991). Rather than outlining these links between the social and the personal, in what follows we will trace contemporary developments in the money culture which are creating the distinctive features of today's spiritual outlook.

Spirituality and Contemporary Capitalism

Relations between the base and the superstructure are themselves not static, nor is the theoretical grasp of them an unchanging monolith. It would be a serious limit in our analysis if we were to leave it with a conception which is primarily rooted in the nineteenth century.

Three current developments, important for our understanding of spirituality today, will be mentioned.

First, the relationship between base and superstructure is now conceived of in more flexible terms. The important point about the social origins of spirituality is that they are to be found in social being; they are rooted in the concrete and material forms of our community life. That does not mean, however, that all spirituality (and everything else in the superstructure) must be tied relentlessly and exclusively to the economic aspects of social life (Larrain, 1979:65). Moreover, the distinction between base and superstructure should be thought of as a contribution to method in social analysis. The question is to distinguish source from outcome in such a way that contradiction and inconsistency become explicable. Economic forms of life such as the rhetoric of economic description, when considered from the reproductive point of view, may be thought of as generating economic practices and relationships. In that case, economics would be attributable to both base and superstructure (Larrain 1979: end of Ch. 2). As with Freud, so with Marx, distinctions between aspects of the structure should be understood hermeneutically not topographically (Larrain, 1979:67; Ricoeur, 1970). We should remember that only the 'scientific Marxists' have interpreted the relationship between base and superstructure in a strictly causal sense. The Hegelian or humanistic developments of the Marxian legacy always tended to approach the problem of cause and effect in the spirit of interpretation.

We need not necessarily conceive of an automobile plant as being entirely of the base while a symphony orchestra is entirely of the superstructure (Castoriadis, 1987:28). The latter may well be run as a business company, with its employees, contracts and capital, its product being music. Indeed, do we not speak of the music industry? On the other hand, the automobile factory will be susceptible to changes in production method inspired by new forms of political life as well as innovations in technology. No doubt the feudal heaven was a projection of the feudal society, and its distinct superstructure, but modern industrial society is more complex. Max Weber's essay demonstrated that theological, religious and spiritual concepts and practices can be influential in the ordering of economic life (Weber, 1902), and it is noteworthy that most of the important western European critical social thinkers of the past half century have been concerned, not with analysis of the base, but with the understanding of the extraordinary vitality and reproductive power of the superstructure (Adorno, 1974; Bloch, 1959; Castoriadis, 1987; Gramsci, 1971; Horkheimer, 1944; Lefort, 1986; Lukacs, 1971; Marcuse, 1968). This is an important point, because if correct it enhances the significance of education.

Cornelius Castoriadis prefers to speak of the *social imaginary* rather than the superstructure. This is the web of symbols, attitudes and beliefs which constitutes the spiritual atmosphere of a society, that which it regards as obvious, because it has never really noticed it. The social imaginary in the thought of Castoriadis is not only constituted by the economic base; it also constitutes, it originates. As it has autonomy conferred upon it, it develops the power to instigate new forms of life and consciousness. Castoriadis provides an example of the construction of a social imaginary in his study of the Sabbath in ancient Israel. 'This terrestrial determination – perhaps real, but already probably imaginary – exported to the heavens is then reimported in the form of the sanctification of the week' (1987:129). The result is that the seventh day is holy. Castoriadis emphasizes the differences between the imaginary, the symbolic and the functional. An icon, for example, is part of the social imaginary when it is regarded as being revelatory, i.e. part of a world in which icons as a class may have revelatory significance. The icon becomes symbolic when a particular icon offers a specific revelation, and it becomes functional when the believer scrapes the paint off it and drinks it as a medicine (p. 131).

An insight into the structure of spirituality is obtained when we consider the intimate and labyrinthine nature of the relationships between the constituted and the constituting aspects of the social imaginary. It is the constituted self who projects the social imaginary in the social context, and when the social imaginary is conceived of as dwelling within the individual, Castoriadis describes it as the 'root imaginary'.

> God is perhaps, for each of the faithful, an 'image' — which can even be a 'precise' representation — but God, is an imaginary social signification, is neither the 'sum', nor the 'common part' nor the 'average' of these images; it is rather their condition of possibility (p. 143).

Thus, such aspects of the social imaginary 'are infinitely larger than a phantasy. They can be grasped only indirectly and obliquely, at once obvious and yet impossible to delimit precisely . . .' (ibid.) The social imaginary is that which unites the invisible odds and ends of images, fantasies, symbols, which holds culture together. The elements within the social imaginary connote almost everything but denote nothing (p. 150). Is this not reminiscent of the impression we gained when we considered the various meanings of the word spiritual in our culture today?

As an example of a real British social imaginary communicated in the form of a children's fantasy we might consider the spiritual world created by the Narnia novels of C.S. Lewis, where everything is governed by deep, inexplicable, magical laws which are inflexible, impenetrable, all embracing and strangely moving at the subjective level. The emotional power is an effect produced by the social imaginary. It originates, although it is also a social and artistic creation.

It appears then that these current developments in understanding the relationship between the spiritual and its social and economic bases not only offer us far richer understanding of the way spirituality works but also present possibilities and themes for education.

The second current development which I wish to emphasize concerns the change in the character of capitalism which has taken place in the last few years. The highly organized international capitalism of the late nineteenth century and the first half of the twentieth century is sometimes called Fordism, because the production line created by Henry Ford in Detroit in 1916 was the outstanding example of this kind of intensive industrial production. The first Ford plant in Britain was set up in Dagenham in 1939. The Fordist method of production was based upon a massive concentration of workers assembling on the one site an enormous number of identical units. Henry Ford is said to have remarked 'people can have the Model T in any colour – so long as it's black'. This system of organization developed under scientific management techniques to produce the lowest unit cost and thus the greatest profitability. The system led to stronger trade unions, strikes, the much discussed monotony and anomie of the work place, a strongly hierarchical management line and so forth.

In or around the 1960s or 1970s a transformation took place into what is now generally called post-Fordism or 'disorganized capitalism', although the latter term could easily be misunderstood. The use of new technology, particularly computers and information technology, has transformed production. The emergence of modern design techniques following upon intensive marketing has enabled relatively small target groups to be provided with products specially designed for them. Small specialized teams working under franchise arrangements have led to a distributed productive environment while the growth of international communications has facilitated an adaptive and dispersed approach to production. A far greater proportion of employees are working on job share or in part-time or short-term contracts while questions of equal opportunities for women, ethnic groups and others have tended to create new assumptions about personal relationships and management policies in the place of work.

The character and the causes of the transformation from Fordism to post-Fordism are under lively discussion and there is no general agreement about either the analysis or the social and political consequences (Hall and Jacques, 1989). But our interest is on the consequences of these developments for the relationship between the infrastructure and the superstructure, with the question of spirituality and its evolution always in mind.

How are these changes affecting contemporary spirituality? We have seen that the nineteenth century analysis understood spirituality as the projection of the industrial base, characterized as liberal capitalism, producing the liberal, individualistic type of spirituality which is still with us. It was emphasized that while the attention of the entrepreneurs was upon the market place, the point of the cycle where the vital transformation of commodity capital into money capital occurred, the true moment of profit taking lay much earlier and deeper in the process: on the production floor where surplus value was extracted from the work force. This point was considered crucial in understanding the difference between industrial capitalism of the nineteenth century kind and merchant capitalism or commerce, characteristic of the centuries preceding the rise of modern industry.

Today, however, there has been a shift of emphasis back towards the market. Interest has moved from production to consumption as being the typical point at which the spirituality of present day society emerges. The distinction between use-value and exchange-value, a fundamental one in critical economic theory, has always been bedevilled by various complexities, but it is now clearer that the value-assumptions of the exchange situation (the market place) are powerful generators of modern spirituality (Hartsock, 1983; Sohn-

Rethel, 1978). For example, the exchange situation in the market creates an illusion of free choice, individual responsibility, acts of decision based upon transfer of ownership and the internalization of imagination as opposed to its outward expression in the arts. All the values and beliefs associated with the model of the so-called 'rational economic man' [sic] are generated in the market place.

That is not all. The emphasis upon consumption supported by marketing to ascertain the desires of the consumers, followed by design itself to create what will satisfy those desires and adaptive technology to create the commodities has brought about other significant changes (Haug, 1986). We may now speak of the spirituality of shopping. The result of this is that the classical distinction between use-value and exchange-value must now be modified by the introduction of a third term: symbolic-value. The use-value of a certain brand label or style of footwear may be no greater than another, similar product which could be bought at a mere fraction of the price. The cash difference is the symbolic-value of the purchase. Indeed, a great deal of marketing today is based entirely upon symbolic-value. Let us take the cosmetic industry. The use-value of a certain underarm deodorant is virtually negligible; its symbolic-value is everything. W.F. Haug has shown how the reaction of men and women to aspects of their own fundamental bodily characteristics (the natural smell of the body, perspiration) has undergone transformations due to marketing and design – the emergence of B.O. as a concept in human relations and the fact that artificially created stimulants have replaced natural sexual triggers for many people.

The basic desires, identities, self-images including life-goals, aspirations for love and sex, and so on, are all manipulated by modern marketing and sales. Wave upon wave of integrated marketing strategies on an international basis cutting across a wide range of products all surge in upon us, supported by nothing but symbolic-value. Consider, for example, the return of the dinosaur to world-wide power, after a lapse of eighty million years. The world of daydreams, of fantasy, the focusing of the excitement of desire, the giving and receiving of names, the construction of friendship, the enrichment of the world of internal objects, the experiences of what satisfies one – the list of aspects of spirituality and its components could go on and on, all related to the consciousness-creating industries of today (Gouldner, 1976).

In order to understand the relevance of this process to spirituality, it is important to grasp the fact that the consumer is an active participant. The older style of industrial production may have been manipulatory; the new style is collaborative. The whole point of market research and design is to find out and deliver what people want. What people want can be affected by all kinds of social pressures, but the result is still consistent with desire. This is why shopping is, for many people, a delightful experience. The energies and fantasies of the spirit at a level above the satisfaction of basic need are caught up in the transforming experience of changing yourself through shopping. It makes you feel good but it never satisfies.

Spirituality and Money

The third point to be made about contemporary developments in the spirituality generated by modern capitalism has to do with money. Although Jean Baudrillard (1975) is probably correct in arguing that political economy based upon the centrality of production is too narrow a base for an adequate critique of modern society, partly because it anticipates a situation of scarcity and need without meeting the spiritual transformations created by affluence and symbolically-induced need, the fundamental insight of the creators of modern economic theory from Adam Smith to Karl Marx was correct: the power of money is basic. Important work in elaborating the spirituality of money has been done by the slightly eccentric but brilliant philosophical economist Alfred Sohn-Rethel. Although he conceives of his work as dealing with the impact of money upon metaphysics rather than spirituality, the importance of what he says for theology and spirituality is clear. The American Mark Kline Taylor is one of the few theologians to have recognized the importance of his work.

Extending Sohn-Rethel's analysis to the explicit religious and spiritual sphere, it would be possible to summarize the history of the spirituality of money from the biblical period until today as follows. Although not unique in its content, the teaching of Jesus about money is striking in its intensity, particularly the contrast made between God and Mammon (Matthew, 6:24; Luke, 16:13). The personification of money in the parable about the two masters, and the parallelism between the service of God and the service of money suggests that there is a spirituality modelled upon money and that the pursuit of money is subjectively realized as a religious devotion. Not until the medieval period did Mammon become an individual demon, and is summed up in Milton's famous description of the fallen angel Mammon contributing to the debate in Pandemonium. With the arrival of the European enlightenment, belief in Mammon waned but the attributes of his deity continued to strengthen. In effect, Mammon goes transcendent and thus invisible. At the same time, his power steadily grows.

We have thus three stages in his development:

1 Under the kinship mode and the tributary mode of money-exchange in the ancient Middle East and in the Graeco-Roman world: awareness is mainly ethical, sometimes personified.
2 During the period of rising European commercialism from about 1200 AD until 1800 AD: with the growing power of accumulated wealth based upon international trade, Mammon becomes a fully fledged demonic power.
3 With the birth of industrial capitalism, money becomes increasingly abstract. Mammon loses his particular concrete image as a deity but is universalized and generalized to become the omnipresent and omnipotent creator of human destiny. Something like this also happens to God and thus the personalized rivalry between the two gods becomes

abstract and invisible. Consequently, their spirituality merges into one subjectivity, incorporating elements of both. This is another basic element in the contemporary crisis of spirituality (Hull, 1992; 1996).

Some Educational Reflections

My starting point here is the stimulating 1985 article by David Hay. Hay argues that the success of Marx and Freud in creating a lack of confidence in religious belief has been such that people today are suspicious of the spiritual. There is a cultural bias against religion so powerful that people are unable to accept their own religious and spiritual experiences. Teachers must provide ways for young people to understand and accept their own spirituality so as to free them for human awareness in the teeth of the cultural rejection of spiritual and religious claims.

I accept this as a sound analysis, but I would like to try to take it a little further. Hay (1985) draws upon the distinction made by Ricoeur between the hermeneutics of suspicion and the hermeneutics of the sacred (Ricoeur, 1970). Hay suggests that in the teaching of religion the hermeneutics of the sacred has been obscured or stifled by the work of the great masters of suspicion. Again, I agree with Hay. However, Hay writes as if he thinks that the inner religious and spiritual experiences which people report offer a more or less uncontaminated source, as if the impact of the hermeneutics of suspicion was confined to the cognitive level or to the sociocultural level, leaving the internal life available for direct communication with spiritual or divine realities. The truth is, it seems to me, that we have to subject the internal spiritual experience to the same hermeneutic of suspicion. Unfortunately, it is not available as an uncontaminated source of spiritual experience. The situation is not just that the somewhat negative thoughts of Marx, Freud and others have prejudiced people against religion. It is more serious than that. After a century of social and cultural criticism we can understand that 'ideology interpellates individuals as subjects' (Althusser, 1971:170). The apparently inner realm of spiritual and religious experience is a construction of the social imaginary, a reification of the social relations of contemporary capitalism producing as its subjective affect the emotions associated with the numinous and the transcendent. The soul does not, after all, offer us a window into heaven but a shop window. I believe that the exciting and sensitive educational methods which Hay and his colleagues (Hammond *et al.*, 1990) suggest are compatible with this extension of their analysis, or could well be adapted to serve the further critical purposes which I am suggesting. The interesting discussion between Thatcher (1991) and Hay and Hammond (1992) about the spirituality of inwardness would have a bearing upon any such adaptation. If the spiritual pedagogy of Hay and his colleagues were combined with the pedagogy of the numinous created by the *Gift to the Child* team (Grimmitt *et al.*, 1991) with its more direct attempt to create a sort of double awareness of both the inside and outside of religious experience, we could be well on the way towards creating educational methods for coping with the complexities and deceptions of contemporary spirituality.

The point is that to the spiritual, his or her spirituality has no outside. It is a world, a cosmos, seen as entire and viewed from the inside without realizing that it is an inside. To the social sciences, on the other hand, the world of spiritual experience has no inside; it is studied comparatively and critically, i.e. from the point of view of the hermeneutics of suspicion. We need educational approaches which combine the inside with the outside. This means that we need to help children and young people both to enter spiritual experience and to leave it; pedagogically speaking, we need both entrance devices and exit devices. The Nottingham and Birmingham approaches of Hay and Grimmitt both contain these elements.

As for the implications of this study for the spirituality of the rest of the curriculum, what it has to say to industrial and economic awareness is all too obvious. Money is a good servant but bad master (Hull, 1995). There are sensitive and responsible people in positions of industrial leadership who increasingly recognize this truth, and experience the corrosive effects upon their own spirituality created by money. At the same time, there are countless ordinary men and women unable to articulate this corrosion, who experience it all the more painfully from the side of consumption and of more pressing human need. The spiritual crisis in education today is due to the fact that we have spent more than a decade in Britain emphasizing the generation and accumulation of wealth, rather than emphasizing the nature of money as a social property to be used to alleviate human need. Money, like spirituality, is essentially a by-product. When sought for its own sake it becomes idolatrous and alienating. When power is used for the alleviation of human need, both spirituality and money are generated.

Paul said that he knew someone who had a spiritual experience, whether in the body or out of the body, he did not know (2 Corinthians 12:2f). This choice, between a spirituality which is embodied and one which is disembodied, remains fundamental for us today, provided always that the body is the suffering body of humanity. An embodied spirituality is one which responds to human need and promotes human solidarity. St Paul also, on another occasion, urged his hearers to present their bodies to God as a spiritual worship (Romans, 12:1f), not to be conformed to this world but to be transformed by the renewing of their minds. If, in our various ways and from our various traditions, we can follow this advice and lead our pupils along these lines, we will do well.

Conclusions

If there is anything in the above analysis, we have discovered why our society expresses ambiguous and even contradictory spiritualities. It is because spirituality is driven by the money madness which grips us today. This conflicts with the spirituality of the religious traditions which emphasize that in order to live a seed must fall into the ground and die. *Children and young people are educated spiritually when they are inspired to live for others.* It would not serve the interests of a consuming society, which depends for the generation of the wealth of the few upon the stimulation of competition and self-centredness in the many, that this should be so. Unable to face the conflict between the demands of Mammon and those of a life of loving service, we all take refuge in inconsistency, self-deception and ambiguity.

Note

I am grateful to the staff of the Cobuild Project in Lexical Computing of the University of Birmingham for providing me with the 252 cases of the word *spirituality* to be found in their data bank of British newspaper and other printed and broadcast materials from the years 1985–1993.

References

ADORNO, T.W. (1974/1986) *The Jargon of Authenticity*, London, Routledge & Kegan Paul.

ALTHUSSER, L. (1971) *Lenin and Philosophy and other Essays*, New York, Monthly Review Press, Essay V.

ALVES, R. (1985) *Protestantism and Repression, A Brazilian Case Study*, London, SCM Press.

BAUDRILLARD, J. (1975) *The Mirror of Production*, St Louis, MO, Telos Press.

BLOCH, E. (1959/1986) *The Principle of Hope* [3 Volumes], Oxford, Basil Blackwell.

BLOCH, E. (1968/1972) *Atheism in Christianity*, New York, Herder and Herder.

CARTLEDGE-HAYES, M. (1990) *To Love Delilah*, Sandiago, CA, Lunar Media.

CASTORIADIS, C. (1987) *The Imaginary Institution of Society*, Cambridge, The Polity Press.

DOUGLAS, M. (1966) *Purity and Danger: An Analysis of Concepts of Pollution and Taboo*, London, Routledge and Kegan Paul.

GOULDNER, A.W. (1976) *The Dialectic of Ideology and Technology*, New York, Seabury Press.

GRAMSCI, A. (1971) *Selections from the Prison Notebooks*, in HOARE, Q. and SMITH, G.N. (Eds), New York, International Publishers.

GRIMMITT, M., GROVE, J., HULL, J.M. and SPENCER, L. (1991) *A Gift to the Child, Religious Education in the Primary School*, London, Simon and Schuster.

GUTIERREZ, G. (1984) *We Drink From Our Own Wells: The Spiritual Journey of a People*, London, SCM Press.

HALL, S. and JACQUES, M. (1989) *New Times: The Changing Face of Politics in the 1990s*, London, Lawrence & Wishart.

HAMMOND, J., HAY, D., MOXON, J., NETTO, B., RABAN, K., STRAUGHEIR, G. and WILLIAMS, C. (1990) *New Methods in RE Teaching – An Experiential Approach*, Harlow, Oliver & Boyd.

HARTSOCK, N. (1983) *Money, Sex and Power: Towards a Feminist Historical Material-
ism*, New York, Longman.

HAUG, W.F. (1986) *Critique of Commodity Aesthetics, Appearance, Sexuality and Advertising in Capitalist Society*, Cambridge, The Polity Press.

HAY, D. (1985) 'Suspicion of the spiritual: Teaching religion in a world of secular
experience' *British Journal of Religious Education*, **7**, 3, pp. 140–7.

HAY, D. and HAMMOND, J. (1992) '"When you pray, go to your private room" – A reply
to Adrian Thatcher' *British Journal of Religious Education*, **14**, 3, pp. 145–50.

HORKHEIMER, M. (1944/1974) *Eclipse of Reason*, New York, Seabury Press.

HULL, J.M. (1992) 'Human development and capitalist society', in FOWLER, J.W., NIPKOW,
K.E. and SCHWEITZER, F. (Eds) *Stages of Faith and Religious Development: Implications for Church, Education and Society*, London, SCM Press.

HULL, J.M. (1995) 'Spiritual education, religion and the money-culture' [An address
delivered in St Andrew's College on 18 February 1995], Glasgow, St Andrew's
College.

HULL, J.M. (1996) 'Christian education in a capitalist society: Money and God', in FORD,
D. and STAMPS, D.L. (Eds) *Essentials of Christian Community, Essays in Honour of
Daniel W. Hardy*, Edinburgh, T. & T. Clark.

LARRAIN, J. (1979) *The Concept of Ideology*, London, Hutchinson.

LEFORT, C. (1986) *The Political Forms of Modern Society*, Cambridge, The Polity Press.

LUKACS, G. (1971) *History and Class Consciousness: Studies in Marxist Dialectics*, Cambridge, MA, MIT Press.

MARCUSE, H. (1968) *Negations: Essays in Critical Theory*, Boston, MA, Beacon Press.

McLAUGHLIN, B. and RORTY, A.O. (Eds) (1988) *Perspectives on Self-Deception*, London,
University of California Press.

PORTER, A.N. (1991) 'Religion and Empire: British expansion in the long nineteenth
century, 1780–1914', [Inaugural Lecture given on 20 November], London, King's
College, University of London.

RICOEUR, P. (1970) *Freud and Philosophy: An Essay on Interpretation*, New Haven, CT,
Yale University Press.

SOBRINO, J. (1988) *Spirituality of Liberation: Towards Political Holiness*, New York,
Maryknoll, Orbis Books.

SOHN-RETHEL, A. (1978) *Intellectual and Manual Labour: A Critique of Epistemology*,
London, Macmillan.

TAYLOR, M.K. (1990) *Remembering Esperanza: A Cultural-Political Theology for North
American Praxis*, New York, Maryknoll, Orbis Books.

THATCHER, A. (1991) 'A critique of inwardness in religious education', *British Journal
of Religious Education*, **14**, 1, pp. 22–7.

THOMPSON, J.B. (1984) *Studies in the Theory of Ideology*, Cambridge, The Polity Press.

THOMPSON, J.B. (1990) *Ideology and Modern Culture*, Cambridge, The Polity Press.

WEBER, M. (1902/1958) *The Protestant Ethic and the Spirit of Capitalism*, New York,
Scribner's.

WELSCHON, R. (1991) 'Ideology, first personal authority and self-deception', *Social Epistemology*, **5**, 3, pp. 163–75.

WOLF, E.R. (1982) *Europe and the People Without History*, Berkeley, CA, University of
California Press.

Chapter 4

Moral Values

Mary Warnock

ABSTRACT: *In spite of the pervasive relativism in our society, there is in fact a very high degree of moral consensus in relation to the 'classroom virtues'. Most parents, whatever their cultural background, want their children to be taught to behave well in social situations; and schools, though they are not the only place where such lessons are learned, can be immensely influential on moral matters. However, there are also many moral issues over which people disagree, especially within the public and quasi-political domain, and the disparity of views in these areas has sometimes been taken to justify teacher neutrality on moral issues generally. It would be unfortunate, however, if the existence of moral pluralism with respect to certain controversial issues were to inhibit schools from teaching pupils how to behave and initiating them into the civilized values of our society.*

We have recently heard a lot about the necessity for children at school to be taught *the difference between right and wrong*. This is a highly ambiguous and somewhat irritating expression. On the one hand it suggests that this is a lesson that can be quickly assimilated and not forgotten, like the difference between organic and inorganic chemistry. On the other hand it also suggests that once learned and remembered, this lesson will have some unique and fundamental importance. Why else should it be taught? But, as the philosopher Hume long ago observed, 'It is one thing to know virtue, another to conform the will to it' (1740: Book 3, Part 1, Section 1). And so those who want this lesson taught at school presumably want a lesson that will affect children's behaviour and not merely add to the stock of their knowledge. Learning the difference between right and wrong, or moral education, is supposed to be a tactical lesson that will change the pupils' outlook, teach them discrimination, and turn them from the paths of crime, if they are minded to follow such paths. In this chapter I shall explore a bit further the meaning of this educational demand, and see, if possible, the extent to which a school, or any other educational institution, can be held responsible for teaching moral values.

The Nature of Values

First, however, I must take a little time to consider what is meant by a *value*. The word has a portentous sound. But its meaning is, I believe, quite simple. What we value is what we either like or dislike (for things are valued on a scale, and there are some things, like health, that we value highly; others, like pain or dementia, that we value in the opposite sense, regard as horrible, and would prefer always to avoid, both for ourselves and others). The crucial word in this definition is *we*. In speaking of values, there is a presumption that humans, and in some cases other animals as well, *share* the preferences so designated. Pain, for example, is something that all animals hate and wish to avoid. There are, of course, values other than the avoidance of pain which may be given priority in certain circumstances; generally speaking, we would expect only humans to have the imagination and foresight to appreciate these long-term values. It follows that as a rule, and as a background presumption, when we speak of values, or of things that are valuable, we are speaking in the public domain. We assume that values are shared, and are capable of being appreciated, if not adopted, by people in general, not just by one person alone. There are obviously cases where we wish to assert an idiosyncratic taste or preference; but generally we incline to speak of this as a preference, not a value; or at least we preface the declaration of our taste by some marker, like 'for my part' or 'I personally'. We do not baldly state that the preference is for something *valuable*.

The publicity of values, their intrinsically shared nature, is of immense importance, and is central to what follows. The belief that to be shared is the essence of a value is based on a yet more fundamental belief, namely that humans are in many important respects alike. It is therefore possible to assert that there are some things hateful, or harmful, to all humans (just as we would probably be happy to say that there are some things hateful or harmful to all cats, and some things that cats, on the whole, prefer and enjoy). The fundamental similarity of humans one to another is what makes it possible for humans to sympathize with each other; and it is the possibility of sympathy that makes morality a feature of human life.

If this were all, if the common nature of human values were generally acknowledged, then the business of teaching these values to children at school would be a simple and uncontroversial matter. Children are not born with moral understanding. They are born capable (most of them) of affection, but not, without teaching, of an awareness of other people as of equal importance with themselves. John Stuart Mill puts the matter thus:

> The pains of others, though naturally painful to us, are not so until we have realised them by an act of imagination, implying voluntary attention; and that no very young child ever pays, while under the impulse of a present desire. If a child restrains the indulgence of any wish, it is either from affection . . . or else because he has been taught to do so (1859).

So at school, when a child is perhaps for the first time away from people he is bound to by ties of natural affection and familiarity, he can be taught that other people exist who are like himself, and whose pains, pleasures and wishes, as well as his own, are part of his proper concern, and of his inescapable heritage. I shall return to this, which I designate the simple view, a little later.

The Problem of Relativism

Let us now go back to the crucial word, *we*. To speak of things that *we* value, as if these were, inevitably, the same things as are intrinsically valuable, or *to be valued*, is manifestly to adopt a particular point of view, privileged so as to claim objectivity. However, there is nothing so universally mistrusted at the present time as this assumption of privilege. The fear of appearing to uphold a universal standard, whether in morals or aesthetics, is itself an almost universal and extremely inhibiting fear. So what is its source? I believe that there is a variety of routes leading to the present timidity about asserting common values. At a comparatively sophisticated level, there is the influence, among the educated, of Post-modernism. This is a doctrine which I suppose had its origins in the consideration of the visual arts, but has spread far more widely. Post-modernism holds, or at any rate suggests, that there is an infinite variety of different possible points of view from which to see any object. No single one is to be preferred to any other. Even the laws of perspective, it has been argued, have been arbitrarily imposed on our representations of the world, and those who are prepared to ignore them have as much entitlement to the claim to represent as those who adhere to them. Such relativism is often used in aid of political creeds. Feminists, for example, have claimed that the so-called laws of perspective themselves were the products of a male consensus, which it is the duty of women to undermine. In wider, more literary contexts, this relativism has led to the view that there is no truth 'outside the text' ('text' being here used to mean whatever is an object of study, literature, history, film, or whatever it may be). There is thus no *true* interpretation, not even an interpretation which approaches nearer to the truth than another. There is your interpretation and mine. If someone embarks on a narrative, purporting to convey the truth, he is in fact inventing the truth as he spins out the narrative. 'Another story, another truth', as Don Cupitt, the Cambridge theologian puts it (1991). For what might be thought to be the world outside the text, to which the text refers, is itself a construction, a view of the 'facts' peculiar to the individual, or perhaps to a group of individuals. The facts have no actual objectivity. There is nothing but the text. Thus the concept of the true withers away. There is your truth and my truth. But no truth true for everyone, or for all time.

Such rampant relativism is sometimes connected with another phenomenon with which we are all familiar, namely the multicultural nature of our society. William Dunning (1993), for example, argues that with the present 'profusion of alternative modes of thinking and consciousness' it is impossible to prefer one point of view to another. All are equally valid. And this brings us nearer to the difficulty of the teaching of values in school. Such teaching is, it seems, inevitably open to the charge of indoctrination, that is the unwarranted imposition on his pupils of the teacher's own point of view. It is domineering; it is dictatorial; it is opposed to freedom and it is, to use a fashionable term of abuse, necessarily *judgmental.* It suggests that some things are better or nicer than others, and some things definitely, and for everybody, nastier or wrong. It seems that, in reflecting on our own history, we have been impressed beyond measure by the horrors of intolerance: we have an ancestral fear of witch-hunts, of religious persecution, of sectarian or racial violence. This in itself is good. It shows an advance in civilization, and a determination to make it possible to live side by side with people whose views and beliefs are different from our own. Given the propensity of all humans to gang up, to regard some people as outsiders and as less than human, one cannot afford to neglect the virtues in the present orthodoxy. Nevertheless I believe that this orthodoxy needs to be examined, before it undermines, as it threatens to do, any possible use of a moral vocabulary within which some things may be designated good or virtuous, others wrong, wicked or vicious, and within which also some people may be told unequivocally that their behaviour is morally intolerable.

The Importance of Shared Values in Moral Education

We need to consider what exactly is meant by the plural society in which we are so often assured that we live. To what extent does the plurality of cultures entail a real plurality of morals? Does respect for the traditions of other cultures entail that we must stand back from all moral judgments? For this is the consequence often drawn, when the question arises of what should be taught to children at school. It is necessary to draw certain distinctions at this point. Let us imagine a typical city primary school at the end of the twentieth century. In any class there will be a wide mix of children of different races, few of whom may be white, or from an even nominally Christian background. Now let us imagine that within this class there is a bully, who makes the life of the other children intolerable, and who has certain particular victims whom he torments. Let us also imagine that there is a thief; and that there is a liar, who will attempt to lie his way out of all kinds of trouble, even at the expense of getting other people into trouble in his place. We can go on with the list: there is someone who always tries to duck his responsibilities; there is someone who habitually uses bad or abusive language, and who has no concept of common politeness; and so on. Faced with these classroom vices, if I may so designate them, which, though here exemplified in the classroom, are real vices not peculiar to children, the behaviour involved really bad behaviour, the teacher will not be in the least inhibited by the varied cultural backgrounds of the pupils. Good and responsible teachers will intervene to put a stop to the behaviour, and moreover, in doing so, will uninhibitedly deploy a strictly moral vocabulary. They will say that it is wrong to tell lies; that bullying is cruel; that one must not harm or give offence to other people. Whether they use the device of saying 'How would you like it if you were at the receiving end?', or other devices for getting the child to comprehend, imaginatively, the equal importance of other people, this is what they will be doing, and this is teaching the difference between right and wrong – teaching that right and wrong are real and applicable, not merely verbal distinctions. In such ways, teachers will be attempting to civilize their pupils, make them fit, that is, to live in society.

It is of the greatest importance to recognize that such civil or societal values are cross-cultural. No-one, whatever their cultural background, or the religious source, if any, out of which their moral convictions flow, can do other than morally condemn people who are cruel to the weak, who pursue their own gain at whatever cost to other people, who care nothing for hurting or merely offending others, who neglect or abuse those for whom they are responsible. If we contemplate what is often referred to as the *breakdown of society*, or the *moral anarchy* with which we sometimes seem to be faced, we should recognize that the thugs and muggers, the vandals and thieves, the violent, the indifferent and the fraudulent do not have a different set of moral values from ours – they have none. They simply do not recognize that there is anything against doing what will get them what they want, except perhaps fear of being caught. This is nothing new. Such passions as greed, lust, violent rage, have always existed, and will presumably continue to exist in humans. This is the truth in the Christian doctrine of Original Sin. Morality is the way in which we learn to control such instincts in ourselves. But for those who cannot control them, the criminal law exists, to act as a deterrent of an external kind, to inhibit people from doing the kinds of things that the morally good person would not do anyway, and so far as possible to protect others from the consequences of the behaviour of those who have no moral sense. If we think of ourselves as members of society, then, and if we think of school as a microcosm of society, it becomes clear that there is within society a wide degree of moral agreement. Children do not automatically know about this or assent to it; so at school, it is the task of the teacher, by example and intervention and the clear use of moral language, to introduce and render intelligible this agreement. The teacher must hope that the requirements of civilized society will be internalized, taken on by the child, becoming a matter of what may be termed *conscience*, so that the power of the criminal law will never have to come into force in his case. School is not the only place where such lessons must be learned; but it is a very important place, in that the classroom and the playground are where so many virtues and vices may find their expression, and the teacher is always at hand, to draw the moral. School should be the breeding ground of the individual conscience, simply because it is, more than the home, a society, and it is within society that the shared values which inform the conscience are predominantly exercised.

Moral Controversies and Teacher Neutrality

To emphasize the wide and crucial scope of moral agreement is to assert what I have called the *simple view*. But, being simple, this view does not do justice to all the facts. No-one could deny that, besides these shared values, common to humans in general, there are also many areas of moral disagreement which may or may not be related to racial or religious differences. However, for the most part, these moral disagreements are over matters that are the concern of the world outside school. I refer to such issues as the role of women in society, abortion, euthanasia, our duty to the environment or specifically to animals, the rights or wrongs of military intervention in foreign countries, whether or not certain drugs should be legalized and countless other moral problems. It seems to me entirely right that such problems as these should be discussed in the classroom, set as subjects for essays or be chosen as topics for formal debate. I am dubious, however, about the merits of introducing them to very young children, as central to morality. Too often children come home from primary school prattling of rain forests or the ozone layer, full of righteous indignation, but, naturally, without any understanding of the political or economic complications of the subject. For all these moral problems, though undoubtedly moral, are also political, or in some cases legal; and it is impossible for very young children genuinely to reach an informed view of them. They are bound to accept the views they are taught, and only gradually, perhaps because of a difference of view between a teacher and a parent, will they come to recognize that these are not matters where everyone agrees about what is right and what is wrong. It seems to me that in the presentation of what one may broadly label political issues, a teacher has a duty to give his own opinion, but to give it *as* an opinion, or as a matter of faith, and, however strongly he feels about the matter, to let it be clearly understood that not everyone agrees with him. We are sometimes told that teachers must appear, or even be, politically neutral. This is a mistake, in my view. Political neutrality can seem frighteningly indifferent. People who are young essentially need the example of those who are not indifferent, but are full of enthusiasms and commitments. But, whatever may be true of political neutrality, in matters of classroom morality, it would be fatal if teachers remained neutral. They have to be definite, judgmental, authoritarian and convinced, ready, as I have said, to use strong and unambiguously moral language. It is hard to get children to see that moral issues may be passionately debated by people who sincerely hold different principles one from another, unless they have already developed a strong commitment to the moral, in other words unless they already have a conscience.

Indeed there is a danger in discussing public, or political, issues with very young children, that the sense of what is morally wrong may be displaced, that badness or evil may seem something from which one is comfortably distanced. The destruction of rainforests may be treated as wicked with safety, because it is far from home; Hitler may be represented as the embodiment of evil – but he is long dead. Questions about abortion or euthanasia or the rights and wrongs of embryo-research are not immediate for pre-adolescent children. (The preference for safety may motivate teachers even more than pupils; it is easy to avoid embarrassment, or too overt moralizing by condemning the distant and the impersonal, rather than what is in front of your nose). And so what is morally wrong may become little more than what characterizes the Baddies in a cartoon story. It is not that stories representing the struggle of good and evil are in themselves harmful. This is far from the case. It is that, if these are the only moral lessons, it may never strike a child that he himself is capable of evil, or subject to temptation. He ought first to learn about temptations to bully, or to take more for himself than his fair share, and then see the global consequences of the lust for power or of greed. And so a love of the classroom virtues must be inculcated first, with its inevitable corollary, the overcoming of temptation to the classroom vices. The simple must precede the complex.

I have suggested that there is a very high degree of moral consensus in the case of what I have designated the classroom virtues. Most parents want their children to be taught to behave well in a social situation, and school can be immensely influential in such teaching, by introducing, probably for the first time, not merely the concept of society but an actual working and living society of which children are a part. I have also suggested that there are considerable areas where moral issues are public and quasi-political within which there is a wide disparity of views, where there exists that moral pluralism of which we are often told, and which has proved an inhibiting factor in the recognition of the plain duty of a school to teach its pupils how to behave. However, it should not be thought that this is the end of the matter, or that moral consensus is not to be sought in the public as well as the private domain, even though here the influences of culture and religion may make detailed agreement between different groups impossible.

The Transmission of Societal Values

In any society, including that of school, government depends upon the wish of the members of that society that order and civilization should prevail, and that people should be free, within society, to get on with their own legitimate business pursuing the values that they have. In any society, as Hume (1748) pointed out, those who are governed outnumber those who either make the law or are appointed (as police or judiciary) to enforce it. If everyone refused to obey the law, the law could no longer be enforced. If no-one had any respect for the courts or the police, or for Parliament as the legislative body, then anarchy would result. Since the forces of law and order are always in the minority, they could be rendered impotent, if everyone chose to disregard them. Society is thus built on faith; a faith that order is preferable to disorder, justice to injustice, peace to violence, government to anarchy, and a recognition of the value of individuals. It seems to me therefore that it is incumbent on a school to teach its pupils these values, the values that are the base upon which society is founded. In particular it is necessary that pupils should be taught that parliament has authority, and that the laws, once enacted, are binding on everyone. Obviously there will be those who do not approve of a particular law. For example, there may be those who believe passionately that the abortion laws in this country at the present time are too liberal. Of course, such people need not themselves have anything to do with abortion; it is always open to individuals to set themselves a more rigorous standard than that enjoined by law. They need not open their shops on Sunday; they may refrain from eating meat, or hunting foxes. They may indeed campaign that the law should be changed on moral grounds. Nevertheless, they should be taught to recognize the sovereignty of the law as it exists. And this will entail that they should be taught to respect both the courts and the police.

One of the most damaging features of society at the present time is the almost universal cynicism to be found at all levels about politicians, judges and the police. It is for this reason, because it gives credence to such cynicism, that bad behaviour, manifest dishonesty, corruption or naked self-interest on the part of these institutions is so greatly to be deplored. Every corrupt policeman, every 'bent' prison officer, every stupid or ignorant judge, every politician who seems to have no serious beliefs or principles, makes it more plausible to argue that 'the system' as a whole is corrupt and self-seeking, and that everyone must therefore go out for himself, disregarding the law. It is quite generally believed today, and especially by the young, that one can never believe a politician, never expect justice in the courts, never trust the police. It is therefore necessary for schools to try, as best they can, to teach what may be called a respect for the constitution, a desire for order, a genuine belief in justice, to countervail against the general cynicism of the time. It will be objected that this would be to place schools in an intolerable position. Every teacher would have to be a conservative; no pupils would be encouraged to be revolutionary, or to wish to change the way things are. This, however, is the reverse of the truth. The way things are has to be changed; and changed by the next generation of policemen, politicians and judges, that is by the people who are now at school. And the changes must stem from a belief in moral values that are shared.

It may well be that the best way to start on such lessons is to get pupils at school to learn in their own society, the school, that people are to be trusted; that not everyone is self-interested or motivated solely by greed or ambition. It may well be that an inspired example of a teacher who believes in order rather than anarchy, in justice rather than favouritism, in keeping promises and fulfilling obligations rather than neglecting them may be the beginning of a love of such values in his or her pupils which will be carried beyond school in the long run. Better still, what is now called a *whole-school policy* may gradually impress on pupils at the school that teachers can be relied on, but also that punishment will follow crime, and that therefore the world is not a jungle, but that civilized values are, here and there, upheld. This, in turn may mean that such values will be internalized, adopted by the pupils for themselves and carried out in due course into the family and the professions.

I would not want to suggest, and I have said this already, that schools are the only source of such lessons. Nevertheless, I do not think that teachers can duck the responsibility they have for the teaching of values. Teaching is an essentially moral transaction. Not only does it demand in the teacher the virtues of hope, patience, honesty and industry; it demands also that such values, and the societal values I have been discussing are handed on, transmitted to the next generation. For to speak of a value is to speak of something common to all humans, and something which we must believe it is our duty to share, if we believe that we cannot live except in a society based on such common values. A student who is unwilling to take on such moral burdens should not, in my opinion, enter the teaching profession.

References

CUPITT, D. (1991) *What is a Story?* London, SCM Press.

DUNNING, W. (1993) 'Post-modernism and the construction of the divisible self', *British Journal of Aesthetics*, April.

HUME, D. (1740/1978) *A Treatise of Human Nature*, in SELBY-BIGGE, L.A. (Ed) 2nd edition, revised, Nidditch, P.H., Oxford, Clarendon Press.

HUME, D. (1748/1963) 'Of the original contract', in *Essays, Moral, Political and Literary*, Oxford, Oxford University Press.

MILL, J.S. (1859) 'Essay on Sedgwick's Discourse', in *Dissertations and Discussions*, London.

Chapter 5

Environmental Values and Education

John C. Smyth

ABSTRACT: *Environmental values divide roughly between those relating to the orderly operation of an ecological system and those relating to human use of it. They reflect tensions between human-kind and nature resulting from rapid human cultural evolution out of phase with natural processes. Values grow from many kinds of learning experience, so tension may also exist between formal education and other influences on learning. These in turn reflect stresses imposed by the nature and speed of environmental and social change. What is learnt is an individualized perception of the environment filtered through past experience and present needs and aspirations. Values range from the utilitarian to the spiritual, and experiences from which higher values grow do not always conform with educational policy. Environmental education should nevertheless foster value development reflecting identification with the ecological system and pride in the skills of living harmoniously within it.*

The Wood

A small oak-wood in early summer: the sky is cloudless and the air still. Near mid-day the birds are quiet except for feeding calls in the canopy. Silence is not complete: all around is a continuous, tiny pattering like gentle rain. The sound is made by the steady fall of faecal pellets from an army of caterpillars feeding on the young oak leaves above. They hit the leaves on the woodland floor and roll off to become part of the soil, where decomposer organisms are constantly at work. From there, nutrients return to the plants. Meanwhile the birds in the canopy harvest the caterpillars for hungry fledglings. *Natura naturans*, nature naturing, as medieval writers once put it. For a little while the human observer feels part of this orderly, working system, a small piece of the larger system which supplies his food and oxygen and disposes of his wastes as best it can. It is an experience to value.

The peace is disturbed by a jet aircraft climbing out of the international airport. This also is something he values, as a quick way of travelling, although he knows well that (among other things) it is polluting the air on which the living system depends. But he belongs also to a human system of far-flung activity which now works faster than ever before: opting out of its machinery might be good for his conscience but damage his effectiveness as a working component. His environmental values, like the systems they reflect, are in conflict.

The value he attaches to the oak-wood is expressed in ecological terms but is not solely born of knowledge. There is also an emotional component which goes back to happy memories of childhood. Other people equally appreciative of the wood will value it for different reasons and yet feel much the same about it. Others again feel differently – those, for example, who value its margins as a quiet place to dump rubbish, and the landowner who hopes that a major developer will get planning permission to swallow it up in a lucrative quarry development. The Secretary of State has had to evaluate the claims of the developers (value to the local economy and employment, value of the product for motorway construction) against the claims of outraged home-owners down the road who value their local green belt and freedom from noise and dust. He has refused the application, but probably the wood played the smaller of parts in his decision.

His neglect of it is not surprising: the wood is not specially valued as a nature site. The criteria for nature reserve status include size (it is quite small), variety of flora and fauna (it is not very old and its occupants are normal for such a wood), rarities (none recognized as yet). Its value to local ecology is as shelter for adjacent fields and as part of the network of uncultivated habitat providing corridors for the movement of wildlife through the area. This is real value but not easy to use for protecting a specific place.

Values in Conflict

Tensions exist here between humankind and nature, and between values re-lating to the orderly working of the living system and to human lifestyles within it. These values are only a few examples surrounding a quite unremark-able corner of our environment, but they illustrate their potential to confuse. They belong to different kinds of interest – individuals, such as the observer or landowner; communities, such as quarry workers, house owners; future generations, such as motorway users, future naturalists; the natural environ-ment itself. Including this last raises a much debated theoretical question, if nature can or needs to be thus recognized (Brennan, 1990): its values could be simply instrumental, acknowledging human dependence on the natural system or its contribution to the quality of life.

The human stakeholders represent different sectors of society with differ-ent functions and priorities – national government through the Secretary of State (good governance, respect for democracy, winning the next election); the government conservation agency (conserving the best available sites within its budget); the business sector (expanding activities, increasing profits, trying to appear environmentally responsible); the local community (maintaining property values, raising standards of living).

The different values are therefore based on different criteria (Berry, 1983) – cost, quantified as money although still poorly related to environmental processes, such as quarry development; usefulness to persons or society, such as air travel, fly-tipping; intrinsic natural worth, an objective quality of the place itself (ecological value); symbolic or conceptual value, such as being part of the life-sustaining ecosphere. All are influenced by factors independent of the locality, the labour market, national transport policy, political affiliations, educational background, social status and therefore also liable to change.

This is quite a simple example of a conflict of environmental values which can crop up anywhere. Personal values grow from different experiences of places and people, influenced by perceived needs, inclinations and ambitions. How they grow reflects the quality of that experience. People need opportunities to develop values, knowledge to back them up and skills to put them to work. They must be able to cope with differences and conflicts between them. Much bigger environmental issues, global warming, ozone holes and the like, attract attention but the beliefs, attitudes and values on which remedial action depends may be rooted in more homely things. Providing for this is the role of education.

Values and Environmental Education

Environmental education grew from international concern about the environment during the sixties. It was defined as a permeating element through all education (Unesco/UNEP, 1975; 1977; 1987), stressing the cultivation of environmental values, as did strategies for environmental care (IUCN *et al.*, 1980; 1991).

Education is used here to cover all those influences on environmental learning which can be guided towards defined objectives. They are found in home and family, friends and peer groups, the community, school and post-school education, work and leisure activities, media and advertising, legislation and fiscal measures. Culture and tradition underlie all of them and are sometimes restrictive. All the influencers interact and vary in their impact between different circumstances and at different stages. Education is a sustained learning experience throughout life in which everyone is both a learner and an educator, whether by precept or example (SOEnD, 1993).

The formal sector sets standards for education, but outside influencers may counter them by observing what society values in practice, from the safety of their own sub-communities. Everyone belongs to one or more of these, defined variously by location, occupation or leisure activity (Nauser, 1993). Routines develop there, enabling people to conform with each other, avoid friction and decision-making, and acquire the knowledge and skills which build confidence to manage daily life. Because they are rewarding they can lead to the co-existence of incompatible values, those espoused and those practised. Such contradictions are, however, too normal to be treated as deficits of the individual (Posch, 1993), although they may indict the system.

Environmental values grow throughout learning, out of beliefs and attitudes derived from knowledge and experience of:

- what the learner has been told (by any of the influencers);
- what has been absorbed through experience (whether designed for that purpose or not);
- what has been actively pursued by the learner in response to inspiration from others or to personal interests and desires.

The third is the most powerful medium, since values stem from role-taking rather than role-playing and real rewards are at stake. Some values grow, many change, some wither and some never germinate, depending on the richness of the process, the balance between conflicting influences, the predilections of the learner (innate or acquired) and the changing circumstances through which life passes. An educator tries to assess the learner's situation and provide the best and best-suited learning experiences possible, taking account of other influences. An educational strategist looks at all the influences on people's learning to identify those capable of guidance and to devise ways of guiding them towards appropriate environmental objectives (SOEnD, 1993).

The learner's response is liable to be influenced by values already acquired. A group of teenagers, for example, were incensed by discovering that their favourite open-air meeting place had been left untidy by weekend visitors. Their view of rubbish changed, however, when they came on left-overs from their own last visit. It brought back happy memories of the occasion and reaffirmed their sense of possession of the site.

Values thus act as part of a filter for new experience, and guide its interpretation. Personal values develop an organic quality by which old values and new are blended into an ostensibly self-consistent (if irrational) system. Such selection is naturally protective; in a complex world we need a reductionist approach just to avoid overload (although it does not prepare us for understanding whole, multifactorial systems, which is also necessary (see Smyth, 1995).

An educator, no matter how fair-minded, communicates with a learner through similar filters; it is almost impossible in practice to avoid selecting and interpreting material to fit a programme and objectives. To think of environmental education (or arguably any other kind) as being value-free may reflect laudable ideals but be a practical non-starter.

Filters raise a question about the relationship of individual and environment. *Environment* means the whole external environment – natural, cultivated, built, social, economic and cultural, and the temporal environment of past and future – not merely some 'green' abstraction from it. It interacts with an internal physical environment of physiological needs and appetites and a mental environment of memories and visions.

We do not value it as we should. The very word *environment* implies something secondary to what it surrounds, yet life is unthinkable without it: we depend on it continuously for the means of life, and we modify it as we live. Together organism and environment operate as a single, inseparable system, described by Patten (1982: 179) as the 'fundamental particle of ecology'. The environmental component of this system corresponds with what Cooper (1992: 168–70) has called a 'field of significance', 'not something a creature is merely *in*, but something it *has*'; it is not 'sharply delineated', and 'despite (or because of) its pervasive role in people's lives, it has rarely been articulated.' We should value its health as an extension of our own. Since it is shared with others, and with other species, its care also enlarges the concept of community.

Filtration processes are part of this single system. The core element is not a passive recorder of environmental data: some environmental qualities are beyond its capacity to perceive (except with instrumentation) but some are ignored (generally as irrelevant), and what is accepted is interpreted on the basis of past experience, context, interest or expectation. Control is thus exercised over experience, both received and sought; perceptions of the environment become constructs from interactions between selected external messages and the internal environment. Actions taken in response are similarly structured. Structured exchanges between organism and environment vary with time and circumstance and between one individual and another in otherwise similar conditions. Thus values attached to this environment, and actions towards it, are referrable to individualized perceptions which may also differ significantly from reality expressed in scientific terms. Educators must be prepared for this.

The Legacy of Nature

The most fundamental tension affecting environmental values is probably between the so-called natural system and the human system; in Berry's well-known phrase (1983) we are both part of and apart from nature. The mismatch may be partly due to behavioral baggage inherited from the past, including biological appetites once necessary to maintain life but now excessive (Smyth, 1977). Humankind is still biologically an animal but progress to our hunter–gatherer ancestors was marked by a huge increase in brain capacity and in the adaptability and complexity of behaviour. Like the tortoise and the hare, biological and cultural (exosomatic) evolution lost sight of each other.

So far as we can tell no other animal species needs values of its own; the choices of action necessary for survival are embedded in a harmonious relationship co-evolved with the environment, predisposed or else acquired by integrated learning processes. Humankind, however, has eaten from the Tree of Knowledge and must now work out its own destiny. So profound is this difference perceived to be that most people, like the Book of Genesis, separate Humankind from Nature with unhappy consequences for their mutual relationship.

For our tribal forebears personal, social and environmental competence were the learning objectives for life as working members of a hunter–gatherer group. But, as cultural evolution proceeded and abilities to alter the environment increased, environmental competence became focused on exploitation and manipulation of resources, which no doubt seemed inexhaustible while one had the skills and the power to acquire them.

Destructive changes followed. Rapid growth and redistribution of population, along with proliferating technology, are now stressors on the human system (Smyth, in press; Smyth and Stapp, 1993). Established structures which insured stability and continuity break down under this pressure; long-term provision for succeeding generations gives way to competitive opportunism geared to quick returns in the short term. Collectively they lead to a widening gap between rich and poor, and to an impoverished system.

Even biological affinity for our own species is confused. When the human is set against other species people tend to give it preference; wildlife conservation workers, passing through the refugee camps of Rwanda on their way to assess damage to the mountain gorilla population, reported troubled consciences (TV report). But when the human is set alongside itself such considerations do not deter either governments or individuals from all kinds of violence, resolve the conflicting values arising from an unwanted pregnancy, nor yet deter animal rights activists from threatening human life.

So environmental value systems are in some disarray. Natural controls no longer guide us, and the human capacity to reflect is not exercised enough. The acceleration of uncontrolled change in populations, habitats and lifestyles is far beyond the capacity of natural systems to adapt to them. Now it seems we are over-reaching our own capacity to adapt, as Lorenz warned us years ago (1974).

The Nature of Environmental Values

Environmental values have no agreed identity; indeed, as the example from the wood illustrated, they are nearly as variable as the people who espouse them. Even committed environmentalists are spread over a wide spectrum, from extreme ecocentrics at one end to extreme anthropocentrics at the other (O'Riordan, 1983), and are not always good at talking to each other. Among educators a similar distance seems to lie between protagonists of ecological criteria and of social justice. Defining the common ground becomes important.

In Maslow's well-known model (1964) values were related to human needs in a 'hierarchy of relative prepotency' – physiological needs, needs for safety, for the exchange of affection, for esteem and for self-actualization. It is easy to relate these to what we know of human origins, to modern life, and to their abandonment under pressure in reverse order. The model suggests to strategists of environmental education where and how growth of desirable values may be cultivated.

Values represent relationships between people and their environment. Rodger (1993) distinguishes these as follows:

- people as users of the environment (utilitarian values);
- people as managers of the environment (utilitarian modified by prudential values);
- people as protectors of the environment (an extension of management, possibly with restrictions imposed);
- people as admirers of the environment (combining consumer approaches with more spiritual attitudes);
- people as respecters of the environment (as possessing its own integrity and value).

Most people exhibit all of these relationships to some degree, and hold corresponding values, but diminishing from first to fifth, reflecting the tensions which were identified in the wood. Four are essentially means to a better quality of life, so values are instrumental. In the last, however, people value the environment for itself, 'a harmonious relationship . . . not only essential for well-being, it is also intrinsic, effortless, spontaneous, natural' (Meadows, 1989).

A sixth relationship might be added, transcending the rift between humankind and nature – people as integral to their environment. A relationship to be real has to be genuinely lived, however, in a functioning part of a working society (i.e. not insulated from the real world). In our society such relationships may be only temporary or artificial, but they were part of the lives of tribal peoples living in much more direct relationship with their resource base (exemplified by the recorded statements of North American chieftains, and of native Australians to-day). They are not wholly inaccessible; many more people, especially young people, should get the chance to spend time exploring this relationship more fully.

What underpins these higher values? The World Conservation Strategy (IUCN *et al.*, 1980) was based on the maintenance of ecological life-support systems, of genetic diversity (now expanded into biodiversity) and on sustainable use of renewable natural resources. It was proactive rather than reactive to problems, and through the concept of sustainable development it combined the human with the natural system. National strategies followed: the Conservation and Development Programme for the UK, in 1983, added a sustainable society and a stable and sustainable economy to its objectives; a New Zealand strategy recognized cultural, spiritual and other non-material needs of society.

Ecological systems are determined by living matter of a distinctive composition, maintaining and replicating itself in a wide range of conditions over the earth's surface. It keeps working by a flow of solar energy through the system and by the continuous circulation of materials between living matter and the Earth's substance. It has a long history of adaptation and evolution. Aldo Leopold (1970) set out for its human members, in his classic land ethic, a first rule for its valuation – 'a thing is right when it tends to preserve the integrity, stability, and beauty of the biotic community. It is wrong when it tends otherwise.'

Photographs of the planet from outer space gave us, in the sixties, a powerful visual image of its finite resources. They also prepared us for the concept of the ecosphere as a unitary system, made familiar by Lovelock (1979) as Gaia. We know that in the geological past this system has come through catastrophic events when much of it was destroyed, and yet it has recovered and continued to grow more complex. As tenants of the ecosphere we should avoid being both cause and victims of the next such episode, but attach high value to processes which keep the ecosphere intact. Since the system, including these processes, is an end in itself, and there seems to be no reason why it should fail were humankind to vanish, they are intrinsic values.

Discussing the kinds of entities which should be accorded intrinsic value Fox (1994) chooses life itself, quoting as its essential criterion the quality of 'autopoiesis' – the primary and continuous renewal by living systems of their own organizational activity and structure. This is helpful since it can be applied to any level of living system from organism to ecosphere, and extends by implication to the conditions on which they depend. A living system can be valued as a working one, with balanced cycles of production, consumption, biodegradation and renewal, rather than as a collection of valued and inviolable organisms. It should also be valued for its capacity to adapt, to change, and evidently to progress.

Fox points out that intrinsic valuation of living systems shifts the onus of justification for exploiting them from those wishing to protect them to those wishing to interfere, 'a fundamental shift in the terms of environmental debate and decision-making' (p. 212) comparable with a legal system operating on a presumption of innocence until guilt is proved, rather than the reverse. In economic terms this calls for values based on what payment one might accept as compensation for a proposed interference rather than on what one might pay to avert it.

How can people come to own such values? Global life support systems may be fundamental to survival but are not easily grasped either by decision-makers and planners or by the voters, tax-payers, shareholders and customers on whom they depend. Indicators of quality are needed which are recognizable in a more homely environment.

Qualities to Value

Qualities associated with a healthy, stable ecosystem include use of resources in tune with productivity, investment in continuity of the system, biodiversity (including variety of habitats, species and gene pools, their equitable distribution, and population sizes sufficient to maintain them), age of the system, variety of age groups within it, resilience to perturbation, specialization and division of roles, mutualistic as well as exploitative relationships, and high information content (both genetic and acquired).

These qualities refer to natural systems but many transfer readily to humanity. They appear as frugality in use of resources, efficiency, economy of lifestyle, such as recycling wastes, energy conservation in houses, travel and recreation, durability of materials, and others familiar to readers of guides to 'green' living. Balancing environmental against social costs is not as simple as people may think, however, on any criteria. Information content is another quality which should be more highly valued: our resources are over-invested in the ephemeral, the spurious, the sensational and the trivial provided by commercial opportunists of the stressed system.

Biodiversity is a special case of Diversity, a quality of everyday life which is in retreat. Monotonous housing schemes, grass from which other plants have been poisoned out, and beds of uniform bedding plants all reflect monotonous ways of life where stress effects are rampant. In the countryside modern systems of agriculture and forestry exhibit a similar trend. Behind these lie the economic benefits of mass production, distribution and labour-saving. Diversity is a quality of life to be valued highly and paid for where necessary. Schemes to promote cultivation of local distinctiveness, for example, by choosing local trees for roadside planting, respecting vernacular building, local crafts, dialects and customs, improve value development as well as local amenity (HM Government, 1994b).

Sustainability is now enshrined as sustainable development in a succession of international policy documents, notably the Brundtland Report (WCED, 1987, p. 8) and Agenda 21 (UNCED, 1992), and in national action plans, such as defined as development which 'meets the needs of the present without compromising the ability of future generations to meet their own needs'. This at once offers a more personal motivation for environmental care, in keeping with a mature system – care for the wellbeing of our grandchildren, and those who follow.

Unfortunately, it also presents practical problems for both policymakers and educators (see Jickling, 1994). It has been described as 'an ideological counterblast to the greens' (quoted by Elliott, 1993: 20) and its use to legitimize continuing development has appealed to governments in both industrialized and developing countries. Its application is, however, elusive; while one can often recognize unsustainability, indicators of sustainability are difficult to define and apply (Carpenter, 1994). On the other hand, use of sustainable, unqualified by what is to be sustained, is seen both as a disguise for retention of a northern affluent life-style and as a green counterblast to development (Smyth, 1995).

The label *Education for Sustainability*, which has become fashionable, is readable as an instrumental approach under-emphasizing intrinsic values. It has, however, the virtue of integrating humanity into the system. Robin Grove-White recently described sustainability (1994a) as 'a *negotiated* concept, an articulation of a new political mood rather than a sharply etched prescriptive tool'. Its attraction lies in additional, associated values. We are urged, for example, to value equitability, justice and reciprocity, applied not only to relationships between rich and poor countries but to ethnic and cultural groups, classes, genders and age groups in all countries. This was the main theme of UNCED; rich countries, for example, are now challenged to redefine progress and prosperity, and to reconsider quality criteria for living standards, both internationally and at home.

IUCN (1991) tried to clarify what should be valued by listing nine Principles of Sustainable Living – respect and care for the community of life, improving the quality of human life, conserving the earth's vitality and diversity, minimizing depletion of non-renewable resources, keeping within the earth's carrying capacity, changing personal attitudes and practices, enabling communities to care for their own environments, integrating development and conservation and creating a global alliance. But work is still needed to show people how to convert these into local practice.

New thinking released by humankind's adoption into environmental conservation policy may have carried environmental values so far towards the social end of the spectrum that mediation is needed. Breiting's 'New generation of environmental education' (1993: 201), seeking harmony with our descendants rather than with nature and placing 'good householding with nature' as a condition, and Sterling's efforts to develop a more holistic, systemic approach (1993; in press) are moving in the right direction.

Educational Values

Educators now have much advice on how to tackle values in practice, from Michael Caduto's guide (1985) to the recent OECD–ENSI project (Environment and School Initiatives, Kelley-Laine and others, 1993). They are, however, exposed to cross-currents. Many environmentalists expect people to be equipped with an environmental book of rules which it will then be their duty and delight to observe at all times. This accords with a current trend among policy-makers to shift education from reflective thought and action to something more instrumental and market-orientated. The readiness of schools to stop teaching such basic skills as cooking and parenthood indicates further distancing from the real world towards an artificial one. Traditional skills may be needed again, and they should be kept in trim as a matter of pride, if not also of direct benefit.

Education is not meant to promote fixed agendas either for environmental management or for social engineering, but to give people the best possible chances to develop as environmental citizens, armed with knowledge and understanding and practised in applying them to real situations. In those circumstances the values will grow by themselves (Posch, 1993). To do this successfully, however, the learning environment must be a good model.

Many formulations exist of what education should achieve. For example, the recent Scottish strategy for environmental education (SOEnD, 1993) included the following on attitudes:

- a caring attitude and a sense of responsibility for the health and well-being of the whole environment;
- a critical attitude to received information, questioning assumptions, cautious about the reliability of personal interpretations;
- a respect for other people's beliefs, and also for evidence and rational argument;
- a sense of community with other people and other living things;
- a sense of continuity with past and future;
- a respect for human potential to work within environmental constraints and to design the future creatively;
- a commitment to contribute personal talents to improving environmental quality.

When an educator can create a good working atmosphere, be a credible model, value the real over the derived, be positive and health-orientated rather than problem and doom laden, and avoid elementary pitfalls such as 'green fatigue', values should grow ('caught not taught'). The importance of field experience can hardly be overstated, whether the field is wilderness or inner city (and the more kinds the better). The approach should be holistic, learner-centred, critical and self-critical, relevant, problem-formulating, normative rather than empirical, affective integrated with cognitive, adaptable, anticipatory, action orientated, exemplary (SOEnD, 1993). These qualities are to be valued through all education (cf. recommendations on education to the Club of Rome, Botkin Elmandjro and Malitza, 1979).

Conclusion

Values are nourished by visions. If we were to revalue our relations with our environment as we should, and then act on them, the emergent lifestyle might be some kind of neo-puritanism (although we would need to guard against its potential for oppression). We would identify ourselves with a system valued for its integrity, its interconnections, the interdependence of its parts. Its processes would have life-costs, products and effects but no by-products nor side-effects. Value and merit would be attached to cultivating personal skills rather than to labour-saving technologies. We would take pride in living sensitively within the system. Educators would value enjoyment and wonder, creativity and far-sightedness, sharing and self restraint as well as knowledge and understanding. Economists would know how to incorporate environmental values in their calculations. And so on. It would be a more civilized approach to both environment and society than they presently get from what passes as civilization, and it might survive.

Writers often call for new values or a new environmental ethic. But Robin Grove-White, once again, was nearer the mark when he wrote (1994b) that the new values

> may well turn out to be rather old values – echoing classical philo-sophical and religious conceptions of human interdependency, of the limits of human capability, and of humankind's place in the scheme of things.

If so, people have been trying to propagate them for a very long time. In 1991, when material on education was being assembled for Chapter 36 of UNCED's Agenda 21, the Gulf War was in full swing. Men were displaying patterns of behaviour which had hardly changed, save in technical sophistication, since Agamemnon sailed for Troy. It says much for human optimism that the little group in Geneva could still urge the adoption of values for an environmentally and socially sustainable world – and that Heads of State at the Earth Summit still signed up to them.

Perhaps values should always be some way out of reach.

Acknowledgments

This chapter has benefited greatly from recent activities in Scotland, notably the Secretary of State for Scotland's Working Group on Environmental Education and the OECD–ENSI Project, and from all who were associated with them.

References

BERRY, R.J. (1983) 'Environmental ethics and conservation action', in *The Conservation and Development Programme for the UK: A Response to the World Conservation Strategy*, London, Kogan Page, pp. 407–438.

BOTKIN, J.W., ELMANDJRO, M. and MALITZA, M. (1979) *No Limits to Learning: A Report to the Club of Rome*, Oxford, Pergamon Press.

BREITING, S. (1993) 'The new generation of environmental education: Focus on demo-cracy as part of an alternative paradigm', in MRAZEK, R. (Ed) *Alternative Paradigms in Environmental Education Research*, Troy, OH, North American Association for Environmental Education, pp. 199–202.

BRENNAN, A. (1990) *Environmental Philosophy: an Introductory Survey*, St Andrews, University of St Andrews and Nature Conservancy Council.

CADUTO, M.J. (1985) *A Guide on Environmental Values Education: Environmental Education Series 13*, Paris, France, Unesco-UNEP International Environmental Education Programme.

CARPENTER, R.A. (1994) 'Can sustainability be measured?', *Ecology International Bulletin 1994*, 21, pp. 27–36.

COOPER, D.E. (1992) 'The idea of environment' in COOPER, D.E. and PALMER, J.A. (Eds) *The Environment in Question*, London, Routledge, pp. 165–80.

ELLIOTT, J. (1993) 'Handling values in environmental education' in *Values in Environmental Education*, OECD–ENSI Conference Report, May, 1993, (Stirling), Dundee, Scottish Consultative Council on the Curriculum, (SCCC).

FOX, W. (1994) 'Ecophilosophy and science', *The Environmentalist*, **14**, 3, pp. 57–62.

GROVE-WHITE, R. (1994a) 'Editorial', *Environmental Values*, **3**, 3, p. 189.

GROVE-WHITE, R. (1994b) Interlocutor's statement, Workshop 2: Society and Culture, in *Values for a Sustainable Future, World Environment Day Symposium*, London, 2nd. June, 1994.

HM GOVERNMENT (1994a) *Sustainable Development: The UK Strategy*, London, HMSO.

HM GOVERNMENT (1994b) *Biodiversity: The UK Action Plan*, London, HMSO.

IUCN (WORLD CONSERVATION UNION), UNEP and WWF (1980) *World Conservation Strategy: Living Resources Conservation for Sustainable Development*, Gland, Switzerland, IUCN.

IUCN (WORLD CONSERVATION UNION), UNEP and WWF (1991) *Caring for the Earth: A Strategy for Sustainable Living*, Gland, Switzerland, IUCN.

JICKLING, B. (1994) 'Why I don't want my children to be educated for sustainable development', *Trumpeter*, **11**, 3, pp. 114–16.

KELLEY-LAINE, K. (1993) 'The environment and school initiatives (ENSI) project', *Values in Environmental Education*, OECD–ENSI Conference Report, May, 1993, (Stirling), Dundee, SCCC.

LEOPOLD, A.S. (1970) *A Sand County Almanac, With Essays on Conservation from Round River*, New York, Sierra Club/Ballantine Books Inc.

LORENZ, K. (1974) *Civilized Man's Eight Deadly Sins*, transl. M. LATZKE, London, Methuen.

LOVELOCK, J.E. (1979) *Gaia: a New Look at Life on Earth*, Oxford, Oxford University Press.

MASLOW, A.H. (1964) *Religions, Values and Peak Experiences*, Columbus, OH, Ohio State University Press.

MEADOWS, D.H. (1989) *Harvesting One Hundredfold: Key Concepts and Case Studies in Environmental Education*, Nairobi, Kenya, UNEP.

NAUSER, M. (1993) 'Environmental concern and the theory of structuration', in STEINER, D. and NAUSER, M. (Eds) *Human Ecology: Fragments of Anti-fragmentary Views of the World*, London, Routledge, pp. 229–47.

O'RIORDAN, T. (1983) 'The nature of the environmental idea' in O'RIORDAN, T. and TURNER, R.K. (Eds) *An Annotated Reader in Environmental Planning and Management*, Oxford, Pergamon Press.

PATTEN, B.C. (1982) 'Environs: Relativistic elementary particles for ecology', *The American Naturalist*, **119**, pp. 179–219.

POSCH, P. (1993) 'Approaches to values in environmental education', in *Values in Environmental Education*, OECD–ENSI Conference Report, May, 1993 (Stirling), Dundee, SCCC.

RODGER, A.R. (1993) 'Values and relationships towards the environment', in *Values in Environmental Education*, OECD–ENSI Conference Report, May, 1993 (Stirling), Dundee, SCCC.

SOEND (SCOTTISH OFFICE ENVIRONMENT DEPARTMENT) (1993) *Learning for Life: a National Strategy for Environmental Education in Scotland*, Edinburgh, HMSO.

SMYTH, J.C. (1977) 'The biological framework of environmental education', *Journal of Biological Education*, **11**, pp. 103–8.

SMYTH, J.C. (1995) 'Environment and education: A view of a changing scene', *Environmental Education Research*, **1**, 1, pp. 3–20.

Smyth, J.C. (in press) 'Education and environment: The challenge of change', Paper presented to the ATEE Conference, Prague, September, 1994.

Smyth, J.C. and Stapp, W.B. (1993) 'Learning to survive with the biosphere' in Polunin, N. and Burnett, J. (Eds) *Surviving with the Biosphere*, Edinburgh, Edinburgh University Press, pp. 244–52.

Sterling, S. (1993) 'Environmental education and sustainability: A view from holistic ethics', in Fien, J. (Ed) *Environmental Education: A Pathway to Sustainability*, Geelong, Australia, Deakin University Press, pp. 69–98.

Sterling, S. (in press) 'Meeting the challenge of education for sustainability: The potential of the systems approach', Paper presented to the ATEE Conference, Prague, The Czech Republic September, 1994.

UNCED (United Nations Conference on Environment and Development) (1992) *Agenda 21, the United Nations Programme of Action from Rio*, New York, UN Department of Public Information.

Unesco and UNEP (1975) *The International Workshop on Environmental Education*, Belgrade, Yugoslavia, Paris, UNESCO.

Unesco and UNEP (1975) *International Conference on Environmental Education, Tbilisi (USSR): Final Report*. Paris, UNESCO.

Unesco and UNEP (1987) *International Strategy for Action in the Field of Environmental Education and Training for the 1990s*, Paris, UNESCO.

WCED (World Commission on Environment and Development) (1987) *Our Common Future*, Oxford, Oxford University Press.

Chapter 6

Democratic Values and the Foundations of Political Education

Francis Dunlop

ABSTRACT: *This chapter is an attempt to break out of the liberal-democratic mould with regard to the values which should form the basis of political education. After an appeal to our experience of values as the positive and negative qualities of 'objects' given in emotionally tinged experience, and to the diversity of democratic regimes, I argue that* democratic values *must be interpreted as the values of our own traditions of political activity. I extend my attack on the liberal democratic approach to value and human nature into a critical discussion of the democratic values most often canvassed by writers of this school. They need to be reinterpreted in the light of a better understanding of the human condition and the incommensurability of values. However, the liberal democratic tradition has preserved some vital features of an adequate understanding of the political sphere. The values revealed here, coupled with the reinterpreted democratic values and the values displayed in political thinking and action, interpreted in the light of our continuing traditions, form the basis of political education. I end with some brief remarks about the general principles for achieving this.*

Since the terms *democratic* and *values* are used in many ways, I had be
start by trying to indicate how I understand them.

Values and Value-experience

Although still very little known in this country, the best starting-point for
philosophical investigation of values is the work of the (mainly) Germ
speaking philosophers of value, who flourished in the first half of this cent
in close association with the early phenomenological movement (for a b
survey, see Findlay, 1970). These thinkers approached their subject ma
with the two questions: what is given (i.e. what are the data of experier

and how is it given (i.e. through what mental acts or operations)? Even if it be true, as is often said, that the users of this method failed, in the end, to attend satisfactorily to questions of *justification*, their work on classifying values, and on the relations that obtain among them, and above all on exhibiting what a 'theory of values' is to theorize about, provide an invaluable starting point for educational thinkers. In what follows I shall draw on aspects of their work, but leave the large question of justification out of the picture. The values I shall be talking about are, then, ineliminable data of experience, and, whatever their metaphysical status may be thought to be, cannot be ignored without producing a radically false picture of human life. This approach is not dissimilar to that of John White in some of his more recent work (for example, 1982:68ff; 1990:23ff).

Values, then, are given as *qualities* of things. We experience the world, and what constitutes it (including persons, events, actions, physical and mental objects – in short, every kind of thing), as possessing positive or negative qualities, or (most frequently) a mixture of the two, as being good or bad (or both) in various respects. Talk of values as such, is, then, essentially abstract, like talk of kinds of things. But values are important to us. Objects possessing value are experienced as attractive or repulsive, admirable or despicable, in countless modes and degrees, but in every case eliciting from the one who experiences them some sort of pro or con response, in which there is an element of emotion or feeling. Hence the essential link with action. Values provide us with reasons for action. This does not mean that the experience of values necessarily results in our doing something in some overt or public sense, since, as in the case of aesthetic values, they may suggest merely some form of silent appreciation, though this is still at least a mental act, capable of being, in Hildebrand's term, 'disavowed'. But it is a characteristic of our experience of values that we feel some sort of response to be required of us; even if the response comes automatically or habitually, rather than being deliberately willed (or withheld), we experience it as in some way appropriate or inappropriate, to be identified with or disavowed (Hildebrand, 1953: Ch. 18).

It seems also to be an ineliminable part of our experience of values that there is more than one type of value. Moral values are fundamentally different from aesthetic values, and the existence of possible borderline cases, let alone the difficulty of establishing theoretically what the difference consists in, does not in the least alter the fact that we are aware of a difference. *Intellectual* values (making up the triad of 'truth, beauty and goodness') are less obviously a type of value distinct from moral and aesthetic values, though a case can certainly be made out. Few have disputed the candidacy of *hedonic* values, or the values of pleasurable and painful sensations, though some have argued that the phenomenon of value takes on a radically different hue in their case. Many have discerned a category of *religious* values (Max Scheler called them the values of the Holy and the Unholy) and also a class of *vital* values, the values and disvalues of flourishing or merely surviving life. These last seem to have something in common with hedonic values but to be given as distinct, since the demands of pleasure and of health frequently clash, and vital satis-faction (in strenuous achievement, for example) may be accompanied by considerable pain. At the very least we need to distinguish sensory pleasures from what the Germans call the pleasures of *functioning* (*Funktionslust*).

Some experience of hierarchy among values seems also to be unavoid-able; hence the common Anglo-Saxon analysis of moral reasons as over-riding other kinds of reasons. Other philosophers of value have drawn attention to the extremely important category of urgency among values, most gener-ally expressed in the moral demand that the abolition of evils must take precedence over the provision of goods. Incommensurability is also part of value-experience; values, for example love and justice, gracefulness and im-pressiveness, cannot be reduced to one another.

One other important point relates to the ultimate status of values. As is well known, many people today talk loosely about 'my values' or 'so-and-so's values', in a way that suggests either that they think all values are relative to the individual (or group) or that they are using the phrase as a shorthand for 'my preferences among (perhaps more or less equal) values', or someone's choices among given values, and the like. The early value-philosophers were aware that certain things meant more to some than to others (at both indi-vidual and group level), but were extremely reluctant to conclude (since it contradicted experience) that all values were relative. Their solution was to think of values on an analogy with the starry heavens; since human beings are inevitably situated in different places, they inevitably see different parts of the whole. Objectivity is preserved, while relativity of experience is accounted for.

The Meaning of Democratic Values

What then of *democratic values*? No-one, as far as I am aware, has ever suggested that these are a type of values in the way that moral, aesthetic or hedonic values are a type. The natural way to take them – and the structure of this book encourages this – is in a departmental sense. Democratic values are the values centrally connected with a distinct department of life, and hence of education, as in religious values, health values, or economic values. They would, then, include both the values of democracy as such, and also the values which must be possessed by things (persons, social conditions, institu-tions, and so on) if democracy is to be possible or sustainable, as well as the values of things (or persons, etc.) which are brought about by democracy.

But to my mind there is something highly unsatisfactory about this. For what is democracy as such? If we survey the number of regimes which have been called democratic we find an enormous variety. No doubt all these re-gimes have possessed some values, and equally indubitably some disvalues, but can we really extract sufficient in common to talk soberly about demo-cratic values in this very general sense? I find this rather implausible.

The point can be made another way by noting that, if we divide up the sphere of values departmentally, we are applying a number of descriptive terms. Even though the word *economic* sometimes denotes a value (as in 'an economic solution'), the term must be used descriptively in the phrase economic values if it is to be of any use. Exactly the same applies to democratic. But its extreme openness precludes its usefulness in this respect. It must be admitted that we often know roughly what certain people mean when, in specific contexts, they complain that people are not being democratic enough. But such uses are highly context-dependent, and the more general and abstract the talk is (as in 'the democratic way of life'), the vaguer these and similar phrases sound. It seems clear that, if the term *democratic values* is supposed to pick out the values of a department of life, we had better substitute the term *political*, which is much less vague than *democratic*.

The Liberal Democratic Ideological Take-over

Unfortunately, philosophy of education in this country (I speak for the United Kingdom only) has in recent years been hag-ridden by the assumption that only a liberal democratic (or 'rational-liberal') interpretation of this department of life is morally acceptable. One writer on education and democracy has even gone as far as to say that she is not particularly interested in what is meant by the word *democratic* – though she uses it fairly freely; what she is really interested in is 'government according to moral principles' (P. White, 1973:228, note 17). Given the diversity of moral principles (and the incommensurability among moral values) and the need to apply all sorts of other (non-moral) principles to the work of government, this drastic move is singularly unproductive. But the important point here is that one tradition of democratic thought is being given a morally privileged position, whereas educational institutions, even if *some* form of democracy can be taken as read, might be expected to point to a variety of forms. Most contemporary liberal democrats would certainly object very strongly were it to be assumed that a particular form of Capitalism was the only morally permissible economic system.

It seems to me that the liberal democrats have largely carried the day because of their utopian strain. One of the main objections to their interpretation of democracy is that it pays almost no attention to what human beings are actually like. If it is, for example, objected that people are not rational enough to consider every decision simply on its merits (which usually means in terms of the rationality-based trio 'liberty, fairness and respect for persons'), it is always said that, even if that is unfortunately true at present, we can change it; if this is countered with the point that this has often been tried, and without much success, it is retorted that we have not tried hard enough. This is a strikingly frequent kind of move and betrays the utopian refusal to accept reality, in this case human reality, as though one could start afresh from the divine drawing-board. This rejection of the actual human condition, together with a failure to grasp the primarily 'embodied' nature of value, and the incommensurability of many if not all values, gives much liberal-democratic writing a desiccated and fanatical quality. Its dogged assumption that all justified values can be derived from the one value of rationality is, as Aurel Kolnai has argued, peculiarly corrupting, since it atrophies our natural sense of values, and draws attention away from the historically situated value-realities around us (see Kolnai, 1995).

However, it cannot be denied that liberal democracy has been the guardian in recent centuries of something enormously important – namely the Judaeo-Christian-inspired value of the individual person. It also lays a vital stress on the general importance of moral values in politics (not to be confused with the claim that the only values needed to settle practical problems are moral ones), and sets up protective limits to political action with its emphatic insistence on constitutionalism. What it conspicuously lacks, as I have implied – at least in some versions – is the idea of ineliminable conflicts among values, institutionalized in the idea of an official parliamentary opposition. Liberal democratic theory by itself incurs the danger of encouraging the One-Party state.

The Importance of Given Political Traditions

In my brief remarks about democracy I have drawn attention to the existence of multiple interpretations of it (and hence of democratic values), and implied that the historical situatedness of human beings, and the existence of value-incommensurability, make the rational liberal claim that, on purely moral grounds, its own interpretation of democracy ought always to prevail preposterous. Despite the fact that the liberal tradition does witness to, and, indeed, preserves, certain supremely important values, we cannot possibly allow a liberal-democratic take-over of the field. On the other hand, to pretend that the field of political choices is quite open – beginning from the time when political education first starts in school – would seem equally preposterous.

We must take our cue here from the fact that values are first given to us as qualities of 'objects'. It is by being confronted with (or told about) acts of injustice, in the presence of someone who is not trying to disguise his feeling-response, that we learn what the disvalue of injustice is, or deepen our abhorrence of it. No doubt we can later imagine acts of injustice, but the disvalue must first be experienced in real examples. Hence we cannot in general learn about democratic values except by engaging directly or at second-hand (never as good, other things being equal) in democracy as we already have it. The liberal democratic yearning for 'a thorough-going democracy' is really quite empty of content, and can have no place in any responsible educational programme.

A related point concerns the general justification of fastening on some *one* form of government as the centre of political education. In the work of Richard Peters we may see, despite the highly abstract justifications actually provided, a firm conviction that the best of our traditions already are (or were) liberal democratic ones, and a (very reasonable) desire to hang on to them, or at least move forward from them (see, for example, Peters, 1966: Ch. XI, sections 1 and 2). Some of his disciples, with their continued insistence that we are 'not democratic enough', breathe a totally different spirit from Peters, and show a cavalier readiness to ditch any tradition that does not measure up to their artificial yardstick (see P. White, 1973; 1983). But the general argument from tradition must be strong, since our public and political selves are largely constituted or formed by inherited ways of behaving. When a country's government repudiates established traditions, and sets out to change things in the name of Reason, countless acts of injustice are done to individual citizens, quite apart from the damage that may be inflicted on the social fabric – that loose framework of institutions which enables individuals to live their private lives. Peters himself, of course, and many of his successors talk rather complacently about our 'tradition of criticism'. But there must be limits to this. Change presupposes continuity. Relentless criticism undermines confidence. In any case the theoretical accounts people give of our traditions diverge from one another. In the end it is traditions or established practices that have the priority. All this strengthens the case for political education's being centred on democracy, but it must start from the actual political traditions we have, not (or not primarily) from some theoretical account of them, let alone from pure theory.

Some Democratic Values Discussed

And so we come at last to the democratic values which should provide the foundation of political education in our schools. I can do no more here than briefly discuss some of those values most commonly put forward as democratic in philosophy of education, and show how they need to be criticized or modified in the light of what we have argued so far about values and human nature. I shall close with some brief remarks about the education of such values.

One of the most general problems relating to democratic values is the clash between the individual and the social, or between the conception of society as composed of atomic individuals (as in most Social Contract theories) whose wills must be rationally aligned, and the conception of society as a solidary community where the 'general will' can and should hold sway. Liberal democracy has, of course, favoured the first, but has itself become lately more aware of the virtues of community, as the social cement holding our society together continues to dissolve. Hence the impression that community has sometimes been tacked on to originally autonomy-centred lists of democratic values. But there is a real tension here, which educators must take cognisance of. The tension can only be intelligently, if partially, resolved where there is an adequate understanding of the human person. Man needs community, of course; persons are social beings. But they are not cattle or sheep, always thinking and willing 'as one' (though there will be something of this at some level of their lives; recall the phenomena of fashion, or the collective sadness after a national disaster). For man has a conscience, moral and intellectual, and must sometimes stand alone (though our moral and intellectual – 'personal' – being must be reared on socially shared foundations).

This interpretation of the human person in terms of *levels* (further explained in Dunlop, 1984; cf. Dunlop, 1991) may also help us grasp the nettle of equality. No sense at all can be made out of a claim that equality is, as such, a value. But, if the origins of the belief that it is lie in the Judaeo-Christian idea that all human beings are equally persons in the eyes of God (all being equally far from God's infinite goodness, and so on), then we may intelligibly locate 'the value of equality' in the purely personal element of human being, and see it instantiated in the equal vote at elections, equality before the law, and the equal right to contribute to the formation of public opinion. But at the vital level of our being, at the level of individual talents, skills, capacities, instincts, and so on, which are all also bearers of value, no plausible case for a value of equality can be made out. To what extent equality of income, opportunity, and so on, will make for the recognition of formal personal equality, is a debatable point; but on the answer to that sort of question depends any value that bestowable material equalities may have.

Liberty is another controversial value, about which one may legitimately disagree. Clearly there is great value in a person's liberation from unjust confinement, and analogous situations, and the sheer formal exercise of free will is an aspect of human dignity, an expression of the value of human personhood. But the whole discussion of liberty (and of the closely related autonomy) in philosophy of education has suffered from the liberal assumption (taken *ad absurdum* by Sartre) that the human person is somehow defined by liberty, and that this primal freedom is unbounded. But the human condition is largely founded on natural and social determinations (not least one's native language), and – since we have no 'natural' outfit of real instincts to prompt our behaviour – must be so. This is by no means the same as claiming that free will is an illusion. But it is to insist that freedom is limited, and that it is always bought at the price of restrictions. One must be bound at one level (by natural dispositions, habits, principles, institutions, laws) to acquire more freedom where it really matters – in the purely personal realm.

Tolerance is also far more problematic than usually realized. This moral quality goes closely with the humble admission that any person (including oneself) may be wrong, that all are in any case of limited capacities (including oneself), and hence that nobody can achieve a God-like view of the Whole, or be a complete embodiment of rationality. But when tolerance is interpreted as the value of 'live and let live' it tends to bring about a reduction of all values to hedonic ones. The idea that I should simply accept everyone's beliefs and preferences *whatever they are*, encourages the idea that beliefs and preferences are in themselves unimportant – merely the expression of subjective whims. The clash here can, to my mind, only be resolved by acknowledging the shared foundational restraints of community (there must be limits to tolerance), but approaching 'the other', in his personal being, with respect and humility. At its best, parliament illustrates this well.

The discussion of tolerance reminds us once again how important it is to keep alive the sense of respect or reverence for high value, and how easily responses to value can be written off as the expression of subjective wants. This decay of a sense of value has been encouraged by the attack on social hierarchies of all kinds. For, however imperfectly (and it always *is* imperfectly) they do it, human hierarchies symbolize value-hierarchies. They are also an essential need of our vital or social being, as the Socialist Simone Weil saw; destroy the old hierarchies and their place will always be taken by new ones. Two related questions then suggest themselves: first, do the existing hierarchies, or some of them, in the long run help or hinder the sense of value? Second, how well do they reflect the multiplicity of value and types of value, and the relations between values? The importance of hierarchy (better, of hierarchies) may be acknowledged without wishing to transform society into a standing army. There need be nothing authoritarian about this acknowledgment of our real natures. Liberal democrats are all too often obsessed by their impatient desire to recreate society on the model of personal being only – without its vital or animal substructure.

An important set of values cluster round the idea of citizenship, including the moral values of responsibility and public-spiritedness. Lying behind it is the idea of participation, the sense of being 'part of the show', with a job to do to 'keep it on the road'. It draws attention to the fact that the people are, at the least, partners in government, to whom the personnel of government are in the end answerable and from whom they must derive their ultimate support and title to govern. Some democratic traditions also strongly connect it with loyalty and patriotism. The former implies a readiness to go on supporting the constitution, or one's party, even when its leaders make mistakes or do things one disapproves of (though, of course, there will be limits to this). The latter, in the sense of 'love for one's country', is often confused with nationalism, and pilloried by some liberal democrats. Clearly the idea of Rationality, as an all-embracing value from which all others are derived, has in the end no place for the particular and personal. This is of a piece with the liberal disregard of human realities. But patriotism does not entail false beliefs about one's country; love of country is a kind of gratitude – one loves one's country because it is one's own, is thoroughly familiar, and has done much to make one the person one is – analogously to filial love. It is of course true that any love for the particular implies relative indifference to what is not part of it: possible hostility, therefore, to the 'out-group'. This very general problem of love can only be solved by distinguishing types and levels of obligation; obviously the moral is, as such, the business of humanity, and expresses the experience of the human race, though actual concrete moralities will be given to the individual as largely constituted by special and contractual obligations to family, friends, employers, colleagues, neighbours, fellow-citizens, and so on, in a range of ever-widening circles of application and diminished urgency.

Other Values in Political Education

In so far as our general concern is political education in a country with democratic traditions, the values just discussed, together with other broad and general values, need to be supplemented with a host of other, mostly lower,
values of political thinking and action, such as the values of timing, leadership,
the formation of public opinion, compromise, imagination, balance, political
will, vision and inspiration, confidence-building, and so on. They reflect the
fact that politics is, in the end, about trying to improve things (inserting the
corporately desirable into the texture of historical reality), not just about deciding what ought to be done. But, in so far as quality of political behaviour,
that is, the way the various institutions of our political life are properly used,
or, alternately, exploited, depends heavily on response to moral value as
such, a general moral education will be an indispensable prelude to it. Unless
we can quite simply trust those who form the personnel of government and
closely influence its decisions, disillusion with politics quickly grows and the
threat of totalitarianism grows with it.

Education in Democratic Political Values

It might seem from what has been argued above that political education would
be best achieved by setting up institutions and practices in schools which
reflected on a small scale the political institutions of society at large (i.e. in
liberal democratic language, 'making schools more democratic'). I have argued
elsewhere that this would be a mistake (Dunlop, 1979). Briefly, our political
institutions presuppose use rather than misuse. Moral maturity is taken for
granted, whereas schools are still trying to develop it in their pupils. Again,
school teaching, or real education as opposed to instruction, requires hierarchy (at least of teachers over taught), whereas political participation – in our
tradition – requires formal 'equality'. If the school is to do its job it must be a
community, where, to a large extent, pupils are being initiated into a common
culture. Thus the scope for 'democratizing' schools in any important sense is
bound to be pretty limited, though there is no doubt room for class elections
to class offices, and for strictly limited political activity at year or school level.

The values of political education, with its foundational moral education,
will have to be handed on in other ways, for the most part. A chapter about
values is not the place to develop a treatment of moral obligation, so this must
be left on one side. But the prime way in which sensitivity to values in general
is developed is by drawing pupils' attention to values, as they are encountered
in historical and literary examples, and the objects of other school subjects,
and in the life of school and society (see also Ch. 5 of Dunlop, 1984). As we
have implied, this inculcation of values is not a merely intellectual matter, not
simply a matter of naming things and having them recalled. The full experience

of values has something emotional about it. Hence teachers must themselves be responsive to values, and not seek to disguise this. They must show values, supplementing the merely intellectual reference by tone of voice, facial expression, gesture and deportment. If the natural hierarchical relation between old and young is not being interfered with by other factors (such as deep-rooted cultural or personal alienation), this must have its effect in time, but is not something easily calculated or controlled. Subject matter can certainly be chosen with a view to its value-illustrative potential but there is little scope for anything in the nature of exercises in value-appreciation. Far more important is the general attempt to develop an attitude of reverent attention to the world, a growing ability to put one's own concerns aside and be simply responsive to the world (and its contents) 'with heart and mind'.

This will, of course, happen fairly naturally if teachers are allowed to relax with their pupils, and do not feel the need to inhibit their usual responses to political and other valuational subject-matter (though it is, of course, vastly easier in the early years of schooling than in the years of adolescence). There is some danger of indoctrination here, but, rather than emasculate educational transactions by making some value-content taboo, schools can try to ensure a balance of political orientation among the teachers of various subjects, or at least of particular classes, and above all ensure that the teachers fully appreciate the virtues or positive values of the traditions they do not actually hold as their own. It is an essential part of all value-education, above all in any kind of democratic tradition, to show how one may do justice to an opponent while not agreeing with him.

It may be objected that I have said remarkably little about 'reasoning' here. The cause is simple. Adequate reasoning, in political, moral and other predominantly valuational contexts, *presupposes* an adequate grasp of values. Value-education, in any sphere, is thus the foundation of reason in that sphere, not its product. (Hence, too, the woeful inadequacy of seeing persons primarily as choosers, or practical reasoners; the crucial prior sphere of receptivity – of taking in the wealth of the world's values – is left out of the picture.) This has long been ignored by educators, mesmerized by the endeavour to subject all values (and choices) to the one single but mythical Rationality. No wonder R.S. Peters and other liberal democrats were accused by various left-wing thinkers of imposing 'knowledge for control' (Young, 1971). These critics of liberal education had an important point. We can accept that while emphatically rejecting their own line. For in the end constitutionalism (which sets strict limits to governmental power and makes its wielders accountable to the people), respect for moral values in public life and for the unique value of the individual person, is, in my own view, far more likely to survive in a more conservative democratic setting (this has little to do with the present Conservative Party!), than a liberal democratic one. But this should form no part of political education as such. It should be clear by now that the ability to be responsive to the values (and, eventually, disvalues) of our traditions is what schools should be promoting in this sphere, and this means values wherever they are to be found. It does not preclude eventual change; but it does provide an essential prelude to rational change.

References

DUNLOP, F.N. (1979) 'On the democratic organization of schools', *Cambridge Journal of Education*, **9**, 1, pp. 43–54.

DUNLOP, F.N. (1984) *The Education of Feeling and Emotion*, London, Allen & Unwin.

DUNLOP, F.N. (1991) 'The Rational-liberal neglect of human nature', *Journal of Philosophy of Education*, **25**, 1, pp. 109–20.

FINDLAY, J.N. (1970) *Axiological Ethics*, London, Macmillan.

HILDEBRAND, D. von (1953) *Ethics*, Chicago, IL, Franciscan Herald Press.

KOLNAI, A. (1995) *The Utopian Mind and Other Papers*, in DUNLOP, F. (Ed), London, Athlone.

PETERS, R.S. (1966) *Ethics and Education*, London, Allen and Unwin.

WHITE, J. (1982) *The Aims of Education Restated*, London, Routledge and Kegan Paul.

WHITE, J. (1990) 'The aims of education', in ENTWISTLE, N. (Ed) *Handbook of Educational Ideas and Practices*, London, Routledge and Kegan Paul.

WHITE, P. (1973) 'Education, democracy and the public interest', in PETERS, R.S. (Ed) *The Philosophy of Education*, Oxford, Oxford University Press.

WHITE, P. (1983) *Beyond Domination: An Essay in the Political Philosophy of Education*, London, Routledge and Kegan Paul.

YOUNG, M.F.D. (Ed) (1971) *Knowledge and Control: New Directions for the Sociology of Education*, London, Collier-Macmillan.

Chapter 7

Values in the Arts

David Best

ABSTRACT: *There are three principal interdependent strands in the argument of this chapter: a) contrary to popular assumptions, values in the arts are fully objective; b) a central characteristic of the arts is that they can offer insights into life-issues and thus the values expressed in the arts can influence attitudes to life generally; and c) the main contribution of education generally is, or should be, to open fresh horizons of thought, feeling and value. It is the objectivity of values which allows this possibility. In this respect, the arts can have a seminal influence on personality development, by offering real alternative possibilities of being. This is the most profound, pervasive, yet widely neglected, potential value of what can be learned from the arts, and by no means only in the formal education system. The almost universal conflation of the aesthetic and the artistic tends to trivialize the arts, and is conducive to the subjectivism which is still so self-defeatingly prevalent among arts-educators. Hence this chapter is concerned with artistic, not aesthetic, education.*

Preface

The crucial but largely misunderstood topic of the values intrinsic to the arts involves almost, if not quite, the whole of philosophy of the arts. I shall outline the questions which seem to me of greatest educational importance and about which there is the most widespread persistent and damaging confusion (see Best, 1993a, for a more thorough explanation of these issues.)

There are three closely related questions which I shall consider:

1   the objectivity of values;
2   the relationship of the arts to life generally;
3   opening horizons of feeling, understanding and value.

I shall approach these principal themes via the generally unrecognized distinction between the aesthetic and the artistic.

Before beginning, it may be worth inserting a cautionary note. A richly rewarding aspect of the arts is that they are so immensely varied in character. It is important to be aware of this, for there is a common tendency to distort or limit this widely varied character in considering the arts in general. This danger is implicit in assumptions and explicit assertions that the arts constitute a generic community. The doctrine of generic arts was until recently gaining ground, and there was a danger of its informing curriculum policy, but it is now, fortunately, largely and rightly discredited.[1]

The Aesthetic and the Artistic

The artistic is still widely, almost universally, conflated with the aesthetic, or at least any distinction between the two concepts is blurred and confused. This confusion is often expressed in the, usually implicit, assumption that the artistic is a species of the aesthetic. The distinction may at first sight appear to amount merely to verbal quibbling, but reflection reveals that it has substantial implications which cannot be adequately considered here.[2] However, I offer an outline, since it is central to the question of values, and it explains why this chapter is concerned with *artistic*, rather than aesthetic, value.

By contrast with the generally assumed conflation, I argue that the aesthetic and the artistic are two distinct, if sometimes interdependent, concepts. The two most important, closely related, aspects of the distinction are a) in general, far more understanding is involved in artistic than in aesthetic judgments; and (b) the failure to recognize it connives in the prevalent trivializing of the arts as involving mere subjective preferences, i.e. the assumption that an artistic judgment amounts merely to whether one likes the work or not.

For example, one may greatly appreciate Indian classical dance without understanding the symbolic movements which at least largely constitute its meaning. In such a case, one's appreciation is obviously aesthetic: it cannot be artistic, since one lacks the relevant understanding. Numerous such examples could be cited from all the arts. This clearly indicates that there are two distinct concepts. Nevertheless, they may be related. For instance, where one does have the relevant understanding, an aesthetic appreciation of the dancers' movements may be part of one's artistic appreciation of the dance performance.

Aesthetic judgments may be made about almost anything. Hence a practical danger of the conflation is that it could be seen as legitimizing a reduction, or even the elimination, of arts teaching in schools. 'Aesthetic education', regarded (unintelligibly) as the development of a general faculty[3], including the arts, could be achieved by taking children on nature-walks, watching sunsets etc., without the unnecessary expense of arts resources, and teachers. That this is no abstract danger is shown by the examples in primary schools cited by Taylor and Andrews (1993).

Beauty

Some years ago a letter was written to a journal objecting to a paper in which I had argued for the objectivity of artistic appreciation. The author objected that my argument was a straw man, since, he insisted, the real issue, which has for centuries been the principal quest of philosophy of the arts, concerns such explicitly evaluative judgments as, 'This is a beautiful painting.'

He was right that this has been the traditional quest of the philosopher, but that quest is thoroughly misconceived. It is the persistent conflation of the aesthetic and the artistic which is the straw man: the traditional assumption that beauty (or, worse, Beauty) is the central issue is integral to it. Despite this still-prevalent assumption (perhaps especially in continental Europe), questions of beauty are usually irrelevant to artistic appreciation. Imagine going to music concerts, plays, art-exhibitions, etc. with someone who says he appreciates these arts, yet who, when asked for his opinion of a work, always replies: 'It is (or is not) beautiful', or some similar comment. We ask his opinion of Shakespeare's *King Lear* and Dostoievsky's *The Brothers Karamazov*, and again he replies: 'They are beautiful.' If this were the only kind of response he made, that would constitute good grounds for believing that he *lacked* the ability for artistic appreciation. One would be bewildered, for example, if, following a powerful production of Shakespeare's *Measure for Measure*, one were to be asked whether the play was beautiful. That may be an intelligible question about some works of art, for instance ballet, but for many it would make little or no sense. Even those with a high regard for Francis Bacon's works are unlikely to regard them as beautiful. Indeed, many artists would, justifiably, regard it as insulting to have their work discussed in terms of beauty. It has been said that beauty is what the bourgeoisie pays the artist for.

Artistic appreciation is rather revealed in the ability, for instance, to discuss, recognize, and propose valid and perceptive interpretations, and to give reasons for what one values in a work. In many cases aesthetic judgments may amount simply to individual preference or subjective taste, as, for instance, in the choice of ice cream, house-decorations etc. These may involve little or no rational or cognitive content. In other cases, such as gymnastics and other sports, valid aesthetic judgments do require relevant understanding. Yet since aesthetic judgments can often be plausibly regarded as expressions of mere subjective preference, to fail to distinguish the aesthetic and the artistic may be to connive in the perniciously prevalent misconception that artistic appreciation is also a matter of mere non-rational, subjective taste or preference, or that artistic values are merely a matter of individual psychology.

Thus, the failure to recognize the importance of the distinction between the aesthetic and the artistic may contribute largely to the trivialization of the potential educational value of the arts.

The Objectivity of Values

Artistic appreciation and creation are fully objective, in that artistic judgments are supportable by reasons which refer to one's understanding of qualities of the object. An objection is sometimes raised which is closely related to, or part of, the deeply embedded misconception considered above, namely that even though judgments of meaning and interpretation may be answerable to rational discussion, these are irrelevant to the central issue, which is that of value judgments.

But this objection is confused, since obviously one cannot make an intelligible value judgment unless one understands the work. Evaluation is inseparable from understanding. For instance, one's evaluation may change, even radically, if one comes to recognize that a work contains ironic or other subtleties which one had previously failed to appreciate. More obviously, some evaluative judgments are incompatible with certain interpretations.

More important, this reveals one of the most wide-ranging and pernicious assumptions of the traditional subjectivist doctrine, namely that value judgments are necessarily merely subjective. This misconception is surprisingly persistent. For even cursory reflection reveals that if it were true that value judgments were mere subjective expressions of individual preference or psychology, then *no* education at all, in *any* subject, would be possible. For to learn any discipline, including, for example, in the sciences and mathematics, is to learn to discriminate what counts objectively as good or bad, valid or less valid, within it. That is, to be educated in any subject or area of knowledge is to learn to grasp and use, practically, its objective criteria of value. One has, for instance, to learn what counts as better or worse reasoning or evidence, and clearly this is to evaluate. One could not have even the slightest understanding of any subject without learning to evaluate by its criteria.

It is of the utmost importance, not only for the arts but for morality and education generally, to eradicate the remarkably prevalent yet seriously damaging misconception that value judgments are purely subjective. For example, in discussion people often say: 'Oh, that's just a value judgment', as if that is the end of the matter, in that value judgments are assumed unquestionably to be expressions of mere subjective preferences, to which the notion of objective reasoning has no application. Yet, on the contrary, so far from being the *end* of the matter, the expression of a value judgment is only the *beginning* since, of course, one can and characteristically does give reasons to support it. One may be mistaken, there may be differences of opinion, but such possibilities necessarily presuppose objective criteria which constitute the sense of such differences and the reasons offered in support.

What creates considerable confusion about, and unnecessary opposition to, the notion that values can be objective is a persistent misconception about objectivity. In arguing that no education makes sense at all, whether in the arts or in other disciplines, without objective criteria of value, I am certainly not contending that there are necessarily absolute values. On the contrary, what I am saying, to repeat, is that the objectivity of value judgments consists in the possibility of giving supporting reasons by reference to one's understanding of qualities of the object. But this answerability to reason does not in the least imply a single definitive interpretation, or evaluation. The sciences are rightly accepted unquestionably as fully objective disciplines. Yet fundamental changes of conception and differences of interpretation occur even in the most soundly established scientific theories. The distinguished mathematician and astronomer Bondi writes:

> I regard the very use of the word 'fact' as misleading, because 'fact' is an emotive word which suggests something hard and firm . . . [Yet] certain experiments that were interpreted in a particular way in their day we now interpret quite differently – but they were claimed as 'facts' in those days (1972).

The philosopher of science, Bronowski, makes a similar point:

> The world is not a fixed, solid array of objects, for it cannot be fully separated from our perception of it. It shifts under our gaze, and the knowledge that it yields has to be interpreted by us (1973).

Moreover, the notion of differences of opinion, so far from supporting subjectivism, actually makes no sense on a subjectivist basis. If you and I disagree, there is a position which one of us asserts and the other denies, and an implicit agreement about what objectively counts as a reason which supports one or the other. Without such a background of culturally shared grounds of rationality there could be no *sense* in the notion of disagreement, or differences of opinion. On a subjectivist basis a disagreement would amount merely to personal preferences passing by each other, and that could not count as disagreement at all. Disagreements, and changes of interpretation, are characteristic of the sciences not *despite* but *because of* their fully objective nature. The objective criteria of any discipline, including the arts and sciences, constitute the sense of what counts as support for the contending positions, and therefore the notion of disagreement would make no sense without such objective criteria.

A persistent source of confusion, then, which distorts the character of knowledge generally, is an incoherently rigid assumption about the nature of objectivity. The deep-rooted conviction is that objectivity concerns absolute and universal facts. This is a source of the prevalent assumption that the arts, and artistic values, are purely subjective, since artistic values are obviously not absolute and universal. The most damaging aspect of this self-defeating assumption is that it continues to be widely canvassed implicitly or explicitly by arts-educators and theorists themselves.[4] It is small wonder that the arts are marginalized in education and society, and that artistic values are dismissed as of no serious significance, when arts' protagonists themselves proclaim a doctrine which carries the inevitable consequence that there is no legitimate place for the arts in education. Yet, sadly, even among arts teachers and theorists, the unquestioned assumption that artistic values are subjective dies hard – indeed, it shows no symptom yet even of a terminal disease.

This deeply confused assumption is part of what I call the Myth[5], of two supposedly distinct and inimical mental realms or faculties – on one hand an objective (in the incoherently narrow sense)/cognitive/rational realm; and on the other hand, a subjective/feeling/creative/personal realm. Value judgments are supposed to be part of this latter category of the subjective.

To put the point briefly, this subjectivist Myth presupposes a grossly oversimple conception of objectivity, which both caricatures the sciences, and consigns the arts to marginalized triviality. It has to be clearly recognized that the sciences, unquestioned paradigms of objectivity, are emphatically *not* concerned with absolute, universal, imagination-free, value-aseptic facts: the arts are emphatically *not* concerned with non-rational, non-cognitive, occult, subjective feelings. The sciences necessarily involve imagination and value judgments, as do the arts: the arts are as objective and rational as the sciences.

Reading Meanings In

A common mistake, which contributes to the assumption that artistic values must be subjective, is to take it that any values attributed to a work of art are merely read in. This would render unintelligible any possibility of valid interpretation and thus of artistic meaning. Yet, on the contrary, what constitutes a valid interpretation is that it is not read in, but is objectively supported by reference to features of the work. To say that a judgment of artistic value is read in to the work is to discredit that judgment: to the extent that it is read in it is invalid. To be valid, illuminating and enriching, a judgment has, for instance, to be supported by the text, the score, the painting, the performance. In this respect there is an exact parallel with the objectivity of the sciences, where a valid conclusion has to be supported by the evidence.

An important aspect of education in the arts is learning to recognize and eradicate readings in, and developing the ability for making and appreciating increasingly perceptive, objective interpretations and evaluations of the works of art themselves.

Associations

A related and equally common misconception is to assume or contend that artistic values consist in personal associations. It is true that in some cases associations may be partly relevant to artistic meaning and value. But obviously not *any* association can be relevant. That I may feel sad when I hear the joyful first movement of a Schubert string quartet, because of its associations with a violinist-friend who died years ago, is completely irrelevant to its meaning and artistic value. Such a response, indeed, could not count as a response of *artistic* appreciation, since it would not be identified by, or logically related to, objective features of the music. Indeed, if it be supposed that all meaning, whether artistic or linguistic, consists entirely of individual associations, then there could be no meaning at all: even cursory reflection reveals the supposition as senseless.

In most cases personal associations are not necessary for the appreciation of artistic meaning and value. Sometimes associations may be required, as, for instance, in a cartoon lampooning Mrs Thatcher. But in most cases such associations, which require prior experience, are not necessary. It is of the utmost importance educationally to recognize that there is a huge range of values which can be acquired through involvement with the arts. Clearly, children learn to understand and respond to numerous life situations through stories, literature, play-acting and so on well before they have encountered similar situations in life. Artistic, moral and other values are implicit in such learning, mainly, at first, through immediate response, and then through reflection. This, as I shall argue later, is the most powerful educational potential of the arts. Part of the reason for this powerful learning-potential is precisely that associations are not necessary for the appreciation of values.

It is true, and important, that a general experience of life is necessary for adequate appreciation of very many works of art, which is why very young children are incapable of appreciating Shakespeare or Tolstoy. Moreover, there may be no sharp distinction between relevant association and general life-experience. Nevertheless, in general, personal associations are not necessary for the appreciation and learning of the values involved in arts-education.

Individuality

A related tendency is to assume that the individuality of response, which is such an important characteristic of involvement with the arts, necessarily implies the subjectivity of values. For example, a good teacher is concerned, as far as possible, with what is right for *each* student, and with the most fruitful and enriching development of each student's individual abilities and potential. Yet, so far from there being any conflict between this concern for individuality, and the grasp of objective criteria of value, it is the objective criteria which give sense to the notion of individual value and potential.

With respect to moral value Bambrough makes the point:

> The fact that a tailor needs to make a different suit for each of us . . . does not mean that there are no rights and wrongs about the question whether your suit or mine is a good fit. On the contrary, it is precisely because he seeks to provide for each of us a suit that will have the *right* fit that the tailor must take account of our individualities

of build. In pursuit of the objectively correct solution of his practical problem he must be decisively influenced by the relativity of the fit of clothes to wearer . . . Similar examples may be indefinitely multiplied. Children of different ages require different amounts and kinds of food; different patients in different conditions need different drugs and operations . . . Circumstances objectively alter cases (1979:33).

Indeed, because of the intrinsic complexity, scope, and need for very sensitive individual judgment, the necessity for rigorous objectivity may be even greater, and may pose greater difficulty, in the arts than in other subjects. Without realizing it, the teacher may be tempted to relax into the self-indulgence of implicitly imposing her or his own kinds of approach to art. But to do so may limit the student's individual development. To help each student to develop her or his *individual* potential makes stringent demands on the teacher's ability to make rigorously objective value judgments.

The confusion here arises from a commendable emphasis on, but a misconception about, the importance of individual response in arts education. The appreciation of artistic value is certainly an individual matter, in that to appreciate fully a work of art one must have experienced and thought about it for oneself. But so far from implying subjectivism, that amounts to a repudiation of subjectivism. For what can experience and thought amount to here if it is not of and about the work? The response is not simply a subjective experience; it does not depend exclusively upon the attitude or psychology of the individual spectator or artist. The point becomes particularly clear when one considers working out one's own evaluations of art. To focus on one's own evaluations, identified by one's understanding of the work, underlines the point that the work must be independent of the spectator. Individual differences of evaluative responses necessarily have, and arise from, limits. These limits are what give sense to the notion of evaluation. Beyond certain limits, one's response could not count as an expression of individuality, but would reveal a lack of understanding. *Not anything* can count as an evaluative response to a work of art; *not anything* can count as a reason for evaluation.

To summarize a central point which requires considerably more elucidation, it is a profoundly misconceived dichotomy – a dichotomy which is created by, or an expression of, subjectivism – to regard artistic values as either objectively in the work of art, or subjectively in people. The personal, individual involvement and response characteristic of the appreciation of artistic values is the appreciation of objective qualities of the work.

Art and Life

The foregoing discussion raises a further, educationally crucial, aspect of the aesthetic/artistic distinction, which reveals the inseparable relationship of the three main strands of my chapter. Let us approach the question by considering again the common misconception that the aesthetic and the artistic are aspects of the same aesthetic concept. For instance, Beardsley writes that:

> many natural objects, such as mountains and trees . . . seem to have a value that is closely akin to that of artworks. This kinship can easily be explained in terms of aesthetic value . . . (1979:746).

This seems to me such a remarkably implausible thing to say that one immediately suspects the influence of a deeply embedded, unquestioned preconception. For how, otherwise, could it be seriously supposed that Bach's *Goldberg Variations*, Ibsen's *A Doll's House*, a Japanese Noh play, and an Indian raga are closely akin to mountains and trees? Is there a kinship between the oak trees in my garden, and the film *Schindler's List*? Can this supposed kinship be explained *at all*, let alone easily? The striking thing is that it never is explained, except by obviously unsatisfactory resort to vague metaphysical notions such as Forms of Beauty, a mysterious transcendent Aesthetic and so on. There is just an unsupported assertion: no reasons are offered for a very implausible claim. Clearly, this is a consequence of bizarre crossing of conceptual wires, i.e. two concepts are being confusedly run together. Aesthetic appreciation of nature cannot intelligibly be regarded as falling within the same concept or category as artistic appreciation of a performance of Chekov's *The Cherry Orchard*, of James Joyce's *The Dead*, of George Eliot's *Middlemarch*, or of the Brahms *Violin Concerto*. Yet the distinction, although obvious when pointed out, is almost universally ignored by arts educators.

The distinction is very far from being a mere quibble. Implicit in it, and in the examples I have adduced to reveal it, is by far the most important issue for the value of the arts in education. To put it starkly, by contrast with the aesthetic, it is a central feature of the arts that they can have a subject matter.[6] For example, through his work, an artist can give expression to an immensely varied range of conceptions of aspects of life generally. Obviously, it would make no sense to attribute this possibility to aesthetic judgments of nature: flowers, autumn leaves, mountains and birdsong, however beautiful, cannot intentionally raise questions about social issues. Thus a further danger of conflating the two concepts is that it contributes to the notion that the arts are entirely autonomous, cut off from the life of society, isolated from significant human concerns. Of course, not all works of art can intelligibly be said to have a subject matter. But it is a central and important possibility of all the art forms. It is this characteristic of the arts which explains their powerful significance in almost all societies. Throughout the centuries, for instance, the arts have raised seminal, influential, often profoundly disturbing, questions on moral, social, religious and political issues. That is, a central aspect of the values intrinsic to the arts is their inseparable relationship to and influence on the life of society.

This characteristic of the arts is poignantly illustrated by the reported visit to Picasso of a German officer during the occupation of France during the last war. He noticed Guernica, which Picasso had painted as an expression of his revulsion at the bombing of the little Spanish town of that name by the German fascists. Impressed by the painting, the officer asked 'Did you do that?', to which Picasso replied 'No, you did.'

In view of this deeply significant possibility, is it not remarkable that there is such a striking ambivalence about the arts? On one hand, as we know to our cost, the arts are commonly regarded as peripheral, expendable in education. It is assumed that they are merely for entertainment, enjoyment or catharsis, from which nothing of significance can be learned. Hence the arts are marginalized in the curriculum.

Yet, on the other hand, the powerful possibilities of learning from the arts are clearly conceded in the frequent nervousness about the arts exhibited by authoritarian régimes. It is all too common for artists to be censored, banned, imprisoned, tortured and executed. *Why*, if there is nothing of significance to be learned from the arts? Mathematics and the sciences, the core subjects, do not normally frighten such régimes.

Does this not show unquestionably that the values implicit in the arts are of profound human significance, and thus that the arts should be given a far more central place in the curriculum?

It may be, as I argued earlier, that the conflation of the aesthetic and the artistic contributes to this trivializing of artistic values, and to the emasculation of their powerful educational potential. It should be emphasized, too, that I use the term *education* in its broadest sense, since through involvement with the arts one can continue to learn, in a deep, humanly important sense, all one's life.

Opening Horizons

I am convinced that the most important contribution of education, in all areas of the curriculum, is not so much to help children and students to acquire facts and useful skills, important though those aspects may be, as progressively to offer an opening of horizons of feeling, understanding in a personally meaningful sense, and equally meaningful discriminations of value. Of course, it may be misleading to imply that these aspects are separate. As I argue throughout my recent book (Best, 1993a), the feelings characteristic of the arts (and the emotions generally) are inseparable from understandings and evaluations: artistic feeling *is* understanding and evaluation.

In opening horizons in this way, the responsibility of the teacher can hardly be overstated. For it may well be that teachers offer the only concrete alternative possibilities of values which children and students ever meet. All too often the child's family, social circle and peer group will be equally infected by popular, conformist clichés of thought and evaluation. D.H. Lawrence wrote: 'Our education from the start has *taught* us a certain range of feelings, what to feel and what not to feel.' Consequently we experience 'false, counterfeit, faked feelings. The world is all gummy with them' (1936:545).

Lawrence was referring not so much to formal education as to the formative influence of the whole ethos of society, whose attitudes and values are taken in much as one breathes the surrounding air. In our day, television, the popular press, much pop music, chat shows, the banal twitterings of disc jockeys and so on purvey an infectiously smothering cloud of shallow cliché emotions and stereotyped norm values. It has been said that Barbara Cartland's romantic novels positively impede an understanding of the human condition. By contrast an enlightened approach to the arts can have a vitally liberating potential.

It should be emphasized that in referring to the important question of opening horizons I mean not simply detached, abstract thought, but the opening of real living possibilities. That is, the learning involved will be not so much, if at all, revealed in statable principle as in a change of values expressed in action; in the attitudes which implicitly inform the way in which one lives.

The emancipatory potential of the arts has never been more vitally needed, in view of the shallow, personally restricting utilitarian values which are being imposed so widely these days. This creates a general ethos in which the only, or at least the predominant, values are materialistic. Education, at all levels, is deeply infected by a miasma of mean-minded managerialism, often to the exclusion or severe limitation of a concern for significant learning – students are explicitly referred to as products, and schoolchildren as 'units of income' [sic]. The arts offer great scope for opening real possibilities of more humanly meaningful and civilized values for living.

Other school subjects, for example history, if well taught, can have a similar personally meaningful, liberating influence. But the scope of the arts is much wider, since the arts can take as their subject matter almost any life-issue.

This underlines the importance and inseparable significance of the first theme of this chapter, namely the objectivity of values. For it is only by developing the capacity to see, and understand objectively, in their own terms, other values that we can expand our horizons. Subjectivism would imprison us inescapably in our prejudices, preconceptions, associations. Coriolanus cries: 'There is a world elsewhere.' There are worlds of values elsewhere which can be available to us and our students, but only through an objective expansion of our horizons of imaginative understanding.

Simone Weil (1968:161) points out how tragically often we *invent* what other people are thinking and feeling. That is, we construe their thoughts and feelings in terms of our own; we impose our subjective values upon them because we have not developed the imaginative, objective capacity to move out from our own preconceptions in order to appreciate what *they*, the other people, think, feel, value. Conversation becomes a dialogue between deaf people.

There is, of course, nothing automatic about the liberating influence of the arts. If, as I argue, the arts can powerfully educate values, then they can be a force for encouraging destructive as well as constructive attitudes. Moreover, some art is cliché-ridden, bland, superficial, and thus serves merely to reinforce the trivial values which are so prevalent in society; such art does nothing to open for students a greater integrity of deeper, more discriminating values, more truthful understanding of life.

In short, the value of the education in the values which can be learned from the arts depends upon the character of the arts taught, and how they are taught. There can be no substitute for sincerely committed, high quality, highly educated teachers. With such teachers there is profoundly meaningful and varied potential in the arts for the education of values, and thus for expanded and enriched possibilities of being.

There could be no more important aim in education.

Notes

1 This misguided notion of generic arts carries the inevitable logical consequence of a single general artistic understanding, i.e. which can be achieved by any of the arts, just as the same muscle can be developed by means of any of various exercises. When spelled out clearly like this, the contention can clearly be seen as senseless, but also dangerous, since it would legitimize a reduction in arts provision. That this is no idle danger is revealed by the fact that the Principal of one college was considering closing the art department on the grounds that the students' *aesthetic education* could be catered for in their dance. And, in the rationale of a proposed degree for arts teachers, another institution stated, 'the days of the separate arts subjects are numbered.' The generic arts doctrine of the *Arts in Schools Project* was cited in justification. For a more detailed refutation of the misconceived notion of the arts as a generic community, see Best (1992a; 1992b; forthcoming).
2 For a more thorough discussion of this important but widely overlooked distinction, see Best (1993a: Ch. 12). For an alternative account, see McFee's splendid book, *Understanding Dance* (1992: Ch. 9).
3 See Note 1 for a similarly unintelligible assumption of a general faculty or understanding. *Aesthetic education* construed (understandably) in this way is, of course, even more senseless and dangerous to the arts (see Best, 1984).
4 See Best (1993b; 1995), where I expose a clear example of an arts educator who is so immersed in subjectivist ways of thinking that he cannot recognize them, and the self-defeating contradictions they impose on his own work.
5 See Best (1993a: Ch. 1) for an account of the Myth, which continues to impose disastrous damage on education generally, not only on the arts.
6 This statement needs some qualification. See Best (1993: Ch. 12).

References

BAMBROUGH, J.R. (1979) *Moral Scepticism and Moral Knowledge*, London, Routledge.
BEARDSLEY, M.C. (1979) 'In defense of aesthetic value', Presidential address at the American Philosophical Association, *Proceedings*, **52**, 6, pp. 723–49.
BEST, D. (1984) 'The dangers of "aesthetic education"', *Oxford Review of Education*, **11**, 1, pp. 159–68.

BEST, D. (1992a) 'Generic arts: An expedient myth', *Journal of Art and Design Education*, **11**, 1, pp. 27–44.

BEST, D (1992b) 'Feast for a dog's dinner', in *The Times Higher Education Supplement*, 31 January, p. 18.

BEST, D. (1993a) *The Rationality of Feeling: Understanding the Arts in Education*, London, Falmer Press.

BEST, D. (1993b) 'Minds at work in an empire of the senses', in *The Times Higher Education Supplement*, 19 February, p. 16.

BEST, D. (1995) 'Educating artistic response: Understanding is feeling', *Curriculum*, forthcoming.

BEST, D. (forthcoming) 'Death of generic arts'.

BONDI, H. (1972) 'The achievements of Karl Popper', in *The Listener*, **88**, No. 2265, pp. 225–9.

BRONOWSKI, J. (1973) 'Knowledge and certainty', in *The Listener*, 19 July, pp. 79–83.

LAWRENCE, D.H. (1936) *Phoenix: The Posthumous Papers*, in MCDONALD, E.D. (Ed), London, Heinemann.

MCFEE, G. (1992) *Understanding Dance*, London, Routledge.

TAYLOR, R. and ANDREWS, G. (1993) *The Arts in the Primary School*, London, Falmer Press.

WEIL, S. (1968) *On Science, Necessity and the Love of God*, Oxford, Oxford University Press.

Chapter 8

Food, Smoking and Sex: Values in Health Education

Michael J. Reiss

ABSTRACT: *School health education generally fails to consider the values it wishes to promote and those that it actually does. After examining education about food, smoking education and sex education, I suggest that only a limited amount of health education takes place in UK schools. Rather, what we have is a form of health training in which little consideration is given to how the intended outcomes of such training relate to the aims of education generally. Health training can do a certain amount of good; more often, though, it has little effect. At its worst, health training can lower self-esteem and increase disaffection with schooling. It can even lead to poorer health, partly because a person with lowered self-esteem is, other things being equal, less healthy, and partly because unhealthy behaviours may be adopted by students as a way of distancing themselves from the values espoused by their schools.*

> Justice is loveliest, and health is best,
> But sweetest to obtain is heart's desire.
> (Inscribed on the entrance of the temple of Leto at Delos.
> Quoted by Aristotle in *The Ethics*)

Introduction

Everyone is in favour of better health, but what precisely should be the aims of school health education and what values should health education seek to espouse and promote? In attempting to answer these questions, I will first outline the values one might expect health education to seek to foster. I will then examine instances of health education in the UK, paying particular attention to education about food, to smoking education and to sex education. These three areas of health education have been chosen because they raise somewhat different values-related issues and at the same time are significant components of school health education. I am interested in seeing to what extent such programmes exhibit the fundamental values one might expect them to. My overall conclusion is that only a limited amount of health education takes place in UK schools. Rather, what we generally have is a form of health training in which little consideration is given to how the intended outcomes of such training relate to the aims of education generally. At best such health training does a limited amount of good; more often it has little effect, failing to interact significantly with pupils; at worst it lowers self-esteem, increases disaffection with formal education and leads to poorer health.

What Values Might we Expect Health Education to Foster?

We can approach this question from two directions. First, by considering health education as a subset of education; second, by considering health education in relation to the values encapsulated in medical and nursing ethics.

By considering health education as a subset of education, we might expect it to promote such values as personal autonomy, respect for persons, impartiality and pursuit of truth (Peters, 1966; Wilson, 1990; Halstead, in this volume). Because the whole subject of values in education is considered throughout this book, I shall not examine these in detail here, though their significance for particular instances of health education will be considered later. We can note, though, that we might expect a debate within health education about the extent to which absolute values exist or whether they are culturally specific; about whether schools should advocate a particular set of values or enable pupils to develop their own; and about how schools should best address a plurality of views among parents.

By considering health education in relation to medical and nursing ethics, we might expect it to operate within a framework of respect for autonomy, nonmaleficence (not doing harm), beneficence (doing good) and justice. These are the four main ethical positions from which medical and nursing practice are generally examined (see Beauchamp and Childress, 1989).

Now it is encouraging, and hardly surprising, that there is a considerable degree of correspondence between the core values espoused, at least in theory, in the two disciplines of education and medicine. From an educational point of view the only one of the four main medical ethical positions which perhaps sounds a little strange is that of nonmaleficence. It could be argued that this is because doctors and nurses have been more aware than teachers of the harm they may do to those in their care, and that educators would do well to include this apparently more modest aim amongst theirs.

Education about Food

It might be thought that health education about food is relatively uncontroversial. After all, it might be posited, surely schools should simply be providing healthy food and encouraging pupils to develop healthy eating habits. There is some truth in this assertion, but it oversimplifies in at least four main ways. First, it fails to acknowledge the uncertainty that exists as to what precisely is *healthy food* and what are *healthy eating habits*. Second, it fails to recognize the fact that the functions of foods and eating are not simply to maintain physical health. Third, it fails to appreciate that many of the values placed around foods and the eating of them are culturally constructed. Fourth, it fails to address the fact that apparent instances of unhealthy eating are patently not being rectified by the current provision of education about food.

Let me illustrate these problems with some examples. We can start with the recent publication of a major piece of research in primary schools by a group of leading science educators involved in the Primary Science Processes and Concept Exploration Project (Osborne, Wadsworth and Black, 1992). As part of the study children in primary schools were presented with a range of foods and asked to identify those which they considered to be healthy. However, the views of the researchers are of more interest than the children. The researchers categorized the food into three groupings – healthy, indeterminate and unhealthy:

Healthy foods were considered to be lettuce, orange, apples, juice, rice.

Indeterminate foods were meat, bread and potatoes. Whilst they can form part of a healthy diet, fatty meat, white bread and chips all have particular health problems associated with their consumption.

Unhealthy foods were sugar, chips, coke, burgers, crisps, sweets and biscuits. (Osborne, Wadsworth and Black, 1992:33)

The fundamental problems with a division of foods into *healthy* and *unhealthy* ones – even if we assume, for the moment, that the aim of health education is to promote physical health – is that such an approach fails to realize that the physical health benefits of a food depend on its overall contribution to a person's diet *and* on the individual characteristics of each of us. There is something patently absurd (one might have hoped) about identifying only lettuce, orange, apples, juice and rice of the named foods as healthy.

The value of a food depends not just on the food but on the one who eats it. For example, people of average weight who take a reasonable amount of active exercise are unlikely to be harmed by burgers and chips, even if eaten regularly over many years, unless they have a quite rare congenital disorder which causes them to have abnormally high blood cholesterol levels irrespective of what they eat. To cite a more extreme case where the particular characteristics of the person eating the food are paramount, most of us enjoy peanuts, but they can be fatal to someone who suffers from anaphylaxis, a condition from which a few people die each year in the UK.

It should not be thought that the example of education about food I have quoted is atypical. A great many biology and science textbooks similarly categorize foods as *healthy* or *unhealthy*. It might be objected that these are biology or science, rather than health education, publications. Unfortunately, the value of this distinction is dimmed by the empirical observation that children usually learn far more about food in biology lessons than they do in health education, PSE or PSHE lessons (personal observation; cf. Whitty, Rowe and Aggleton, 1994).

A related problem of much teaching about foods is that it fails to acknowledge the academic uncertainty that exists about the subject. True, good evidence exists to show that a shortage of certain items in our diet can be harmful – for example insufficient vitamin A can lead to blindness, insufficient vitamin C results in scurvy, insufficient protein leads to kwashiorkor and insufficient energy intake results in marasmus (starvation). However, the evidence that an *excess* of certain items in our diet can be harmful is far less clear cut. Take, for instance, the assertion that a high level of saturated fats in the diet is associated with an increased risk of coronary heart disease. Yes, there is now good evidence that, in a number of Western countries, including the UK, people who end up with coronary heart disease are more likely to have high levels of saturated fats in their diet. However, this does not mean that cutting down on the level of saturated fats in your diet will necessarily decrease your risks of suffering from coronary heart disease. In particular, if you exercise sufficiently and are not overweight, you can probably eat saturated fats to your heart's content.

So far we have not challenged the assumption that education about food should promote physical health, or, to be more exact, longevity. On reflection, however, it is immediately clear that if one of the major aims of education is to enable people to maximize their longevity, we should also try to stop them from participating in a wide range of leisure activities (including swimming, mountaineering and skiing), travelling by car, choosing dangerous careers or acting selflessly (for example, rescuing strangers from fires). Incredible as it may sound, much of school health education fails to acknowledge that life consists of rather more than trying to live for as long as possible. This is despite the fact that almost all the health education materials regularly used in initial teacher training and INSET include open-ended exercises in which participants debate the concept of health, almost invariably concluding that health is more than the absence of disease (for example, Williams, Roberts and Hyde, 1989).

Now this is not, of course, to deny that while the quality of life is important, enjoyment of good health requires that one be alive. Given this, it is most unfortunate that those eating habits that possibly do most to lead to premature death and to decrease the quality of life are still rarely addressed in school health education. I refer to anorexia nervosa, bulimia and other eating disorders.

Anorexia nervosa is a condition in which people do not eat enough even though they have access to food. From a national perspective, 90–95 per cent of all sufferers are female, usually in the 15–25 year age range. Often a person with anorexia is extremely interested in food but an obsession with her figure causes her to eat less and less and to lose more and more weight. In the UK probably one in 200 women aged 15–25 will suffer from the disease. There is not a single cause, but expert counselling often reveals deep-seated psychological problems for the person or her family. Anorexia starts a defence against these problems, but then gets out of hand. Some 50 per cent of people with anorexia recover within two to five years.

Estimates as to the total frequency of eating disorders are uncertain, but the majority of women spend a large proportion of their lives attempting unsuccessfully to diet, while probably over 10 per cent have what may be described as serious eating disorders. For anyone who goes on to develop an eating disorder most school education about food is, at best, completely irrelevant. This is because such education is predicated on an assumption that factual knowledge about food is sufficient to result in good eating habits. Accurate knowledge about food is, of course, necessary, but in no way sufficient for healthy eating habits (cf. Booth, 1994). It is also salutary to note that Dee Dawson, who runs a residential clinic for anorexic and bulimic teenagers, believes that the way the UK media reported the specimen meals listed in the 1994 Committee on Medical Aspects of Food Policy recommendations will lead to more cases of teenage anorexia (Young, 1994). It is still the case that school health education about food is far more likely to stress the consequences of overeating that the harm resulting from what might be called *miseating*. Presumably this is in large measure because it is easier to teach about overeating than about anorexia, bulimia or compulsive eating (cf. Buckroyd, 1989).

Two final problems with much health education about food are that it fails to acknowledge the cultural significance of food, and that it overestimates the power of the individual to change her or his eating habits. The cultural significance of food manifests itself in the way what we eat reflects our ethnicity, our nationality, our religion, our social class and our age. Further, most school children have little control over what they eat. Gill Combes has pointed out the extent to which health education is highly individualistic in its emphasis on individual responsibilities, attributes and skills necessary for achieving health (Combes, 1989). This is particularly true of a person's eating habits. Few of us eat most of our food on our own. Are 14-year-olds supposed to tell the adults giving them their food at home that the whole family is to change its diet? The notion is unrealistic, particularly when the diet preached in most health education textbooks requires access to large amounts of fresh fruit and vegetables, involves meals that take quite a long time to prepare and generally appears upper-middle class.

Smoking Education

In many schools the bedrock of health education has been smoking education. Smoking education is more accurately termed 'anti-smoking education' since the aim is, almost without exception, to stop pupils from smoking. Consider, for instance, the recent Health Education Authority book *Smoking Policies in Schools* (Health Education Authority, 1993). This publication does not dither as to its aims:

> In December 1989 the largest-ever integrated attempt to tackle the epidemic of smoking among young people in England was launched. The programme, coordinated by the Health Education Authority with the Department of Health and the Department for Education (formerly the Department of Education and Science), aims to reduce smoking significantly among young people. (Health Education Authority, 1993:7)

No waffle here about the aim being to promote student autonomy; the aim is straightforwardly one of beneficence. Similarly, at a National Health Education Conference in November 1994, I heard the speaker at a Keynote presentation state that smoking, unlike alcohol or sexual health was 'a black and white issue'. Her declared aim, as a full-time professional worker in health promotion, was to reduce the number of people smoking. Health promotion, with its stand of beneficence, arose as a movement alongside traditional health education. It is concerned with the creation of a physical and socio-economic environment which fosters health. Although there are various interpretations of health promotion, a common central feature is the belief that health improvement requires political action to effect structural changes (Tones, 1986; 1991). There is currently a major move in Europe towards health-promoting schools.

However, a number of objections can be raised to beneficence being the over-riding aim of smoking education. First, is the aim of beneficence compatible with the wider aims of education? Second, how unequivocal is the evidence that smoking is bad for your health? Third, what are the value judgments implicit in the promulgation of this doctrine? I shall address each of these in turn.

Is Beneficence Compatible with the Wider Aims of Education?

Beneficence is indeed compatible with the wider aims of education, provided it is seen as an interim stage. Just as a parent determines much of the behaviour of a young child for its own good (instructing it not to touch a stove, for instance), so a teacher, acting *in loco parentis*, may validly instruct a pupil for his or her own good. However, beneficence needs to recede in prominence as a child ages. People do not remain at schools for the whole of their lives. Part of the role of a school is to enable its charges to live in the world beyond school. The 1988 Education Reform Act asserts that the curriculum for a maintained school needs to prepare 'pupils for the opportunities, responsibilities and experiences of adult life' (Great Britain, Statutes, 1988:1). This entails,

---

THE AIMS OF FOREST

1. To maintain the right of adult individuals to freedom of choice and in particular their rights to personal pursuits such as tobacco smoking.

2. To assist in educating the public, smokers and non-smokers alike, on all aspects of the smoking and health controversy.

3. To resist all unwarranted interference in this field, and in particular to counter biased allegations and exaggerated propaganda from whatever source.

4. To protect the travelling smoker from unfair discrimination in public transport and to ensure adequate provision of smoking accommodation of similar standards to that provided for the non-smoker. Equally to uphold and acknowledge the rights of non-smokers through courtesy and consideration.

5. To make representations as and when necessary to government at all levels and other organisations on behalf of the tobacco consumer.

6. To maintain the independence of FOREST to express views to this end.

Figure 8.1:   The aims of FOREST (Freedom Organisation for the Right to Enjoy Smoking Tobacco.
Source: Application Form of FOREST, 2 Grosvenor Gardens, London SW1W ODH.

inter alia, allowing pupils to explore, in a safe educational environment, the reasons why people do certain things. Ironically, many school health education programmes give pupils more of an opportunity to look in a balanced way at the reasons why some people use solvents and other illicit drugs than at the reasons why some people smoke.

Is Smoking Bad for Your Health?

That smoking is bad for your physical health is agreed by the overwhelming majority of doctors and health education experts. However, it is worrying that what evidence there is on the benefits to one's physical health of smoking never appear in school materials. For example, consider the book published by the Health Education Authority (1993) which lists five pages of resources. Included amongst these are such titles as '*Towards a smoke-free generation*', 'Seven ages of moron', 'How to become an ex-smoker' and '*Smoke-free Europe series*'. None of the publications listed argues the other side of the case.

The main organization that exists to protest against what it describes as the 'anti-smoking industry' is FOREST (Freedom Organisation for the Right to Enjoy Smoking Tobacco). Its aims are given in Figure 1. FOREST is an organization, part of whose funding comes from companies involved in the manufacture and sale of tobacco. It is not, on its own, an impartial organization, but its resources, when used along those produced by ASH (Action on Smoking and Health) and other anti-smoking organizations, can help to ensure a more balanced education.

One of the arguments put forward by FOREST is that there is increasing medical evidence that an inverse relationship exists between the risk of developing Alzheimer's disease and the number of cigarettes smoked. This would mean that nicotine intake, though associated with a decrease in life expectancy, may be associated with an improved quality of life before death. Articles describing the benefits of smoking to physical health have now been published in a large number of reputable, refereed journals including *The Lancet, British Medical Journal, British Journal of Psychiatry* and *New Scientist.*

My intention in all this is not, of course, to argue that school health education should advocate smoking, but that it has a duty to be accurate about the health consequences of smoking. I fear that some people do not like the fact that what may once have seemed to be totally unambiguous – namely that smoking is bad for physical health – is now less clear cut.

What are the Value Judgments Implicit in the Message that you Should not Smoke?

It might seem odd to suggest that the message 'you should not smoke' is value-laden. However, it is for a number of reasons. For one thing, in asserting this, schools are passing judgment on those people, including parents and guardians, who smoke. For another, smoking is increasingly a working class phenomenon. Diatribes against smoking, particularly when delivered by middle-class teachers, are increasingly likely to be unconsciously perceived as an attack on the values of the home. Graham (1976) and Combes (1989) have explored exactly why it is that some people smoke. They argue that smoking 'can serve a healthy function' (Combes, 1989:71). For example, in Graham's study:

> The smoking of one, or several cigarettes, appears as a way of delineating periods of the day as both a time for relaxation (putting the feet up) and a time for social intercourse (having friends in). These are times when the harassed mother can temporarily escape from the exactions of full-time motherhood. During such interludes, the children are expected to entertain themselves, for the mother is not oriented to them but to herself or to her peer group. The existence of these periods was considered essential by the individuals if they are to keep 'their strength up' and perform their role with equanimity.
>
> (Graham, 1976:403)

In other words, even if smoking is physically unhealthy, it may not be unhealthy.

None of this should be taken to negate the health arguments against passive smoking. In March 1988 the UK Government's Independent Scientific Committee on Smoking and Health concluded that several hundred of the lung cancer deaths in non-smokers could be attributed to passive smoking. In addition, the irritant effect of tobacco smoke is widespread while there is some scientific evidence that passive smoking increases the risk of coronary heart disease in non-smokers. I am unaware of any arguments to suggest that health (in the broadest sense of the term) is improved by passive smoking; indeed, most non-smokers dislike tobacco smoke. There are, therefore, convincing ethical arguments for asserting that smokers have a responsibility not to smoke in the presence of non-smokers, while employers have a responsibility to provide a smoke-free environment for their workers. This is not the place to go into the practical resolution of these issues, but it is worth noting that all workplaces in the European Union must provide smoke-free rest facilities by 1996.

Sex Education

Of all the topics within health education, sex education is perhaps the one that is most obviously value-laden. For years criticism that too much of school sex education takes place in a moral vacuum has come from a number of corners. In particular, religious groups have frequently been suspicious of much of the sex education taking place in schools. For example, an agreed statement by members of six major UK religions concluded:

> The religious perspective on sexual behaviour and relationships should be fully and properly presented. Often it is either disregarded or treated in a casual manner. For example, homosexual acts are sometimes presented as something entirely natural without any mention that from the religions' point of view they are regarded as other than normal and physically and spiritually harmful . . . Sex education should always be set within a clear moral framework. Too often the sex education given in schools conceals value controversiality and under the guise of openness imposes determinant values on pupils at variance with their own family and religious beliefs.
>
> (Ashraf, Mabud and Mitchell, 1991:6)

So what should be the overall aims of school sex education? Three main ones can be suggested: the development of personal autonomy, the promotion of responsible sexual behaviour, and the internalization of accepted norms. I shall look briefly at each of these in turn.

The Development of Personal Autonomy

Harris (1971) and Jones (1989), both writing from a philosophical perspective, have argued that sex education should promote rational sexual autonomy. It is generally agreed that rational personal autonomy is exhibited by people who act intentionally, with understanding and without external controlling influences that determine their actions (cf. Haworth, 1986). A considerable amount of school sex education does indeed aim to realize these conditions. Good sex education can increase relevant knowledge, help students to make their own decisions about their sexuality, help them develop assertiveness skills and bolster their self-esteem (Reiss, 1993).

The Promotion of Responsible Sexual Behaviour

Construed narrowly, autonomy says nothing about how we should behave to one another. Most moral philosophers, particularly since Kant, hold that others should be treated as of equal worth to oneself, and one of the aims of sex education is often held to be the promotion of responsible sexual behaviour. However, precisely what constitutes responsible sexual behaviour is more problematic. One can say that sexual relationships should be caring and non-exploitative, but how precisely do such worthy words translate into specific behaviours and lifestyles? For instance, are only monogamous sexual relationships responsible? And what about sexual relationships outside marriage and homosexual relationships? Any answers involve making value judgments. It is perhaps for this reason that few sex education materials written from a secular perspective give answers to such questions. Rather they prefer to raise the issues and encourage informed discussion.

The Internalization of Accepted Norms

Some schools see their aim to be to encourage pupils to adopt particular values. For example, many Roman Catholic schools intend their pupils, *inter alia*, to hold that sexual intercourse should be practised within marriage without the use of artificial contraception. A school with a particular religious affiliation is not, of course, disqualified from the need to prepare its pupils for life in a society where many people do not share its views. However, it has been argued that a school that adopts a particular religious framework for its moral ethos can still embrace such liberal educational values as the development of autonomy in its pupils (McLaughlin, 1992). At the very least, though, the promotion of a particular religious viewpoint opens a school to the risk of unjustifiable indoctrination. On the other hand, of course, a school which operates within a predominantly agnostic framework may equally run the risk of unjustifiably indoctrinating its pupils. Just as health education can, often unwittingly, be racist (Pearson, 1986) or sexist (Baker and Davies, 1989), so it can be what might be termed *religionist.*

What Happens in Practice?

The reality of sex education in the UK generally differs considerably from the ideal. Surveys of young people show that most schools provide little effective sex education beyond a minimal biological knowledge of conception, contraception and physical changes at puberty (Allen, 1987; Ray, 1994; Shuster and Osborne, 1994). Reasons for this presumably include the uncertain place of sex education in the curriculum, the absence of a widely agreed framework for sex education, pressures on the timetable, a lack of confidence among many teachers in dealing with controversial and sensitive issues, and a plethora of apparently contradictory advice from national government.

Conclusions

Too much health education fails to examine the values it intends to promote. Katherine Weare points out that education differs from training in that training can be characterized as encouraging people to acquire a set of pre-set beliefs, habits and values. Granted this, much of what is presented as health education is, in reality, health training (Weare, 1992). Health training can do a certain amount of good; more often, though, it has little effect and fails significantly to affect pupil attitudes or behaviour. An occasional lesson parading the virtues of fibre or the vices of cigarettes generally achieves little. At its worst, health training may lower self-esteem and increase disaffection with schooling. It can even lead to poorer health, partly because a person with lowered self-esteem is, *ceteris paribus*, less healthy, and partly because unhealthy behaviours may be adopted by students as a way of distancing themselves from the values espoused by their schools.

Teachers of health education need to reflect on the values they seek to promote. It is easy to say that schools should enable their students to develop the values of personal autonomy, respect for persons, impartiality and the pursuit of truth, but how can this be achieved in health education? Teachers of health education need to be factually well informed about the area in which they are teaching, able to implement a range of teaching methodologies to enable learning, and capable of analyzing the values they seek to promote. A demanding set of criteria! And yet, unless these criteria are met, health education is unlikely to be both effective and morally justifiable.

References

ALLEN, I. (1987) *Education in Sex and Personal Relationships: Research Report No. 665*, London, Policy Study Institute.

ASHRAF, S.A., MABUD, S.A. and MITCHELL, P.J. (1991) *Sex Education in the School Curriculum – the Religious Perspective: An Agreed Statement*, Cambridge, Islamic Academy.

BAKER, C. and DAVIES, B. (1989) 'A lesson on sex roles', *Gender and Education*, **1**, 1, pp. 59–76.

BEAUCHAMP, T.L. and CHILDRESS, J.F. (1989) *Principles of Biomedical Ethics*, 3rd ed., Oxford, Oxford University Press.

BOOTH, D.A. (1994) *Psychology of Nutrition*, London, Taylor & Francis.

BUCKROYD, J. (1989) *Eating Your Heart Out: The Emotional Meaning of Eating Disorders*, London, Macdonald Optima.

COMBES, G. (1989) 'The ideology of health education in schools', *British Journal of Sociology of Education*, **10**, 1, pp. 67–80.

GRAHAM, H. (1976) 'Smoking in pregnancy: the attitudes of expectant mothers', *Social Science and Medicine*, 10, pp. 399–405.

GREAT BRITAIN, STATUTES (1988) *Education Reform Act 1988*, Ch. 40, London, HMSO.

HARRIS, A. (1971) 'What does "sex education" mean?', *Journal of Moral Education*, **1**, 1, pp. 7–11.

HAWORTH, L. (1986) *Autonomy: An Essay in Philosophical Psychology and Ethics*, New Haven, CT, Yale University Press.

HEALTH EDUCATION AUTHORITY (1993) *Smoking Policies in Schools: Guidelines for Policy Development*, London, Health Education Authority.

JONES, R. (1989) 'Sex education in personal and social education', in WHITE, P. (Ed) *Personal and Social Education: Philosophical Perspectives*, London, Kogan Page, pp. 54–70.

McLAUGHLIN, T.H. (1992) 'The ethics of separate schools', in LEICESTER, M. and TAYLOR, M.J. (Eds) *Ethics, Ethnicity and Education*, London, Kogan Page, pp. 114–36.

OSBORNE, J., WADSWORTH, P. and BLACK, P. (1992) *Processes of Life: Primary SPACE Project Research Report*, Liverpool, Liverpool University Press.

PEARSON, M. (1986). 'Racist notions of ethnicity and health', in RODMELL, S. and WATT, A. (Eds) *The Politics of Health Education*, London, Routledge.

PETERS, R.S. (1966) *Ethics and Education*, London, George Allen & Unwin.

RAY, C. (1994). *Sex Education Highlight*, London, National Children's Bureau.

REISS, M. (1993) 'What are the aims of school sex education?', *Cambridge Journal of Education*, **23**, 2, pp. 125–36.

SCHUSTER, V. and OSBORNE, A. (1994). *A Survey of Young People's Views of their School Sex Education*, Cambridge, Cambridge Health Promotion and AIDS Services.

TONES, K. (1986) 'Promoting the health of young people–the role of personal and social education', *Health Education Journal*, **45**, 1, pp. 14–19.

TONES, K. (1991) 'Health promotion, empowerment and the psychology of control', *Journal of the Institute of Health Education*, **29**, 1, pp. 17–26.

WEARE, K. (1992) 'The contribution of education to health promotion', in BUNTON, R. and MACDONALD, G. (Eds) *Health Promotion: Disciplines and Diversity*, London, Routledge, pp. 66–85.

WHITTY, G., ROWE, G. and AGGLETON, P. (1994) 'Subjects and themes in the secondary National Curriculum', *Research Papers in Education*, **9**, 2, pp. 159–81.

WILLIAMS, T., ROBERTS, J. and HYDE, H. (1989) *Exploring Health Education: Materials for Teacher Education*, London, Macmillan / Health Education Authority.

WILSON, J. (1990) *A New Introduction to Moral Education*, London, Cassell.

YOUNG, S. (1994) 'Anorexia warning after health report', in *The Times Educational Supplement*, 18 November, p. 2.

Chapter 9

Values and Education Policy

Richard Pring

ABSTRACT: *An examination of the values underpinning governmental education policy in recent years draws attention to a
potential clash of values between the pursuit of intellectual excellence and the emphasis on vocational preparation. After a critical
examination of both sets of values, the chapter argues that there is
a need to look more fundamentally at what it means to educate
the 'whole person' and suggests that this may best be achieved
through the incorporation of vocational values within liberal
education. Finally, the argument is placed in the wider perspective
of a social philosophy which, sadly, militates against the liberal
values which are intrinsic to education.*

Introduction

There has been a deeply rooted feeling that schools are failing children and
the community. This is reflected in the belief that schools are not preparing
young people adequately for the world of work; that students are ill-prepared
psychologically for an unpredictable future; that standards of academic attainment are too low; and that too many lack even the basic skills of literacy and
numeracy. So many dissatisfied people add up to a strong pressure for reform.
Hence, the range of educational legislation over the last fifteen years, the most
significant of which was the Education Reform Act of 1988.

In the late 1960s, the Black Papers argued that standards in schools were
falling and that there was a need to return to more traditional values which
had been neglected in the pursuit of equality through the creation of comprehensive schools. The *equality* of the many had undermined the *quality* of the
few. Social aims had replaced those of intellectual excellence. The Black Papers represented one kind of traditional value – values located in the subject
traditions of the sciences, arts and humanities which embodied a notion of 'the
perfection of the intellect'. Standards were protected in well-established subjects, performance in which was assessed by formal examinations (see Cox
and Dyson, 1969).

Academics were not alone in expressing concern over standards. Employers were critical, too, though they appealed to other measures of success, namely, relevance to the world of work. *Utility* should have a place in schools, and what is taught should relate more closely to economic needs, as these are defined by employers (see Confederation of British Industry, 1989).

Criticism did not go unnoticed by government. Future policy was reflected in the speech of the Prime Minister, Mr Callaghan, at Ruskin College Oxford in October 1976. The theme was about the 'preparation of the future generations for life'. Education needed to be more 'relevant': first, in the provision of the basic skills which many school leavers lacked but which industry needed; second, in the development of a more positive attitude towards industry; third, in greater technological know-how; fourth, in the development of personal qualities. This speech set the tone and the agenda for the reform of education and training which has proceeded apace during the last fifteen years. Thus, in introducing the second reading of the Bill for Educational reform, Mr Baker felt able to say:

> Our education system has operated over the past 40 years on the basis of the framework laid down by Rab Butler's 1944 Education Act, which in turn built on the Balfour Act of 1902. We need to inject a new vitality into that system. It has become producer-dominated. It has not proved sensitive to the demands for change that have become ever more urgent over the past 10 years. This bill will create a new framework which will raise standards, extend choice and produce a better educated Britain (Hansard, 1987–88:771).

But already we can see a potential clash of values: between, on the one hand, stress upon intellectual excellence indifferent to vocational preparation, and, on the other, emphasis upon relevance to the workplace; between, on the one hand, importance attached to liberal values, protected within an independent academic tradition, and, on the other, a shift from producer dominated control of what should be learnt to that of the consumer or, indeed, of government; between, on the one hand, the status accorded to theoretical and intrinsically worthwhile studies and, on the other, the need for more practical and relevant programmes of learning.

It is this potential clash of values which I wish briefly to explore in this chapter – in particular, how different traditions, representing different sets of value, might be reconciled. Such a task takes us into the area of ethics certainly – after all, we are questioning what knowledge is of most worth; but it also raises questions in social philosophy concerning the authority with which different people seek to control the education and training system. It is not simply a matter of what is worthwhile. It is also a matter of who decides what is of most worth.

The chapter, therefore, is divided as follows. First, I spell out what seem to be the educational values as these are expressed within a particular tradition of liberal education. Second, I look critically at these – in particular at the rather narrow interpretation of liberal education which leaves so many ineducable. Third, on the other hand, I argue against the vocationalizing of education which is reflected especially in the reforms for those who are classed as less able. Fourth, there is a need to look more fundamentally at what it means to educate the whole person – where the 'best that has been thought and said' might be reconciled with the vocationally relevant. Finally, I shall place all this in the wider perspective of a social philosophy which, sadly, militates against the liberal values which are intrinsic to education.

Liberal Education

Lord Quinton, in his Victor Cook lecture, describes what in his view is the relation between culture, education and values. By culture he especially refers to 'high culture', namely, 'the summit of intellectual achievement, measured by established intellectual and literary values' (Quinton, 1992:14). In this, he refers with approbation to what Arnold describes as 'the best that has been thought and said' and to Eliot's 'interest in, and some ability to manipulate, abstract ideas'. The job of the teacher, *as educator*, is to introduce the learners to this world of ideas and to initiate them into the best that has been thought and said.

There is, in other words, an independent educational tradition, the result of critical thinking, scholarship and research, which transcends economic or political need. Rather than *serving* the worthwhile life, such a tradition is constitutive of it. And the teacher, in introducing the young learners to that tradition, will value a canon of literature and art which that critical tradition has picked out and selected as illustrative of the best. 'That canon defines what one ought to have read and understood, at least in reasonably large part, if one is to count as an educated person' (1992:11). We need to explore a little this idea of liberal education, especially as Quinton sees it to be endangered by those who impose more instrumental purposes upon education – either those of meeting economic needs or those of promoting social goals such as that of a more equal society.

One major criticism of the liberal ideal is that it promotes a particular set of values – 'the *best* that has been thought and said' – which is not shared by a great number of people. Who is authorized to say what literature everyone should value or what history everyone should study? One of the dangers that Quinton identifies to his idea of the educated person is a kind of cultural relativism in which the teacher is deprived of authority in promoting what is objectively worthwhile.

One way of defending such values – those values pertaining to the studies which everyone should pursue if they are to be counted amongst the educated – is to locate them among the necessary conditions of acting and thinking as a distinctively human being. Thus the intellectual disciplines at their best not only help to develop the capacity to think and to reason; they are constitutive of that capacity. To think at all is to think scientifically, historically, mathematically, morally, aesthetically and so on. To introduce children to particular literatures is to introduce them to a way of thinking, reflecting, criticizing, appreciating constitutive of what it means to think. And to ask the question 'Why are these studies worthwhile?' is tantamount to asking seriously why one should learn those things which enable one to answer the questions which puzzle one.

Hence, essential to the liberal tradition is a belief that certain studies and activities are intrinsically worthwhile; they require no utilitarian justification; they partake in a tradition of critical thinking, which is constitutive of the life of the mind we have inherited and which raises us above the purely animal mode of existence, making us distinctively human. Such intrinsically worthwhile activities do not depend for their value upon the pleasure or support which they receive from a consumer. Standards are not defined in terms of popularity in the market place. Indeed, education must be *producer dominated*, because the producers are the experts, the authorities, able and authorized to define what count as standards within the different forms of knowledge or intellectual disciplines or aesthetic traditions.

Education, therefore, has been understandably producer-dominated. The universities particularly have defined what areas of knowledge and understanding are important for young people to learn and what, within those areas, needs to be selected. It is in such places that Oakeshott's 'conversation between the generations of mankind' takes place, directed only by the conversation itself (see Oakeshott, 1972). Universities, and schools guided by the universities, initiate the next generation into that conversation – enabling it to listen to and to appreciate the voices of poetry and of philosophy, of science and of history. The selection of what should be contained within the conversation, and the definition therefore of what is worthwhile, are part of that conversation. They arise, not from the fiat of a Secretary of State worried about the usefulness of what is learnt, but from within a tradition of scholarship and critical enquiry. Indeed, the 'best that has been thought and said' is that which has survived such critical scrutiny.

We need however to remember the chief characteristics of this idea of liberal education. There are authorities, sustained in the main by universities, which define and maintain those studies which are intrinsically worthwhile and the intelligent pursuit of which constitutes the educated person. The value of such studies has nothing to do with usefulness. Indeed, they are best pursued in a context separated from the distractions of the world of business and economic activity. There is a time and a place to enjoy the world of romance before one enters the world of precision – and of earning a living.

Problems with the Liberal Ideal

The liberal ideal is attractive. It challenges the purely instrumental view of education in which the value of what is studied is defined solely in terms of economic or social usefulness. It focuses upon what is distinctively human – the capacity to think, to reason, to reflect, to value and to appreciate. Education is the initiation into those forms of thought which enable one to live this distinctively human life. It requires no further justification. Universities therefore should never be in hock to government. The spirit of criticism and of scholarship must never be twisted by economic or social pragmatism. The research agenda must arise from problems within the disciplines, not from problems which others (government, say) require answers to.

I do not want to reject this liberal ideal. Indeed, it expresses an important truth at a time when the independence of that tradition of critical enquiry, of scholarly pursuit of the truth wherever that pursuit might lead, is being challenged and put in jeopardy. And yet, at the same time, I wish to be critical of it. Quinton, reflecting upon the expansion of higher education and no doubt upon the shift in standards as these accommodate a wider range of academic achievement, says, 'If what has hitherto been taught only to a few is the best there is, why should it not be made available, as numbers expand, to a larger number?' (1992:16).

There are two reasons why this liberal ideal, and the values which it embodies, have provoked criticism. First, despite the broadening and empowering influence which it claims, it is still seen by many to be, in fact, rather narrowing. The emphasis upon traditional subject areas, upon the value of particular content irrespective of whether the learner finds value in it, upon the authority of the teacher rather than upon the interests of the learner, has led to the disdain for the practical, the doing and the making. There is the kind of dualism, which Dewey (1916) argued so strenuously against, between theory and practice, between the academic and the vocational, between thinking and doing. In focusing upon the world of ideas, it has ignored the world of practice – the world of industry, of commerce and of earning a living. Partly in criticism of this liberal ideal, the Royal Society of the Arts (RSA) produced its Capability Manifesto:

> There exists in its own right a culture which is concerned with doing and making and organising and the creative arts. This culture emphasises the day to day management of affairs, the formulation and solution of problems, and the design, manufacture and marketing of goods and services (RSA, 1980).

The second and connected reason for criticizing the liberal ideal is that it writes off so many young people as failures, indeed as ineducable – those who do not come up to the standards which define the educated person within the academic traditions of the specific subjects. Such young people may well have their intellectual curiosity; they may well take life seriously as a moral undertaking; they may demonstrate a great deal of practical intelligence and wisdom in personal relations. But, in failing the initiation tests of academic success, they are not regarded as educated. Their voices are not acceptable within the conversation between the generations. To paraphrase Quinton, the expansion of education lies in giving to the many what once was the prerogative of the few – without much adaptation to the needs or interests of those who are less capable of or who are less motivated by academic success.

The consequence has been in the past a division between the few who have been selected as capable of receiving a liberal education – the pursuit of knowledge for its own sake through an academic curriculum – and those who enter adult life either on job-related training schemes or as unskilled workers prepared only for relatively unskilled work. The former are capable of being educated; the latter are not.

But this is seen to be unacceptable. First, the country cannot afford to have so many rejected as ineducable. A highly competitive economic world needs a more broadly educated and capable workforce. Narrowly focused training is not good enough. But, second, each person has the capacity to develop intelligence – to learn how to think more effectively, to feel more sensitively, to engage more practically, to relate to others more wisely. We need a broader vision of liberal education which does not reject as unimportant such capacities.

Vocationalizing the Liberal Ideal

One solution has been to vocationalize the liberal ideal. The Department of Employment's 1981 White Paper, *A New Training Initiative: A Programme for Action*, set the agenda:

> The last two years of compulsory schooling are particularly important in forming an approach to the world of work . . . The Government is seeking to ensure that the school curriculum develops the personal skills and qualities as well as the knowledge needed for working life, and that links between schools and employers help pupils and teachers to gain a closer understanding of the industrial, commercial and economic base of our society. (1981: para. 12)

And many of the developments over the last few years have implemented that agenda, striving after greater economic and social relevance in the curriculum. But the implications of this have not been fully grasped. Certainly there is much sense in raising questions of relevance and utility. One of the many benefits which people want to see from education is that of being able to earn a living. How one works, and what occupation one works in, affect profoundly the quality of life. But vocational preparation is not in itself the same as being educated.

First, vocational preparation is often associated with preparation for specific jobs; one acquires the competences needed for doing a job effectively. As such that preparation does not have to pass any *educational* tests – it need not empower the individual to think or to reason or to evaluate. Indeed, a good vocational preparation for certain jobs may require just the opposite, namely, the termination of curiosity, the dulling of creativity, the unquestioning acceptance of authority.

Second, the goals of learning derive no longer from within the different disciplines of enquiry but from an analysis of the jobs which have to be done. The authorities are not the academics or the teachers; they are the employers. Vocational teachers, therefore, deliver someone else's curriculum; they are the experts on the means to the achievement of goals, not on the goals themselves.

The distinction between educational and vocational aims is important, the former referring to those activities which are intrinsically worthwhile, the latter to those which are economically or occupationally useful; the former referring to an engagement between teacher and learner, the outcomes of which cannot be clear, the latter to outcomes which the employers have specified. These differences are not necessarily incompatible. A *useful* activity, such as making an artefact to sell, can also be educative, developing skills and critical powers which help constitute a worthwhile form of life. Activities which produce the outcomes defined by employers might nonetheless be chosen by teachers because, as well as leading to those outcomes, they also embody values which are educationally justified. The well-trained carpenter may be so taught that he or she comes to appreciate aesthetically the artefacts produced.

Nonetheless, there are dangers that, in the pursuit of vocational relevance, the values of a liberal education might be undermined. A concern for the economically useful can jeopardize those activities which, however educationally valuable, have no obvious occupational relevance. It is not without significance that, in the reform of the National Curriculum, the humanities and the arts have become optional from the age of 14, whilst the sciences and the mathematics remain compulsory. And yet is it not through the arts and the humanities that young people are encouraged to explore what it is to be human and what constitutes a worthwhile form of life?

More significant, however, is the shift in language through which the educational enterprise is described and evaluated. The language of *specific outcomes* enters the account of education such that the transaction which takes place between teacher and learner becomes instead the relation between *input invested* and *output expected*. Education becomes one amongst several commodities competing for customers on the open market. Value is measured by performance indicators spelt out in terms of economic relevance. Questions about educational goals give way to questions about means to non-educational ends. Academic judgment submits to bureaucratic audit. Knowledge and understanding, imagination and creativity are reduced to the standardized language of competences – thereby glossing over key distinctions in the description of the life of the mind which education aims to foster. Teachers no longer deliberate about the aims of education as part of their professional responsibility; instead they deliberate about the means to achieve externally imposed ends as part of their craft.

The seriousness of this shift of language is yet to be acknowledged – namely, the adoption of metaphors from the world of business in place of those which have normally described that transaction between teacher and learner as together they try to make sense of, to find value in or to examine critically. Hence, the effort by the National Council for Vocational Qualifications to reduce the complex life of learning to lists of competences. Hence, too, the attempt to separate the product from the process of learning, assessment from the curriculum.

Making compatible the educational and the vocational aims of learning should not require the impoverishment of education itself. But it does require revisiting what we mean when we talk about educating the whole person. Possibly the problems we encounter arise from an unexamined idea of education. And it is significant that the reforms of the curriculum have been accompanied by so little exploration of these deeper ethical questions.

Educating the Whole Person

Education is an evaluative term. We talk about educational *activities* or educated *people*. In doing so, we claim that those activities or those people are in some sense good, that they meet certain criteria which merit approval, that they are deserving of praise, that they embody certain values. In other words, education refers to the development of valued activities and persons.

Those values relate to what we regard as distinctively human. There are many other sorts of values – many activities to which we attach value (such as eating and drinking and lying in the sun) which we do not necessarily regard as educational. The pleasures that they bring are not valuable from a distinctively human point of view. The qualities which they engender are not regarded as forming the person in a distinctively human way.

But other activities are. These are generally activities which help form the intellect and the capacity to think and to reason. Such activities are educationally valuable if they lead to the person being able to think and reason more effectively and intelligently. The educated person is distinguished by a well formed mind, able to engage knowingly and intelligently with a range of problems.

R.S. Peters, therefore, defined education as the initiation into worthwhile activities, such activities being worthwhile because they provide a 'cognitive perspective', a capacity to know, to understand, to engage critically and intelligently from a broadly balanced point of view. Certain activities are educational because they, rather than others, provide this perspective. Other activities would not be educational because, if anything, they dull the mind and lead to boredom, limit the capacity to think and narrow the person's vision; they hinder the critical faculties (see Peters, 1966).

There are several points we need to remember at this stage. First, education is an evaluative term which applies to activities. Second, the evaluation of these activities is parasitic upon our idea of an educated person – someone who possesses certain qualities of which we approve. Third, these qualities are what makes the person distinctively human and yet which need to be learnt. Fourth, such qualities – such distinctive human qualities – are normally associated with the capacity to think, to know, to understand, to reason.

There will always be disagreement over the idea of an educated person – over the precise qualities that we should promote and over the kinds of knowledge and understanding which we should regard as important. And these controversies are deeply embedded in ethical questions which are the very stuff of philosophy. The answers will reflect particular moral traditions, particular ethical standpoints. For that reason any educational system must always be able to accommodate disagreements about ends to be pursued. It must always find room for different moral traditions and provide support for their respective understandings of the educated person. Education must never be handed over to government which too often seeks uniformity when there are no grounds for consensus, and which too often promotes an idea of the educated person determined more by political and economic than by moral considerations. Indeed, there is a danger that government may fear too much education in this broadly liberal sense. After all, there may be limits to the number of people that society can tolerate who have the capacity and disposition to reflect seriously about political issues and about the economic and social goals which government establishes.

Being human and becoming more so is what is picked out by the concept of the educated person. What then are these distinctively human qualities essential to being more fully a person?

First, a person is capable of knowing, of understanding, of reasoning. To grow as a person is to acquire those differentiated forms of knowledge through which experience is organized and made sense of. To be a person is to have a mind, and to have a mind is to have the capacity to enter into the different forms of knowing through which each of us is able to understand the physical world, the world of personal and social relations, the world of moral ideas and moral ideals, the world of beauty and of imagination. In the absence of that capacity – characterized by concepts, ideas, forms of judgment, modes of enquiry – then the capacity to act in a distinctively human way is extremely limited.

Second, one distinctive form of understanding is that of appreciating oneself and others as persons – as distinct centres of consciousness with the capacity to think, to reason, to criticize, and to feel. This is by no means a trite point. Such a form of understanding can be poorly developed. Too often one lacks the imagination and the disposition to appreciate things from another's point of view. A narrowness of experience and of vision precludes an awareness that others might not see things and feel about them in the same way as oneself. One might lack the concepts and ideas through which a more impartial examination of an issue might be conducted. Furthermore, even the understanding of oneself as a person might be very limited. Young people, for example, may have little capacity to reflect upon their own understandings, reactions and feelings. And they may have little respect for those understandings, anyway, not having confidence in them, believing that they are of no account. 'Know thyself' is an educational imperative – a distinctively human ability which needs to be learnt through criticism, support and engagement with others.

Third, persons are able, if appropriately encouraged and supported, to exercise control over the general direction of their lives – to contemplate the 'ends worth living for', as well as the means of achieving them. Such a concern for the quality of life provides a moral dimension which is distinctively human, but which needs to be learnt – through exposure to 'the best that has been thought and said', through critical discussion about forms of life and the values inherent within them, through the formation of habits and dispositions which embody those values, and through role models and examples. This moral dimension requires strength of vision and strength of will – the formation of the mind both in terms of the capacity to think about ends to be pursued and in terms of the determination to pursue those ends despite distractions and obstacles. Such a moral dimension rises above the do's and don't's of moral rules; it is concerned too with the ideals which inspire and motivate; and it is connected to a sense of personal worth and dignity which enables young people not to be limited to immediate satisfaction but to have confidence in aims which transcend the mere pursuit of pleasure and usefulness.

Fourth, persons such as I have described – whose ability to know and to understand the physical, personal and moral worlds requires nurturing and support – exist necessarily within a social framework. The ideas that we have, the language we use, and the values whereby we live are initially acquired from others – parents, peers, the school, the wider community. Too much stress upon individual autonomy has tended to conceal from educational discourse the essentially social nature of being a person, and the obligations, therefore, of people to contribute to those social relationships if they are to receive the support for their personal development which they need. Such a social context embraces not just those people with whom one interrelates on an immediate and personal level, but also the institutions, which are the products of previous generations' struggles and achievements and which incorporate their own values. Such a social context includes, also, the products of the deliberations of others long since dead – in books, film, art and ritual. Being a person entails a participation in that social context, and to be more fully a person is to engage with it critically, actively. It requires political and social awareness. And it requires those social skills which enable that participation to take place. A fully human life requires participation through deliberation and decision making in those social conditions which shape the life of individuals.

In sum, therefore, to be a person is to have those forms of knowledge through which one is able to understand the world and make sense of experience; it is especially to be able to recognize oneself and others as persons –

as distinct centres of knowledge and feeling; it is to have the capacity and disposition to take responsible control over the direction of one's life, especially
the values worth pursuing; and yet, at the same time, it is to have internalized
the essentially social context of those individual capacities – recognition in
theory and in practice of the interdependence with previous and present generations in the acquisition of those different forms of knowledge, of the understanding of one's own humanity and of the moral traditions through which
one is enabled to deliberate about ideals and qualities of life to be pursued.

It is difficult to divorce such a view of the educated person from one who
is vocationally prepared, because the sort of work one does is such an important part of the kind of life one is choosing to live, the power one has to direct
that life towards particular ends, the capacity to exercise responsibility and
control over one's own affairs and the contribution one might make to the
social and economic welfare of the wider community.

It is the aim of liberal education to do just that – to initiate the young
learners into those forms of thought and feeling through which they might
make sense of the world and act responsibly and knowingly within it, and
through which they might find their vocation in life. But in doing so such
education must attend to the full range of qualities and understandings and
skills which, through learning, enable young people to become persons in a
fuller sense. Furthermore, since being a person is not confined to the academically able, and since the qualities and understandings and skills stretch beyond
those which characterize the academically successful, liberal education must
be more than an initiation into the concepts and principles and modes of
enquiry of a few selected subjects. It must address those personal and social
qualities which enable the young person to live productively and responsibly
within society. It must in that sense be vocational. There is more to being
educated – that is, to being formed as a serious and intelligent person – than
reaching the attainment targets of the National Curriculum.

Foremost, certainly, is the importance of intellectual development – the
capacity to think, to reason, to understand, to be critical. Such a capacity needs
to reflect the logical structures through which public understanding of physical,
personal, social and moral experience is organized. However, this must not be
confused with the acquisition of 'inert ideas', disconnected from the personal
thinking which is effective in how one sees and acts upon the world. Teaching
is a matter of making intelligible and *significant* those ideas, let us say, in
science or in the humanities, which come in an impersonal form. Teachers are
the mediators of a cultural tradition to young learners who are, as it were, on
the outside of those public traditions. They need to be initiated – and that,
more often than not, is made possible through the transaction which takes
place between teacher and learner. Intellectual development requires *making
personal* the understandings which are embodied in different intellectual disciplines but which too often are presented in an impersonal form.

However, that intellectual development must not be confined to theoretical and academic learning. There is practical intelligence – the ability to 'do'

effectively and wisely, the *know how* which cannot be captured in the *know that* of propositional knowledge. Such practical intelligence needs to be developed in the doing, rather than in the abstraction from practice, though critically and reflectively. One learns *how* to be a politician or a parent or a worshipper, helped no doubt by reading, but first and foremost through the endeavour, critically supported by others, *to be* a politician, parent or worshipper.

Such an education would develop self-reflection – the capacity to examine one's own motives and ideas, to understand oneself as a person, to examine the values which guide one implicitly and to ponder alternative goals. Such a capacity does not come easily, since it struggles against the easy distractions of a busy social world. It is a capacity which needs encouraging and nurturing. It requires, too, a belief in oneself – a sense of being worthy of self-reflection.

There is a need also to develop in young people a social and political awareness such that they learn how to participate in those institutions and communities which shape their lives and affect the sorts of people they become. It is a matter of shifting the balance from individual excellence to one defined in terms of active and intelligent membership of communities, in which their identities are formed.

This more vocationalized education is to be contrasted, on the one hand, with an academic tradition linking liberal education with a narrow form of academic success, which excludes the majority as ineducable or as failures, and, on the other hand, with a narrow form of vocational training aimed at the acquisition of job related competences. Rather does it focus upon the qualities and capacities, the skills and the understandings, which enable all young people to live valuable, useful and distinctively human lives. Such an education is not a pipe-dream. Many teachers, concerned with the education of all children, not just for the academically able, have striven to translate such educational aims into curriculum reality. The Technical and Vocational Education Initiative was one such attempt within a tradition of prevocational education. Sadly, it is a tradition which has been ignored in the various reforms of the curriculum.

The Social Context of Education and Training

I have implicitly identified three competing traditions: an academic, a vocational and prevocational. Of course, this is a simplification. The academic tradition can be taught in a vocationally relevant way; the vocational tradition can be liberalized. But on the whole the influence of such distinctive traditions is reflected in the three track system which is emerging post-16 and which some would wish to start much earlier – represented by A Level for some, General National Vocational Qualifications for others and National Vocational Qualifications for the rest.

These different traditions reflect different values concerning the nature and the purpose of learning. But the most important question lies not in whether those are the right values but in who should decide what those values should be. In the liberal tradition, as that has been briefly described, such people would be the academics, those who had already been initiated into the conversations which constituted the different intellectual modes of enquiry. In the vocational tradition, it would be the employers who supposedly know the competences required for doing a job well. But who are the authorities in the more broadly conceived education where we seek to develop the whole person, not just the academic qualities? Has the government any special wisdom here such that it can define what successful learning is to be?

The teacher is essentially the mediator of cultural traditions – in the sciences and in history, in poetry and in philosophy, in the arts and in religion – through which the important questions, which all persons ask or are capable of asking, are explored. Too often that culture remains impersonal – stuck on as if with sellotape, of no personal significance to the young learner. But it is the job of the teacher to help the young learner to see significance in such texts and artefacts and to be more understanding of and responsible for their own lives as a result. The teacher therefore must have expertise in that which is to be communicated and in the mode of understanding and motivation of those to whom those cultural traditions are being transmitted. Such an expertise lies in enabling all young people to find value where there is lack of interest, inspiration where once there was boredom, meaning where there once was ignorance.

The control of education, therefore, cannot ignore the expertise and the authority of the teachers and the academics, since it is they who, professionally, are participating in the deliberations about the quality of life as it pertains to learners and as it has been explored through literature and history, through philosophy and the arts. As Morrell argued in his reflections upon the establishment of the Schools Council:

> Jointly, we need to define the characteristics of change – relying, whenever possible, on objective data rather than on opinions unsupported by evidence. Jointly, we need to sponsor the research and development work necessary to respond to change. Jointly, we must evaluate the results of such work, using both judgement and measurement techniques . . . Jointly, we need to recognise that freedom and order can no longer be reconciled through implicit acceptance of a broadly ranging and essentially static consensus on educational aims and methods (Morrell, 1966).

Morrell rightly identified the problem, which gave rise to curriculum exploration and reform, as the 'crisis of values' – the lack of consensus over the aims of education or what counts as an educated person. Such lack of consensus reflected a deeper lack of consensus over moral values and the quality of life to be striven for within society. But the answer to the problem was not to impose a consensus, not to assume that there was no fundamental disagreement. Rather it was to recognize it and to institutionalize the deliberations about what was worthwhile. There can be no certainties in these matters, but there can be deliberation and there can, as a consequence, be commitment to those values which seem most reasonable to pursue following such deliberations.

Sadly this has not been accepted in the reforms of the last few years. The advisory bodies have been abolished; the Schools Council closed down; Her Majesty's Inspectorate as an independent critical voice emasculated; the countervailing influence of local education authorities enfeebled; the language of education impoverished; the curriculum imposed by politicians; the inevitably perennial deliberations over what is worth learning foreclosed.

References

CONFEDERATION OF BRITISH INDUSTRY (1989) *Towards a Skills Revolution*, London, CBI.

Cox, C.B. and DYSON, A.E. (1969) *Fight for Education: A Black Paper*, London, Critical Quarterly Society.

DEPARTMENT OF EMPLOYMENT (1981) *A New Training Initiative: A Programme for Action*, London, HMSO.

DEWEY, J. (1916) *Democracy and Education*, New York, Free Press.

HANSARD (1987–8) *Parliamentary Debates: Commons*, **123**.

MORRELL, D. (1966) *Education and Change* (The Annual Joseph Payne Memorial Lecture, 1965/6), London, College of Preceptors.

OAKESHOTT, M. (1972) 'Education: the engagement and its frustration', in FULLER, T. (Ed) *Michael Oakeshott and Education*, New Haven, CT, Yale University Press.

PETERS, R.S. (1966) *Ethics and Education*, London, Allen and Unwin.

QUINTON, A. (1992) *Education, Values and Culture*, Victor Cook Lectures, University of St Andrews.

ROYAL SOCIETY OF THE ARTS (1980) *Education for Capability*, London, RSA.

Part II

Education in Values

Chapter 10

Voicing their Values: Pupils' Moral and Cultural Experience

Monica J. Taylor

ABSTRACT*:* *Statutory inspection of pupils' moral and cultural development and official guidance documents have prompted schools to review their values education intentions. Yet little attention has been paid to pupils and their own part in affective empowerment. In this chapter pupils give voice to their values encounters, and have their own values perspectives in their perceptions, accounts and actions acknowledged. Their voices allow us to hear what values they actually experience in the school ethos, aspects of the curriculum and relationships with teachers and peers. They also identify the out-of-school influences of parents, communities, and the media on their moral and cultural learning. We learn what pupils value in school – the good teacher, the loyalty and trust of friends and learning together in community. Issues of articulation, interpretation and evaluation are raised in making judgments about values statements, educational opportunities and experiences.*

Our Charter

Children should not be beaten up.

Children should not be looked upon as lesser human beings.

Children should have a secure home.

Children should be fed properly.

Children should be taught to defend themselves.

Children should not be discriminated against when applying for a job.

School children should be let out for a time.

Children should be heard and believed.

Children should not be kept away from their friends their parents are against.

(Displayed in a classroom of a mixed, inner city, largely multi-ethnic 11–18 secondary school)

Values – Intentions and Inspection

This pupil charter sets out several fundamental moral rights which are a pre-condition of, or should be an integral part of education. As such it demands standing equal to that of a parents' or citizens' charter. That certain pupils needed to state these basic values is a salutary reminder that for some such 'rights' are by no means automatic. So the school, family and community contexts offer qualitatively diverse starting points for evaluating pupils' values. Yet a prevailing social concern about moral values – heightened by exceptional horrific acts, such as the murder of James Bulger by two primary school pupils – has resulted in schools, as a focus for the community, being expected to take a stronger lead in values education and to compensate for the ills of society as a whole.

In the early 1990s British schools have been exhorted to develop values statements. The White Paper, *Choice and Diversity*, recommended that 'any school should include a clear vision of the values within it, and those of the community outside' (GBPH of C, 1992: para 1.30). The erstwhile National Curriculum Council's discussion paper, *Spiritual and Moral Development*, suggested 'The ethos of the school may be apparent through a statement which sets out the values the school intends to promote and which it intends to demonstrate through all aspects of its life' (NCC, 1993:7). School values are explicit in brochures for prospective parents, as well as a range of internal policies and curriculum documents. Paradoxically, schools' espoused values are not always obviously reconcilable with the overarching value of the entre-preneurial marketplace which they have been obliged to adopt. Some schools have made a virtue of necessity in advertising their partnership with parents; as School C (a virtually white, rural, mixed, 11–18 school) claimed in its bro-chure, 'the real strength of the school is in sharing problems with parents'. Parents choose schools not only for academic results but also (and perhaps mainly) on the ideological value or belief basis of the education offered, ac-cording to criteria of gender, ability, faith and social class (see Marfleet, Chapter 12). 'While many schools share common values, they will differ in others, and those differences are critical in affecting parental choice.' (NCC, 1993:8). It is assumed that the stated values of the school, and those of its pupils' parents and of the surrounding communities are in concert, or at least are not antipathetic. Sometimes this is not so.

Following the profile given in the Education Reform Act (GB Statutes, 1988) to the spiritual, moral and cultural development of pupils, guidance documents from the NCC, such as that on the whole curriculum, on certain cross-curricular themes, such as citizenship, and on spiritual and moral development, have advocated approaches, topics and values. Brief quotations illustrate aims and inherent tensions:

> The education system ... has a duty to educate [the] individuals to
> think and act for themselves, with an acceptable set of personal qualities

and values which also meet the wider social demands of adult life (NCC, 1990a:7).

Pupils should be helped to develop a personal moral code and to explore values and beliefs. Shared values, such as concern for others, industry and effort, self-respect and self-discipline, as well as moral qualities such as honesty and truthfulness, should be promoted . . . (NCC, 1990b:4).

The task of schools, in partnership with the home, is to furnish pupils with the knowledge and the ability to question and reason which will enable them to develop their own value system and to make responsible decisions on such matters (NCC, 1993:5).

NCC guidance to schools on moral development was forthright about the list of moral values schools should include: 'telling the truth; keeping promises; respecting the rights and property of others; acting considerately towards others; helping those less fortunate and weaker than ourselves; taking personal responsibility for one's actions; self-discipline.' Importantly it also recommended that school values should reject 'bullying; cheating; deceit; cruelty; irresponsibility; dishonesty' (NCC, 1993:4). Morally educated school leavers should, among other qualities, be able to 'articulate their own attitudes and values . . . develop for themselves a set of socially acceptable values and principles, and set guidelines to govern their own behaviour' (p. 5).

Although study of these sources reveals differences of emphasis on certain values – and in one case the misguided assertion of 'moral absolutes' – their central thrust has served as the foundation of many schools' values statements and curricular goals. Above all, the significance and urgency of this aspect of schools' educational remit has been greatly influenced by the statutory requirement that OFSTED inspections report on the spiritual, moral, social and cultural development of pupils (as well as their behaviour and discipline, welfare and guidance) (GB Statutes, 1992). The fact that this ranks alongside three other key areas of inspection – quality of education, educational standards and management of educational resources – suggests that in principle some value (if not equal value?) is being placed on these educational aims.

Not surprisingly, OFSTED has experienced difficulty in deciding what counts as *development* (GB OFSTED, 1994a). Thus the most recent *Handbook for the Inspection of Schools* has refocused on 'opportunities' offered by the school and 'how the pupils respond to that provision' (GB OFSTED, 1994b, Part 2:22), including 'whether pupils are developing their own personal values'. The *Handbook* sets out evaluation criteria, evidence and a code of conduct for inspectors. Pupils' views about school and their learning, are to be taken into account. In the section 'Relations with Pupils' (Part 3:25), sensitivity to pupils' social and learning environment ('treat pupils on all occasions with courtesy and respect'), is curiously mixed with negative, unsympathetic assumptions ('pupils may feel no moral obligation to co-operate'), and cautions ('in no circumstances question individual pupils on their own'). Inspection also involves consulting parents about whether they are 'happy with the values and attitudes which the school teaches' (Part 3:33).

The *Handbook* distinguishes spiritual, moral, social and cultural development. Of the moral and cultural development of pupils it says:

> Moral development is concerned with pupils' ability to make judgments about how to behave and act and the reasons for such behaviour. It requires knowledge and understanding and includes questions of intention, motive and attitude. Pupils should be able to distinguish 'right' and 'wrong' as matters of morality from the use of the words right and wrong in other contexts.

> Cultural development refers to pupils' increasing understanding and command of those beliefs, values, attitudes, customs, knowledge and skills which, taken together, form the basis of identity and cohesion in societies and groups . . . (Part 4:86).

Forming a judgment about pupils' development involves discussions with staff and governors, analysis of school documents, and observations of lessons and of the life of the school to determine whether pupils:

> feel free to express and explore their views openly and honestly, and are willing to listen to opinions which they may not share;

> are developing their own personal values and are learning to appreciate the beliefs and practices of others;

> ask questions about meaning and purpose;

> develop their understanding of spiritual, moral, cultural and social issues and [to] further their own beliefs, character and behaviour which help them to approach problems rationally;

> develop wider interests, social skills and community awareness . . . (Part 4:16).

With the exception of these gleanings from official documents, notably little attention in both school developments and inspection has been paid to the true clients of education – the pupils themselves – and to their part in affective empowerment. What values do they take from the school, its ethos, and the informal curriculum of relationships with teachers and peers? What do pupils perceive as the other main influences on their values? What do pupils' values appear to be in the school context?

These questions form the three empirical pupil-oriented core sections of this chapter, grounded in over ten years' research, seeing and listening to pupils' moral and cultural experience in school. The pupils' voices derive from an ethnographic project on personal and social education (PSE) and pastoral care in relation to multicultural antiracist education in four secondary schools of varying ethnic compositions, chosen to investigate the translation of their policies into practice (see also Taylor, 1992). The case studies, over two school terms, which included analysis of school documents and teacher and governor interviews, focused on Year 9 pupils, and involved pupil–pursuit exercises, classroom and lunchtime observations and semi-structured pupil interviews (group, individual and with a friend). A total of 86 pupils (fifty-two boys, thirty-four girls, partly due to School N being a boys' school) participated in interviews, some up to three times. The pupils came from fourteen self-ascribed ethnic origins.

Our conversations aimed to allow for the expression of pupil narratives and to encourage exploration of and reflection on their moral and cultural experiences of education in multiethnic settings. By telling their own stories pupils gave voice to their values encounters and, in so doing, had their own values perspectives in their perceptions, accounts and actions acknowledged. Through the pupils' voices, we hear their perceptions of the informal curriculum of their schooling – the school's values rhetoric, teachers' behaviour and pupils' experienced reality – and are allowed an insight into some of their values. Some of the more articulate voices resound. Pupils' self-reports reveal moral and cultural awareness, a sense of fair play, and, in some cases, exemplary actions which suggest that more opportunities need to be made for pupils to take and demonstrate responsibility for self-development and that of the school community.

School Values – Are They Shared Values?

Education cannot and must not be value-free . . . At the heart of every school's educational and pastoral policy and practice should lie a set of shared values which is promoted through the curriculum, through expectations governing the behaviour of pupils and staff and through day to day contact between them. Every attempt should be made to ensure that these values are endorsed by parents and the local community (GBPH of C, 1992, para 8.3:37).

Although they operate within a partly secular, multicultural pluralist society, lacking in explicit values consensus, schools, by their very nature, have to rise to the challenge of offering – often to both pupils and parents – guidance which is values-based. Pupils' experience of values through the content and process of their schooling is mediated by the religious and élitist values inherent in the educational system itself, the political imposition of certain values, and new values related to cultural pluralism, technological advances and on-going social change.

Little is known of the process by which schools 'agree to core values which are acceptable to all' (NCC, 1993:7), but recently governors, teachers, parents and sometimes pupils have debated policy development. Even if a school has evolved a values statement and a set of linked, specific rules, which these educational partners agree are necessary to the functioning of the school as a learning community, in putting values into practice it is likely that they will not be interpreted or implemented consistently by all teachers, or even by one teacher from time-to-time. So to what extent is there a shared understanding of, common practice in, and genuine commitment to upholding the school's espoused values? From the pupil's perspective – one of participant observer with varying degrees of delegated responsibility and influence – we learn what values they actually take from the school ethos, aspects of the formal curriculum and relationships. Are these the values that the school intends?

School Ethos

The brochures of the four case-study schools' included among their general aims some relating to pupils' personal, social and moral development which emphasized 'respect for others and the community in which the child lives'. A statement in School N's brochure (boys 13–18 school, in a county town, with about 25 per cent minority ethnic pupils from a range of backgrounds) was typical:

> The school aims to help and encourage each boy to:
> - develop a reasoned set of attitudes and beliefs;
> - develop personal qualities of mutual respect, tolerance and understanding, essential to harmonious relationships in a multicultural society.

Ask secondary school pupils, 'What values do you think the school stands for?' and you are – initially at least – more likely than not to be faced with a blank look. Pupils lack familiarity with school aims, though they are used to discussions about values issues in the school's pastoral approach and PSE. School values are not conceived of in the abstract. Pupils' expression of their experiences is concrete, rooted in the perceived particularities of actual school life. On reflection, some Year 9 pupils said:

> A community spirit, that's a favourite. That's the one Mr M [the head] likes (Kate, School C).

> . . . it likes you to keep your manners . . . most kids in this school will open doors . . . they won't close the doors in people's faces . . . I think it tells you how to give respect to people . . . And . . . you have to come in the proper uniform (Giovanni, School N).

> They always try to push you one step further which is quite helpful (Stephen, School N).

Like in the brochures it might say its not sexist and that, but in some lessons it is (Satwant, School F).

It's a place where teachers know that they've got the power to boss us about, so they just do it. They don't treat us right, and I suppose that's not a value really, but that's one thing (Purminder, School H).

Well, it depends what the pupil is like. If the pupil is hard working then they don't need much to develop them so they keep on going with them, whereas if a pupil doesn't try hard then they just leave them alone, they don't do much (Harjinder, School H).

Curriculum Contributions – PSE, RE and Collective Worship

Although the whole curriculum of schools contributes to the development of pupils' values, 'by consciously highlighting, for example, ethical issues or enlarging pupils' experience or cultural vision' (GB OFSTED, 1994b, Part 4:17), certain aspects of the formal curriculum and school life, such as PSE, religious education and collective worship, are often seen as having a special influence (see Edwards, Chapter 13). Pupils, however, expressed mixed views on their value, often depending on individual teachers' awareness and skill. Although some pupils welcomed the more discursive, interactive approaches characteristic of PSE, dealing with such topics as racism, human rights and citizenship, as an opportunity to 'put your views forward', others thought it was 'too personal'. PSE, did, however, promote learning together in the form group. Some young people found that RE extended their awareness of religions and cultures, but some from faith backgrounds other than Christianity observed that, in teaching about Sikhism, for example, 'they stick to the main things – the 5Ks – that everybody knows', and they wanted instead to discuss bi-cultural issues. Collective worship was usually seen as a time for moral homily, rather than developing religious awareness or spiritual insight. However, for some minority ethnic pupils an acknowledgment of and respect for their cultural and religious backgrounds was demonstrated in a whole-school assembly which involved community members in celebrating the Sikh festival of Baisaikhi:

We felt that everybody knows about our religion now and nobody should pick on us because it's our religion the way it's their Christianity, isn't it? So they should be variable with each other. Like we don't go around saying to Christians like 'your religion's this and we're going to do this to it'. Like we should be equal with each other. We listen to their point of view about Christianity. They should listen to ours as well, not just ignore ours, because that's when Asian people feel left out (Daljinderjit, School H).

Relationships – Respect and Fairness

The salience of the informal curriculum often outweighs the formal curriculum in its influence on moral and cultural learning, as illustrated by two values frequently mentioned by pupils – respect and fairness.

Respect

School F's Code: The 4 Rs

Self Respect: appearance, attendance, homework, doing your best.

Respect for Others: conduct, other cultures, feelings, other points of view.

Respect for the Environment: not walking on grass, no litter, no graffiti, no vandalism.

Respect for the Law: property.

In School F (an 11–18 mixed comprehensive with an almost equal mix of white and Asian (Sikh and Muslim) pupils) respect was recognized as the ground from which relationships have to start. Whether or not respect exists between a group of pupils, or pupils and a teacher is strongly affected by the first few moments with a class – an encounter preceded by the influence of reputation.

> You should respect the teachers, but if the teachers respected you you're more likely to respect them. A lot of the teachers don't respect you for what you are, they treat you like little kids (Lyndsey, School H).

Some pupils – perhaps those with difficult experiences of school – take a more immediately demanding approach, expecting the teacher to show respect as a precondition for their relationship. Complaints about lack of respect are usually related to the teacher being in authority rather than an authority.

> *Kate:* One or two teachers treat you like in primary school again, like you're not adults . . . One or two of the younger teachers they don't tell us to shut up, but we do it out of respect because they don't degrade us, they don't like really put over their authority.
>
> *MJT:* What makes you respect them?
>
> *Kate:* If they give me respect. No one gets respect from me without earning it (School C).

Demonstrated reciprocity is also a key element of respect:

Once Mrs W said no one should eat in lessons. But the next day Mrs W had a packet of strong mints beside her. She eats in lessons. This is what we don't like . . . The teacher walks out the classroom and goes and makes himself a cup of coffee and then he comes back and starts drinking it (Kiran, School F).

Fairness

Fairness, or more likely unfairness, manifest in many forms, is a central values concern of pupils in school life. Pupils frequently report discrepancies in teachers' behaviour, and in the way they fail to implement rules consistently or treat pupils equally:

One instance was today in PE. John got told off after he threw a javelin. He took about two steps and Miss had said its dangerous to walk because there's some other people would still be throwing. She told him to sit on the bank and then a few moments later I did the same thing. She told me off but didn't tell me to sit on the bank. She never excluded me. She doesn't like John much (Phillip, School H).

According to other pupils, from Year 7 John had a reputation of being 'a trouble causer', though by Year 9 he only did so 'occasionally'. Thus they implied teacher expectation was an influential factor.

Some pupils might appear to get more favoured treatment on account of their personal characteristics:

Rajinder: Like if we wear slogans on our T-shirts, right, Jamie always wears one but she doesn't tell him off. But when someone else is wearing one, right, and Jamie's not wearing one then she tells them to take it off. But if Jamie's wearing one and another person's wearing one she doesn't say anything to that person 'cos she knows that Jamie's wearing it. I think that's not fair. She should be equal to all children.

Purminder: I think, 'Well he's coloured, but why's she different to us?'. But I think it's just him (School H).

Purminder had learned that it is wrong to jump to conclusions in complicated cases; she was unsure whether the teacher was discriminating on grounds of race, as this was not consistently applied. The teacher may have been more concerned to avoid a confrontation with an assertive and popular Afro-Caribbean boy, thereby probably invoking wider social discord in the peer group.

Another complex episode involved an Asian teacher, a white girl and an Afro-Caribbean girl:

> *Lyndsey:* It was pretty unfair . . . He just happened to pick me and
> Miranda to pick on. He usually picks on me. In all the
> lessons with him I am the first one he starts shouting at to
> be quiet.
>
> *Miranda:* The only reason we were talking was that he wasted our
> time at the beginning of the lesson. He came in really late
> without telling us where he'd been. So the class said 'Don't
> stop talking when he comes in.' So Ranjeet and Amandeep
> started giggling and I started to laugh at the way he was
> shouting and he told Lyndsey to get out and she goes 'Me
> or Miranda?' and he says 'Both of you!' But Ranjeet and
> Amandeep were laughing and he didn't say anything to
> them (School H).

According to other pupils, the teacher said that he had 'to make an example of them', which may have been a way of re-establishing control after a series of disruptive incidents. In fact the situation had a longer history. To these girls it was inherently unfair, not only that they alone should take the blame for a collective act in response to the teacher's absence and failure to explain, but also because they had not received reciprocal support from Ranjeet and Amandeep, with whom they had previously demonstrated solidarity, as Lyndsey explained:

> They got sent out in Geography because they were talking and we
> knew that we were talking as well so we got up and stuck up for them
> and went out with them . . . but they didn't bother to stand up for us
> and say that it was them as well, so we were a bit angry with them.

Conversely, a curious but common source of complaint of unfairness is when the whole group of pupils are held to account or are penalized for the apparent misdeeds of the few or one.

> One boy was clapping and saying things and the teacher came round
> and blamed the whole class and we got kept in (Alan, School N).

In School H an historic episode affected the social life of the whole school:

> One thing that really is getting us, they had a disco once and a girl got
> drunk and that and they've banned all the discos ever since. I mean
> its not fair – if the teachers are there its their responsibility to see that
> no one takes any in. And if they do, they can't expect the whole
> school to suffer for one person (Purminder, School H).

Sometimes individuals get blamed unjustly for acting out of self-defence, or defence of their property:

I was walking upstairs and someone was behind me and lifted my skirt up and I screamed. And he [the teacher] goes that it was my fault and I shouldn't have done it. I tried to explain, but he didn't listen and gave me a detention and started shouting at me (Kerine, School F).

Paul Cleaver, he touched my bag. And before the teacher had said 'All be quiet' . . . so I thought he was nicking something out of it. So I told him 'Paul get out my bag!'. And Mr R goes 'Right, you got a detention.' And I said 'No, I haven't. It wasn't my fault.' And now my parents have got to come in and see him about it and see what happened (Christian, School C).

School C took its liaison with parents on pastoral matters rather too seriously for some pupils, who found the involvement of parents 'overeactive'. Others objected to the school's intervention in encouraging them to 'make friends again'. Some complained about the school's jurisdiction extending out of school, even when a member of staff was involved – 'dinner ladies are like the mafia' and 'they are not civil, they treat you like animals':

They think they've got a right to tell you off outside school. There's a dinner lady that has a go at me. I went outside school and said something to her. They got me in the next day and said, 'What did you say to that dinner lady? You shouldn't say that.' It was outside school so I don't think they should have done that (Rebecca, School C).

Out-of-School Influences on Pupils' Values

The values of the homes and communities in which pupils live, their interests and the media are major influences on their personal development, especially in early adolescence. They may outweigh those of the school, or operate discordantly from, and in parallel to it. Young people are engaged in a continuous process of exploring, making sense of, and arriving at their own beliefs, attitudes and values, testing them out against the views and actions of peers, parents and significant others and TV.

Learning from Parents and Communities – Identity and Independence

In developing their own identity and independence, pupils recognized above all influences of family and friends, but also a need for support to cope with pressures. Some, however, lacked a close family relationship:

My Mum doesn't take that much interest in the sorts of things I am doing . . . she spends more time with other people than she does with me and my sister, it annoys me a lot . . . I can't tell my Dad things. It's like he's not my Dad any more really. I'm not as close to him and that's a pressure for me (Beverley, School C).

I have to do my work by myself without any advice really so that sort of gets to you sometimes . . . I get nervous inside . . . It's just the atmosphere that I'm involved in at home as well. Because I've got to do everything on my own and I'm not really sure because there's nobody to ask (Harjinder, School H).

Others were encouraged by their parents, although high expectations could also be a pressure:

I get pressured from my Mum because she wants me to be something that I don't particularly want to be. She expects me to be good all the time and always work hard at school. She gets disappointed when I don't do well (Lyndsey, School H).

I think my parents want us to grow up so that we do get respect from other people and not just be ignored . . . They suggest that I treat people well so that they'll treat me well in return. Be kind, fair, honest (Mizan, School N).

Some pupils were concerned about racism in the community around school and of parents and saw these as affecting pupils' attitudes:

I think it's the parents' fault for not teaching them, and then sometimes the parents are bad themselves like that. Like Davina's Mum, she doesn't like Indians or blacks, she swears at them, she kicks them (Jamie, School H).

My Dad is racist and I am trying to get him over and tell him that it is wrong (Alan, School N).

For some young people community languages and/or the beliefs and practices of their religion are central to their identity and the way they perceive and live their lives. Like many Asian pupils, Purminder was trying to have the best of both worlds: 'In school you might think I'm dead Westernised, but I still want to stick to my traditions.' This involved negotiating complex and delicate boundaries at home and in school:

My English friends say 'I've done this, or I've done that, or I've got that' and I go home and say 'Can I do this?' and they say 'No' and it gets me dead angry. They act as if they were still in India. The main reason is because other people are going to talk . . . I don't hear my Mum gossip about anybody else, but my Gran does.

At school I sort of face up a bit more than at home. I suppose I am a bit harder at home. I answer back. At school I try to keep discipline otherwise they're going to say your parents haven't actually taught you much. And without my parents really saying anything I know what to do. I don't want to give a bad impression about my religion and that to everybody, so I don't answer back at teachers, try not to. If me and my friends mess about teachers say that's what Asians are like.

However, some white pupils were also conscious that their beliefs and practices did not fit with the secular life stances of their peers:

Well, religion is sort of important to me. I have to go to church every Sunday because my Mum makes me so its sort of been forced on me . . . It sometimes gets a bit boring, and I don't actually talk about it a lot at school as I said it the other day and they all thought, 'Why do you do that?', because I'm probably the only person who goes regularly . . . I've been confirmed and stuff, I've been going for ages . . . But I sort of believe a bit more because my Grandpa died this year and it sort of helped (Claire, School C).

By comparison, some pupils in their out-of-school lives were dealing with cultural and social conflicts which gave them a wider first-hand experience of morality and the law.

We used to live in a white area and the white people used to come round and throw their rubbish in our garden and break eggs. One day my uncle got cross and beat them with a stick. We told the police and they didn't do it any more, but we have moved now (Ali, School F).

There was a riot in the street. This girl I punched her nose and she had bruises all over her and she had to go to hospital. It got took to court. But I just got a caution in the end because I was too young . . . I'm not proud of doing it, just glad that I got away with it in the end. I didn't break her nose, another girl did. All these social workers kept coming out to me. Said, 'I think she understands she's done wrong' (Debbie, School F).

Some young people felt their lives to be quite pressurized, as they had to balance variable homework demands with domestic responsibilities, caring for siblings and sometimes working in family businesses or a part-time job. Quite often school friends are not seen at home. But several of the Asian pupils, especially the girls, seemed to have strong friendships and community ties. Many pupils were involved in interests outside the home – football, Scouts, Mosque, choir, community language classes, and so on – through which they implicitly or explicitly encountered values. Some of these interests serve to promote not only personal and social development, but also a growing awareness of being a member of several communities with differing values. On the other hand, pupils' out-of-school interests were sometimes solitary, contrary to expectation, revealing characteristics and dispositions, such as caring, which the school environment did not always allow them to demonstrate: 'I grow minature trees. It takes me about an hour to water and feed them' (Robin, School C).

Learning from the Media – Rights

Two pupils connected bullying and intimidation by a teacher in school (regretably such treatment was reported in each school) with what they had seen on TV in a way which helped them understand their rights:

Glen:	I don't know who it was, but somebody was like being told off, and Phil Murphy was laughing behind him . . .
Giovanni:	I told Phillip a joke, and Phillip was laughing, and he just turned round and hit Murphy in the face.
MJT:	Who hit him?
Giovanni:	Mr P. That's why I feel a bit scared of him sometimes, you don't know how he's going to react . . . Sometimes he'll say things like 'Ring your parents I won't care' . . .
MJT:	Did that boy ever complain when he was hit?
Giovanni:	No, he didn't.
Glen:	He felt like nothing would happen to him [the teacher]. But I saw on TVAM today that teachers can't hit you. And we can do 'em.
Giovanni:	And we can say things because we're supposed to have 24 hours notice before we have a detention. So if we haven't then by law we're only allowed to stay at school for about 15 to 20 minutes, and Mr P says, 'I don't care about your parents, I'm still keeping you after school.'

These boys had learned from TV about their right not to be physically abused, but, like many others, had not been empowered by school to make the most challenging complaint of all – against the authority of a teacher. No doubt their reluctance was underlined by their recognition of the ambiguity of the situation: the boy had drawn attention to himself by laughing at his friend's joke, which was probably misinterpreted by the teacher as a further attack on his authority.

By contrast, in School C pupils were more proactive and invoked their form tutor's support:

A group of us have been to him already. That is if we don't like the teacher or they have been unfair to us. He gets the teacher in and talks to them about it (Robin, School C).

Education aims at developing young people's critical reasoning skills and responsibility and a rights based culture has been growing. So it should be expected that pupils become more critical, less accepting of their school experiences and more proactive about change.

What Pupils Value

Privileged access to pupils' values depends on what they choose to disclose to a relatively trusted stranger as meaningful to them in the school context. Thus pupils' values have to be inferred from what they say they value and the episodes they recount to support their values stances.

The Good Teacher – Consideration and Professionalism

The good teacher – the teacher who is respected and valued by pupils – has several qualities. The Head of Year 9 in School H was universally respected and liked by pupils who saw him as someone reliable to whom to turn for help:

I would go to Mr J. He's a safe teacher, he is. He's brilliant. He's funny. He's fair. He listens to your questions or problems (Nicholas, School H).

Listening is one of the most valued qualities of a teacher – but is all too often lacking. Listening is especially important because 'they don't know the other side of the story' or 'the full story'. Above all, as pupils in all four schools strongly averred, the good teacher listens to the pupil's explanation without obvious preconception:

When you're in trouble he doesn't like shout down your throat, he'll discuss it sensibly. Like some teachers they'll get angry and everything and they don't listen to what you've got to say and they just do what they want to do. They don't listen to what happens in the start, whereas Mr J is there to listen to you (Daljinderjit, School H).

Matthew, testified to the importance of learning self-discipline through dialogue with a respected form teacher in School C:

I'd rather them leave it up to us to decide what we've got to do and if we carry on then discipline us. But first of all when we do things

I reckon they should talk to us. Because when I let off extinguishers . . . they talked to me loads of times and I thought, 'Well, isn't this enough?', 'cos they were going to do more . . . I won't do this again because I've learnt my lesson.

Dean (School N), who also claimed to have become more responsible in Year 9, felt he had learnt to listen to other points of view and develop his own because:

if you have a discussion with a teacher and they listen to what you have to say and you have a discussion with someone else you tend to do the same thing.

The good teacher is also valued for professionalism. Pupils are keenly aware of and dislike a lack of professionalism:

In Year 8 I did about 20 books – these SMP maths books – and in my report she wrote I completed one book (Kiran, School F).

Professionalism includes being sensitive to individual pupils' needs and abilities:

Hayley: Mr S, I reckon he's really good he is. He understands he does. Like I reckon he knows a lot about each person. He's really nice.
Debbie: He comes and sits next to you and tells you what work to do.
Hayley: If you don't understand it and if he's talking to someone else he goes 'I'll be with you in a minute' (School F).

Teacher explanation of intended actions is valued by pupils, as is consultation about the learning process. As with the need to take racist incidents seriously and deal with them sensitively and fairly, so the teacher, in negotiating ground rules and boundaries, may need to act against race and gender bias in forming an integrated learning commmunity, as two examples show.

Endip: There's one [teacher] she chose these two girls to choose the teams, right. There was an Indian one side and an English girl the other. The English girl chose all the English girls, and the Indian chose all the Indians.
Satwant: But she [the teacher] goes 'In the whole time that I've been at this school I've never seen that!'
Endip: She goes, 'Sit down, I'll sort it out.'
Satwant: She made them mix up.
MJT: What did you think about that?
All: It was good.

Satwant:	The Asian girl she had mainly Asian friends and so she chose all her friends, that's why.
MJT:	So you think she didn't necessarily choose those who were good at rounders. So if that was you, you'd choose a mix of people, would you?
Satwant:	Yes, I would.
Endip:	I'd choose the best ones (School F).

Mrs D is against racism and sexism, but in the first three months of this year we all sat in rows, boys on one side and girls on the other side. Miss said she wasn't going to have it and she wanted boys and girls to sit in the middle. And we volunteered and it's been like that ever since. That actually brought us together – we were talking and doing stuff in groups (Harjinder, School H).

Friends – Loyalty and Trust

Around Year 9 pupils easily fall in and out of friendships. 'The person I was going around with, I was ill for a week and a half and by the time I got back she had gone off with somebody else' (Claire, School C). Trust and loyalty are much sought after qualities in friends, as, to a lesser extent are similar ways of thinking and interests.

Their being there when you need them, always there, that's what I value most (Glen, School N).

As Amit and Dean, two friends interviewed together in School N, said of one another:

Amit:	He will stick by you even if everyone else is picking on you. He will say 'Don't listen.'
Dean:	He's someone you can call on to tell your troubles to, someone you can talk to who won't go and tell every one else. Someone you can trust.

By contrast, pupils were open and quick to disclose the personal and social circumstances of their own and other pupils' lives. In the first group interview in School F, seven pupils of mixed gender and ethnicity, reported that two Asian girls in their form had social workers; one was 'having a bad time at home', not being properly fed and cared for; and the other had 'cut someone's hand with a carving knife. She doesn't like talking about it.' They knew because 'she knows she can trust us', but saw no lack of trust or disloyalty in telling me, 'I don't think Kiran would mind telling you, Marm, we haven't told no one in school about it.'

The same group also disclosed an instance of pupil extortion and injustice, when pupil loyalties were severely strained:

> *Sukwinder:* Sher Khan, the boy who's left . . . lost his walkman but he made us lot pay for it. We never done it but he blamed us. So he made me, Parminder and Gurmanjit pay for it. Gurmanjit had to pay £10, me £5 and Parminder £5.
>
> *Hayley:* If he never done it he bashed them, Marm.
>
> *Endip:* Even if you tell teacher he still gets on to you and threatens you. He was hard and he had bottle.

Learning Together – Responsibility and Tolerance

Asked 'What was the most important thing you learned this year?', some pupils made claims like 'social behaviour' or 'to be responsible and get on with each other'. Many recognized that peer pressure could change or mislead them. Some motivated and achieving pupils resented the disruption of others. A few pupils were learning to be self-corrective:

> I can be a bit talkative and disruptive, but if I want to I can work well . . . I was just thinking about when the exams come the trouble they'll be if I don't work, so I just started to buck up a bit . . . I decided it for myself really. I knew that I was going the wrong way really so I just changed while I could (Giovanni, School N).

Sometimes learning occurs because of omissions by other members of the group, as when pupils asked their form tutor to loan dinner money:

> He's not unfair about lending out dinner money. Because if he hasn't got enough money he says so. And if people don't bring their money back the next day when they're supposed to he doesn't lend any more out . . . So the person who hasn't paid back is holding up everyone else (Christian, School C).

The pupil group itself can offer overt peer correction. After an episode when a lighter had been placed near a girl's hair the form tutor had summoned the link police officer, who, as the pupils characteristically humorously said, 'let them off with a light warning'. Nevertheless from this outsider some understood that:

> *Matthew:* Having a lighter in school is quite a serious matter . . . if they did that in the real world they could get had up.
>
> Claire: Because if they had a lighter by her hair it could have gone up . . .

Rebecca: But it didn't . . . it never . . .

Matthew: Rebecca – it doesn't matter what it didn't do, it's what it
could have done!

Off timetable, out-of-school learning experiences, such as participating in
activities on residentials, can be the most powerful in learning together, as
some of the boys in School N testified. They 'learnt more about teachers' and
about their peers 'in a different way'.

> You learnt to work with people easier and you know more about the
> people than before . . . I saw that some of the lads who act really hard
> and things when they are at school they showed that they will help
> you if you are in trouble or things while you were there, but they
> wouldn't do that if you were in school because there's like other kids
> watching them. I learnt to trust people more, which is the main thing
> (Alan, School N).

While abseiling pupils learnt from the teacher's example 'She was really
scared. But she did it. She went first. If she hadn't done it some of us might
not have done it.' Indeed, Glen had himself been scared and had been 'amazed'
to find that Stephen, whom he had not thought of as a friend, had helped him
down. In fact he, too, was scared of heights. But Stephen dismissively said, 'I
just talked to him and explained that I knew what his situation was and he was
alright after that.'

An encouraging finding from the research was that pupils in these
multiethnic schools at least accepted and mostly positively liked such an environment, which they saw as important for getting to know each other as
people with characteristics influenced by ethnicity, culture and race.

Mizan: I think having different races in the school helps the pupils
to understand about each other's cultures.

MJT: How do they do that, just by being together, or is it things
they learn, like in Humanities?

Mizan: It's being together and also learning from each other.

Mizan had in mind an impressive Muslim visitor to the school who spoke
about Islam. He and three white boys chose to do an RE project on Islam
'because they found it interesting' and 'they were also asking me about ideas.'
He thought it was beneficial 'because if it carries on going people will be in
one group and not divided and separated.'

In these multicultural settings a few young people had developed a degree of moral and cultural maturity, characterized by tolerance. Though tolerance can be too passive a value in such schools, where active intervention is
often required to uphold basic rights and respect for personhood, these young
people demonstrated tolerance founded on first-hand experience, awareness

and an active will to learn together in community. In holding this value, as it turned out, their learning in school had been complemented by that from their parents, to 'stick up for your rights' (Satwant) and 'that we are all equal' (Stephen).

> We've all got to live in this world and we've all got to be friends and neighbours, so we should get along with each other instead of making racist remarks. You just make other people's lives a misery (Satwant, School F).

> I think a human being is everybody who lives in this world. I think we have a responsibility to ourselves and anyone else to not make fun of anybody or put them down because of racism. We're all on the same planet so let's make use of it . . . (Stephen, School N).

Values – Articulation, Interpretation and Evaluation

Key concepts in making judgments about values statements, putting them into practice in provision of educational opportunities and experiences, and pupils' ability to benefit from them in developing their own values are: articulation, interpretation and evaluation. These permeate consideration of school inspection and pupils' reports.

In contradistinction to official school evaluations, this chapter gives the loudest voice to the pupils themselves. By speaking out about their moral and cultural experiences they demonstrate their articulacy and perceptiveness, as well as concern for the quality of their learning environments. Thus they voice their values. In the face of pupils' episodic accounts, the sceptical reader may wonder about objective canons of reliability, validity and generalizability. But it is more appropriate to consider whether pupils' narratives have authenticity in school life and salience for them and their peers. Thus, when pupils see disclosure in conversations as too personal or risky, they may talk about events as if they happened to others. The researcher in school over an extended time can begin to know some pupils, their biographies and behaviours, and has the opportunity to triangulate observations and accounts from several sources. As some pupil reports reveal, episodes and encounters are often far from clear cut, instead ambiguous, ripe with unexplored levels of interpretation and meaning. Pupils themselves question situational ambiguity. In evaluating their moral and cultural development allowance needs to be made for the notorious judgment-action gap. In common with most adults, pupils in their developing maturity often demonstrate the difference between expressed values, attitudes and beliefs and behaviour, between what they say, expect from others and what they themselves do. They also show that, given opportunities, they can enter into a self-correcting moral and cultural learning community.

In this light, articulation, interpretation and evaluation of opportunities for pupils' moral and cultural development offered by schools is no simple task. Whereas some schools have set out their values statements, these largely remain at a level of bland generality and, for the most part, have to be interpreted by individual teachers without the benefit of whole-school in-service training. Disparities of implementation can too easily occur. What clearly counts as 'considerate behaviour', 'taking responsibility', 'showing respect' in the everyday experience of school life? Where are the school portfolios to review levels of moral and cultural attainment?

Similarly, the criteria for inspection require unpacking for greater specificity, not least so that schools may have a clearer sense of the basis of evaluation. The gravest concern with inspection is that quick judgments have to be made on audio-visual bites of school life – no more than, and quite probably not as much as, the episodes recounted by pupils in this chapter – by a team who may not have discussed, in any detail, the criteria for their judgments, or seriously engaged in attempting to reconcile conflicting perceptions and interpretations. These, in turn, are translated into fairly anodyne but potentially influential comments (not least for parents) in an OFSTED report. This fails to do justice to the rich cultural and moral texture of the values interplay of school life. The *Handbook for Inspection* warns inspectors against allowing their own views to 'colour judgments' and about conflating culture and religion, and ethnicity with religious belief (GB OFSTED, 1994b, Part 4:16). Nothing is said about the insidious issues of perspective differences due to social class and inequalities of power.

There are several potential values tensions inherent in governmental and school values statements: between the personal and the social; the school, the family and community; and, perhaps most significantly of all in the school context, between developing skills of critical inquiry and argument and dispositions towards fairness, caring and commitment. Can schools and teachers accept and respond constructively not only to inspectors' criticisms of provision, practices and relationships, but also to those voiced by pupils as a result of the educational process in which they develop independent reasoning skills and make judgments based on their own emerging beliefs and values? Are schools two-way learning communities, able to learn from the pupils' everyday ethnographic experience and evaluation?

Satwant: they've got a responsibility to teach and also to help the children out. That's what it says in the brochures.

Saria: We understand all the children, that's what it says. But they don't even ask us anything, so how are they going to understand us?

Acknowledgments

The voices heard in this chapter were those of pupils interviewed in a research project sponsored by the Economic and Social Research Council 'Multicultural/

antiracist policies: pastoral care/ personal and social education issues'. I should also like to acknowledge the contribution of Rani Dayaramani who participated in this research.

References

GREAT BRITAIN, OFSTED (1994a) *Spiritual, Moral, Social and Cultural Development. An OFSTED Discussion Paper*, London, OFSTED.

GREAT BRITAIN, OFSTED (1994b) *Handbook for the Inspection of Schools*, London, HMSO.

GREAT BRITAIN, Parliament, House of Commons (1992) *Choice and Diversity. A New Framework for Schools*, London, HMSO.

GREAT BRITAIN, Statutes (1988) *Education Reform Act 1988*, London, HMSO.

GREAT BRITAIN, Statutes (1992) *Education (Schools) Act 1992. Chapter 38*, London, HMSO.

GREAT BRITAIN, Statutes (1993) *Education Act 1993. Chapter 35*, London, HMSO.

NATIONAL CURRICULUM COUNCIL (1990a) *The Whole Curriculum. Curriculum Guidance 3*, York, NCC.

NATIONAL CURRICULUM COUNCIL (1990b) *Education for Citizenship. Curriculum Guidance 8*, York, NCC.

NATIONAL CURRICULUM COUNCIL (1993) *Spiritual and Moral Development – A Discussion Paper*, York, NCC.

TAYLOR, M.J. (1992) 'Learning fairness through empathy: pupils' perspectives on putting policy into practice', in LEICESTER, M. and TAYLOR, M.J. (Eds) *Ethics, Ethnicity and Education*, London, Kogan Page.

Chapter 11

Vision, Values and Virtues

Jasper Ungoed-Thomas

ABSTRACT: *The focal point of education should be the vision of a school. Vision most appropriately arises within an established understanding of what is meant by school. Vision needs to be, for schools, a 'high' word. Authentic vision promotes right action and aspiration for the future. It also gives schools a secure and justifiable sense of direction. While vision may be shared, it is essentially a personal matter. The validity of any vision is best established through discussion and observation of its effects. The vision of a school is sustained by national values, and by values specific to its circumstances. There can be difficulties in identifying and substantiating these. Ultimately, a vision will only be authentic where it is integrally related to the practical objectives, or 'goods' of schools. These are that students should learn to good effect about persons: the curriculum, community and citizenship. The first virtues of these are respect, truth, fairness and responsibility. It is these virtues which should be seen as the vision of a school.*

The focal point of education should be the vision of a school. Such a vision is, in essence, to do with the idea which one may have of a school: an idea in this sense being, to quote Samuel Coleridge (1830), 'that conception of a thing . . . which is given by the knowledge of its ultimate aim.' So, for example, T.S. Eliot, in discussing the *Idea of a Christian Society*, said that his concern with contemporary society was not 'primarily with specific defects, abuses or injustices but with the question what – if any – is the idea of the society in which we live? To what end is it arranged?' (1939:8).

The Idea of a School

Possible ideas of a school, of the end to which it is arranged, are limited by what is meant by *school*. At first sight it might seem reasonable to assume that we all know what we mean when we talk about a school, and that we all mean the same thing. However, as the song says, 'It ain't necessarily so'.

There is a fairly widespread tendency to define school in terms which reflect individual and particular attitudes towards education, whether explicit or implicit. For example, Ivan Illich, anxious to attack the whole notion of school, described it in such a way as to emphasize those compulsory, authoritarian aspects of school which he disliked. For him, school was 'the age-specific, teacher-related process requiring full time attendance at an obligatory curriculum' (1973:32). A school is, self-evidently, not a process. It does not necessarily, though it does usually, require full-time attendance. And even today the curriculum is very seldom, if ever, fully obligatory in any type of school.

Each historical period tends to perceive school in terms of those types of institution which most characteristically, if not best, reflect what is sometimes called the *Zeitgeist*, or the spirit of the age. Thus, for many generations in England it was usual to understand what a school was by reference to religious institutions. It was commonly held that, at the very least, a major purpose of a school was to help scholars become good Christians. To this end teachers, if male (which they overwhelmingly were), were frequently ordained, much of the curriculum was concerned with theological matters, and the chapel was a focal point of school life. Indeed, many schools were almost indistinguishable in appearance from religious houses, with their places of prayer, cloisters, dorters or dormitories, closes, kitchens, fraters or dining halls, libraries, lodgings for the head or principal and even wine cellars. Care of souls, or pastoral care, was in theory if not always in practice, a major preoccupation. And the school was often subject, formally or otherwise, to ecclesiastic visitation. In such circumstances it was not always easy to distinguish at first sight a theological college, a seminary or a novice house from a simple school.

It does not require deep probes or archaeological instincts to discover strong remaining traces of such views of what a school is. Early religious educational foundations continue to attract support, as do more recently established Anglican, Roman Catholic and Non-Conformist schools. Furthermore, the existence of schools for those of Jewish, Islamic and other faiths helps more generally to reinforce the notion that education should be grounded on theological principles.

Today's culture is not, however, predominantly influenced by religious thought. More powerful are the philosophies of free markets, industry and commerce. It is ideas from such sources which now very possibly exert the greatest influence on what we consider a school to be. Although it is seldom spelled out in such straight-forward terms, not least because the notion might be less than appealing to many teachers, students and parents, the most characteristic contemporary paradigm of a school is a factory. At its apex is the senior management team, deploying such techniques as line management and total quality control, and concerned to compete effectively in the market place. To this end, budgets are kept and scrutinized by accountants, press officers try to ensure a positive public image, and performance indicators are put in place to monitor output variables. Above all, there is concern that the product,

that is the student, should be delivered effectively and efficiently in accordance with the requirements of the various customers, for example, employers,
government, further and higher education and parents. And it is hardly necessary to emphasize that all this is more than likely to take place in a structure
virtually indistinguishable from one designed for the purposes of light industry: there are the same flat-roofed, anonymous, beige exteriors, the same administrative suites and offices, the same multi-purpose internal spaces, the
same utilitarian neglect of civilized amenities and comforts.

Factories, religious institutions, and indeed any other models for schools
which might come to mind, are in fact simply analogues. As such they can
offer us insights into what schools may do, or what they may be for. They may
even help us to understand the values which underlie our approaches to
education, individually or as a society. Alternatively, they may, fairly or not, be
open to various criticisms. It could be argued that certain characteristics, crucial to the nature of some analagous bodies, are at best irrelevant and at worst
hostile to what schools are about. For example, religious institutions may be
seen as properly concerned with indoctrination, insofar as they are committed
to certain dogmatic positions; but indoctrination is not justifiable as an aspect
of any educational activity. As for factories, they must be committed to the
delivery of product; but to equate students with products would be dehuman-
izing, and so inimical in principle to the nature of education.

How best, then, can a school be defined? Clearly, it must be described in
its own terms. Inevitably, various approaches could justifiably be suggested.
However, for present purposes, I will take it that a school is a particular
institution, in a particular place; that it houses a community of young people
and adults whose shared intention and responsibility, within the context of
education, is the pursuit and achievement of learning; and that it offers such
learning to students from infancy to the point where they leave school, usually
for further or higher education, vocational training, employment or other
occupation.

Vision

The vision, the idea of a school, its good, the end to which it should be
arranged, these then necessarily occur within the sphere of meaning which we
attach to *school*. As for the understandings which we can have of the concept
of vision itself, these may vary. Vision can be interpreted as meaning the
ordinary act of seeing; for example, an optician may tell me that the vision in
my left eye is deficient. It can also, while referring to something perceived
other than by ordinary sight, relate to everyday, material matters. Thus, the
management of a vehicle manufacturing company may announce that it has
a vision of producing so many cars a day, all achieving certain standards of
quality.

Vision, however, has generally tended to be more of what has been called a high word. It can call to mind something seen distinctly, vividly in the imagination, something quite possibly inspiring, perhaps even sublime. Vision of this sort, though, may also have negative connotations. It could be taken to be fanciful, or unrealistic, or, to use the word in a pejorative sense, mystical. Such vision would be a mirage or an illusion.

For schools vision should be, for the most part, a 'high' word with all the opportunities and dangers which such use implies. The dangers are only too familiar. It is easy to depict a vision; and not all that difficult to display it in glowing colours. Many headteachers, at least those with the relevant talents, do so frequently in brochures, at speech-days and on other occasions as the chance occurs. But such visions, unless they arise from personal conviction and are related to school life in all its diversity, complexity and sheer intractability, are more likely to undermine than to support the quality of education. Vision which is hopelessly distanced from actuality, and so which there is no realistic hope of successfully pursuing, is liable to breed a sense of failure, even cynicism; and vision which is relevant but ignored in practice can seem hypocritical.

Authentic vision is, however, of critical significance for schools. In the first place, it should help inform and guide the moral development of students. There is a necessary connection between real vision, as contrasted with fantasy, and moral behaviour. If we are to develop fully as persons we can hardly manage in the absence of a moral vision. As Iris Murdoch has put it, 'truthful vision prompts right action'; moreover, 'we can only move properly in a world that we can see, and what must be sought for is vision' (1992:303).

Real vision is as vital to ensuring the quality of education in the psychological as in the moral spheres. Young people, no less than adults, are faced with personal stresses, family problems, and from time-to-time, outright tragedies and disasters. Confidence that these may be survived and coped with can grow where there is belief that a better world can exist, can indeed be created. As Bettelheim has concluded, drawing on his clinical work with children, 'Only hope for the future can sustain us in the adversities we unavoidably encounter' (1978:4).

So, in education, vision needs to be interpreted as a high word. As such, it can offer an ideal of what a school should be. It should help to give schools a continuing, secure and permanent sense of what they ought to be doing. Further, vision should enable schools to respond to society's changing hopes for the future and consequent expectations of education in the light not only of the current ideas of theorists, politicians, economists, business people and others, but also of more lasting considerations. Vision should, in fact, provide schools with a means of looking forward with some assurance, whatever the various and immediate demands being made in the name of an unknowable future.

Where high vision is absent, schools can pay a considerable price. There is a natural tendency for structure, procedure, management and so forth to be given too high a priority, to degenerate from means into ends. Important though such matters are, they can, if clumsily handled, suffocate spontaneity, inspiration and delight in schools – the very things which bring teaching and learning alive, make it of value. Indeed, without a view of the goal of their aspiration, schools can become dispirited, and allow what they are doing to deteriorate into a treadmill of routine. It is in such schools that teachers and students alike appear to lack a sense of either purpose or direction. At worst, classroom work becomes a bore for all concerned, students misbehave or simply fail to turn up, and teachers can become dispirited and obsessed with discipline.

How does one decide who appropriately might perceive a vision? Vision, like spirit, is no respecter of precedent, protocol or authority. It may come to anyone, at any time. It is also personal. Of its nature, it appears to individuals. It is very doubtful if it can truly be perceived by any corporate entity, as such: at most, it can be seen by persons who are members of such an entity. We need to be on our guard where it is claimed that an organization or a group, for example, school management or government has received a vision.

That visions are seen properly by individuals has significant implications. It is identifiable human beings, not the spokespersons of associations, who observe, explain, communicate, inspire, can be questioned, who are answerable. Vision described by an institution is anonymous in origin, at best a mirage designed to offer comfort, at worst a device intended to promote hierarchical control.

If vision, rightly, remains personal, it will probably although not necessarily, tend to differ from one person to another. Varying experiences, values, hopes and circumstances are all liable to influence perceptions of what is desirable. Thus, a young teacher in a suburban independent school may well have a different vision from that of a head-teacher of an inner city comprehensive, while a local Labour councillor is likely to have a different view from a member of a Conservative policy unit. Moreover, different visions, once articulated, are liable to attract different followings.

We could thus be envisaging a scenario, where a thousand flowers are blooming, where some may clash, and where many may be fighting for survival on the same ground. One possible response to such a situation would be to accept a counsel of despair and assume that chaos is bound to reign. Alternatively, one could go to the opposite extreme and, taking a Platonic stance, argue that vision implies that there is an ideal form of a school, the reflection of an ultimate Good, which is in the last analysis the only logically possible, single and correct notion of what a school should be.

However, while it is, I suppose, just conceivable that a kaleidescope of contrasting visions could enliven our educational horizons in perpetuity, or that *a priori* reasoning might ultimately establish one true and universally agreed idea of a school, it is surely reasonable to take a rather different approach. One could plausibly argue that discussion and experiment should help to sort out the stronger, more tenacious and adaptable, better rooted, more realistic views, from those which have, for whatever reason, less durability and worth.

Accordingly, in putting forward the vision of a school, probably the best approach, and in any case the one I shall adopt, is simply to describe and to argue for it as best one can. As far as I am concerned, I am more than content that the worth of a vision should be established through the processes of rational discourse.

Values

It is values which sustain vision. A school is, essentially, concerned with values. But from where do these values come; and how does one identify them? They must surely derive, in the first place, from those held to be important by society. This is, of course, a widely held view and one which is articulated from time-to-time by those concerned with national educational policy, and more generally by those with an interest in the moral well-being of the country. When Home Secretary, Kenneth Clarke declared at a press conference that, 'Schools must promulgate the values we as a society want to pass on to the next generation' (Clarke, 1993).

The values of a school also need to include those which are identified by itself as being of particular importance to its specific circumstances. Rural, inner-city and suburban schools, fee-paying and state schools, selective and comprehensive schools, schools serving mainly single or multi-ethnic communities, schools with, and those without, religious foundations, all are likely to hold values particular to their own needs, and so which are likely to differ to a greater or lesser extent from one school to another. It is as important that schools, in their aspirations and practices, reflect locally determined values as that they take on board those considered to be of national significance although there may well turn out to be a considerable overlap between the two.

One does not have to look either hard or long to find various values identified and discussed which are believed to be important for the whole of our society. Despite the pluralist nature of the country, it is relatively easy to find a degree of apparent agreement over what they are. The range of those which appear to be most frequently mentioned is indicated by Isaiah Berlin in *Two Concepts of Liberty* (1969:170) where he talks of liberty, equality, justice, happiness, security and public order; and by the Archbishop of York, John Habgood (1987), who has discussed a 'cluster of principles around the notion of human worth', in particular personal freedom and responsibility, and choice and solidarity.

Those who speak of national values with education particularly in mind also tend to cover similar ground, albeit with the sort of distinctive tone which tends to be heard when people are referring to children. Her Majesty's Inspectorate has talked of those 'values and qualities in pupils which will result in attitudes characteristic of a good citizen in a democratic, humane and free society . . . reliability, initiative, self-discipline and tolerance' (Department for Education and Science, 1985: Para. 103); and the chairman of the National

Curriculum Council, said that he would expect the school his children attended 'to have a clear vision of the moral values which it and society hold to be important. These include trust, fairness, politeness, honesty, and consideration to others' (Pascall, 1992:3).

Individual schools may identify or reveal in various ways those values which, for whatever reason, are of particular concern to themselves. They may be published in official aims, having been reached by discussion or not; they may become apparent through the expressed or implicit attitudes of staff; they may be part and parcel, intentionally or otherwise, of organizational arrangements, teaching methods and curriculum planning.

But how are the values held to be important by society to be identified, and to be adopted by schools? Given the degree of apparent consensus it might seem that the easiest and most obvious thing to do would be to draw up a list which contained those values which appeared to enjoy the strongest national support, and to expect or require schools to promote them.

Unhappily, such a straight-forward approach could well lead into various troublesome entanglements. For a start, what exactly would be the mechanism by which a view was expressed about those values which are held dear by society and which should be taught in schools? Individual ministerial initiative? Guidance following widespread consultation with all those interested? A paper from the relevant quango? Any combination of these? It is possible that no such approaches would result in harmony or consensus. Moreover, values chosen in this way might turn out not to fit easily in every respect with central educational purposes and activities; and it is possible that schools could resent being dictated to on such matters.

There are also other difficulties of a more fundamental nature. As Isaiah Berlin has pointed out when discussing values, 'We are faced with choices between ends equally ultimate, and claims equally absolute, the realisation of some which must inevitably involve the sacrifice of others' (1969:168). This is clearly a substantial point. How far can liberty and responsibility, freedom and equality, choice and solidarity, even honesty and consideration for others be satisfactorily reconciled?

Such questions are of course familiar, not least to those with an interest in theology, or in moral and political philosophy. One well-tried way of dealing with them is, not to leave them to stand in isolation but, as John Habgood (1987) has argued, to place them within 'a complex, balanced system of principles'. This solution, however, merely lifts a curtain on a vista of further complications. Thus, it could be that a collection of values identified as important for schools might be enabled to achieve a mutually coherent relationship through being rooted within the value systems of, for example, one or other of the Christian theologies, or of other faiths, or of particular political philosophies, or of groups or movements such as environmentalism, feminism or anti-racism, which have their own perspectives and cultures. However, within different value systems particular values, both on their own and in relation to others, can readily take on varying hues of meaning, attract dissimilar emotional charges and be rated as more or less significant. So, equality will resonate differently in the minds of a free-marketeer and a feminist; while the connections between freedom and responsibility are likely to be interpreted in contrasting fashions by an orthodox Jew and by a Humanist.

Virtues

So how, taking account of these various pitfalls, can one identify more precisely those elements which should form the vision of a school?

In the first place, we need to scrutinize our terms. The concept of value is commonly used in any discussion of the moral purposes of schools. It is conventionally taken to mean something which is, in itself, worthy of esteem. So far, I have followed that usage. From now on, however, I will need to be more specific. 1 intend, therefore, to use the concept of *virtue*. Of course, both historic and contemporary debate surround the notion. Nevertheless, and not least for educational discourse, it is of considerable use.

MacIntyre (1985) has proposed a particular approach to interpreting the meaning of virtue. In its essentials, I will follow this. It places due emphasis on the cultural contexts and social traditions within which notions of virtue arise and develop. It does not, however, adopt a stance which is either necessarily relativist in moral terms, or which denies the significance and integrity of the idea of a person. It is, in fact, a perception of virtue which is consistent with and supportive of the idea of a school as I have discussed it.

MacIntyre understands virtues as human qualities which must satisfy certain conditions specified at each of three stages. Any attribute or disposition which fails to meet all of these conditions cannot be properly called a virtue.

At the first stage, virtues are those qualities necessary to achieve the ends (together with related standards of excellence) which are intrinsic to and implied in a very broad range of established, and at least in part co-operative, worthwhile human activities. These activities are called by MacIntyre *practices*. They include the maintaining of communities, such as families, sport, agriculture, architecture, scientific and historical enquiry, art and music, and so on. Education would clearly also count as such a practice.

At the second stage, virtues are those qualities necessary to sustain us in our personal search for the good. At the least, the ends here envisaged would not preclude humanist, rationalist or theological ideas of ultimate value. At the third stage virtues are qualities, whether exhibited in collaborative endeavour or personal quest, which are dependent for their vitality upon a particular condition. This is that any worthwhile human goals – which, of course, virtues are involved in attempting to achieve – 'can only be elaborated and possessed within an ongoing social tradition' (1985:273).

We have now established the criteria of the concept of virtue. Next, bearing in mind that in MacIntyre's terminology education may be called a practice, we can ask what should be the chief practical objectives of education. Once we have established this, we can go on to identify the related virtues.

Education in schools should be concerned with certain major goals. It should intend to ensure that students learn, and learn to good effect, about persons, the curriculum, community and citizenship. Schools should be concerned with persons. Much of the curriculum necessarily ought to deal with a study of the nature of human beings, for example, in the humanities, English, some sciences, and courses or topics dealing with personal and social education. Equally importantly, schools must be concerned with persons as learners, as students, as leavers or graduates, as teachers and other members of staff, as parents, as governors, and so forth.

Schools obviously have to be concerned with the curriculum, – that is, knowledge and understanding, together with the related attitudes and skills, of the particular disciplines of which a given course of study is an articulation. The immediate and main focus of any school's activities ought to be the curriculum.

Schools have no choice but to be concerned with community. It is within this context that teaching and learning occur. Without community there could be no school. Schools should be concerned to enable students to participate effectively and constructively as members of the communities to which they belong now, and to which they may in the future belong. And schools should be concerned with citizenship. This may be seen as membership of that community which is identified as the state. Education has to prepare students for the political, legal, economic and moral aspects of life as a citizen.

It is generally taken for granted that these practical educational goals have moral features, and that therefore ethical procedures must be followed, if they are to be achieved. But this is not necessarily so. The educational objectives identified can be seen as value free, or more specifically as not incorporating or predicating the practice of any, or any particular, values.

Learning about persons can leave open the question as to how they should be perceived, for example with respect, or at worst as beings to be disregarded, manipulated or used for one's own or some other purpose. Learning about the curriculum does not, of itself, imply that knowledge should be offered within a particular interpretative framework, or that it should be justified with regard to any given criteria or authority. Learning about community and citizenship does not have to require that the student should value these ideas as such. The practical objectives of school need to be morally supported. If they are not, they will be eroded. A school would be destined to fail if it regarded with indifference or contempt persons, evidence, community and citizenship.

So, from where can this moral support come? In general terms, it should arise from the ethos of a school, itself influenced by the nature of education as a moral activity. But this, while necessary, is not sufficient. Each practical objective has a related first virtue. If the practical ends of schools are to be achieved, they must be supported by knowledge and practice of the relevant virtues.

We are now able to enquire: what are the first virtues of education? The answer, given the way the argument has developed so far, must be that they are those qualities which will help all concerned, whatever their particular roles, to engage positively, creatively and productively with the fundamental concerns of schools. In other words, in MacIntyre's terms, the key virtues are those qualities necessary to achieving the essential good or goods of education.

With persons, the first virtue has variously been described as care, concern, charity, love, respect. Of these closely related notions that which probably fits best in the world of education is respect. The teaching of respect for others is not only one of education's more important objectives, but in its absence little, if any, real learning can take place. The first virtue in relation to the curriculum is truth; and to community is fairness. As John Rawls has put it,

> Justice is the first virtue of social institutions, as truth is of systems of thought. A theory however elegant and economical must be rejected or revised if untrue; likewise laws and institutions no matter how efficient and well-arranged must be reformed or abolished if they are unjust (1972:3).

Finally, it would be hard to show that responsibility was not a first virtue in relation to citizenship. A citizen has various rights and duties in relation to other citizens, and to the state. If these are ignored, or not exercized responsibly, then the structures and relationships of the society in which the citizen lives will, no doubt only gradually, but nevertheless inevitably, begin to erode. Accordingly, the possibilities both of maintaining stability and of constructively promoting change, will diminish. In the last analysis, an irresponsible citizen makes nonsense of the idea of citizenship.

However, if these virtues are to have real substance for schools, further conditions must be met. First, the first virtues should be learned, taught and developed with reference to cultural traditions which provide them with meaning, context and history. If considered in isolation virtues degenerate into disregarded labels, the origin and purpose of which are only recalled partially, if at all. Second, the first virtues should be interpreted and understood in such a way that they can help individuals, and in particular students, in the search for their own personal ideal of the good life. Virtues would have little strength if allowed to remain ethereally detached from the contingencies, anxieties and aspirations of daily existence.

Third, the very nature of the first virtues requires that there should be no attempt to impose them, but that students should be encouraged themselves to evaluate the worth of the virtues in theory and in practice. Virtues may be perceived, not only as means, but also as ends. Thus, each of the key virtues should be seen both as helping in the achievement of given practical objectives, and as being of educational worth in themselves. Accordingly, students should be encouraged, as an integral part of their education, to develop the key virtues in all their activities, throughout their school lives.

Further, the virtues should also be seen as having relevance to existence more widely, and as being generally applicable; which is to say, that it should make equally good sense to observe them in the varying circumstances of private and of public life, and of those often tricky areas where they overlap. Students need to learn strong virtues which can hold good, and can support them throughout their lives, in whatever they may be doing, and wherever they may be doing it. Of course, students will need to realize that such virtues cannot be practised simplistically, and that thought and care are necessary if they are to result in appropriate behaviour in different situations. However, it is a major responsibility of schools to make sure that this is something which students know and understand.

To conclude: the goods of education can be, and often are, understood in mainly pragmatic terms. However, they cannot be enjoyed or secured where the related virtues are ignored. Equally, those same virtues ought to be seen as being worthwhile in themselves. Schools, therefore, should be concerned with the teaching of virtues for their own sake, as well as for the educational results their exercise can bring. The knowledge and practice of the first virtues are absolutely essential for the successful conduct of education.

Respect for persons, truth, fairness and responsibility are then the educationally necessary first virtues. It is these which should represent the vision of a school. Of course, there are other virtues, which individual schools might hold. These, however, assuming they were educationally justifiable, would necessarily be either supportive of or related to the key virtues. Thus, schools might refer to the virtues of co-operation, of discipline, of tolerance, of hard work, of compassion, of honesty, and so on. However, it is the key virtues which should sustain and guide every school. It is the vision of them which should illuminate and sustain the studies, relationships, organization and social attitudes of a school; and which should receive the support of society.

References

BERLIN, I. (1969) 'Two concepts of liberty', in *Four Essays on Liberty*, Oxford, Oxford University Press.

BETTELHEIM, B. (1978) *The Uses of Enchantment*, Harmondsworth, Penguin.

CLARKE, K. (1993) *Dealing with Juvenile Offenders* (Press Conference), London, Home Office, March 1993.

COLERIDGE, S.T. (1830/1972) *On the Constitution of Church and State*, London, Everyman.

DEPARTMENT OF EDUCATION AND SCIENCE (1985) *The Curriculum from 5 to 16* (An HMI Series), London, HMSO.

ELIOT, T.S. (1939) *The Idea of a Christian Society*, London, Faber and Faber.

HABGOOD, J. (1987) 'Ethical principles for when the going gets tough', *The Independent*, 6 June.

ILLICH, I. (1973) *Deschooling Society*, Harmondsworth, Penguin.

MACINTYRE, A. (1985) *After Virtue: A Study in Moral Theory* (2nd Edition). London, Duckworth.

MURDOCH, I. (1992) *Metaphysics as a Guide to Morals*, London, Chatto & Windus.
PASCALL, D. (1992) Speech to the Religious Education Council of England and Wales, 7 May.
RAWLS, J. (1972) *A Theory of Justice*, Oxford, Oxford University Press.

Chapter 12

School Mission Statements and Parental Perceptions

Andrew Marfleet

ABSTRACT: *With the legal requirement for schools to declare their values in their prospectus, there has been an upsurge in school mission statements. Denominational schools have been given ample help in the task of constructing such statements, though common schools are now feeling their own way in the process: their statements of official values are beginning to reflect the influence of market forces in education. Parents choosing schools may well look at statements in prospectuses and other policy documents, but they are swayed by many other factors, too. Social, ethnic and religious backgrounds make a difference, and it is probable that more parents are taking the school's perceived ethos and what they know of its academic performance into account. But it still too soon to say how influential official statements are in the process of parental choices or indeed whether the statements are a reliable guide to what happens in schools.*

Choice and Diversity

Parents in England, it seems, have 'a right to know'. They are told in the Parent's Charter that 'every school must publish a prospectus every year which describes its achievements and what it has to offer' (Department for Education, 1994a:7). It must contain statistics on the performance, attendance and destinations of pupils, but more than this: prospectuses also explain 'the aims and values of the school and its approach to teaching' and how schools 'provide moral and spiritual guidance for their pupils' (*ibid.*).

The right to a free prospectus was established in 1980; what is new is that it must contain a statement on values and ethos. The prospectus is also now the direct responsibility of the school governing body. The Regulations (Great Britain, Regulations, 1993) and Circulars (Department for Education, 1993a; 1993b; 1993c) that gave effect to this were a direct result of promises made to the House of Lords in 1992. As I describe elsewhere (Marfleet, 1995), these regulations, like the amendments to the 1992 Act, that require inspectors from the Office for Standards in Education (OFSTED) to report on 'the spiritual, moral, social and cultural development of pupils' (Great Britain, Statutes, 1992), were not initially part of Government policy. Those who drafted the amendments and the bishops and peers from all sides of the House who spoke up for them were more concerned about allowing a genuine pluralism in school values to flourish than with encouraging traditional values or a return to basics. There is evidence that the pressures that were put on the Government in the Upper Chamber came as a result of lobbying from those who hoped to see, eventually, new Christian or Muslim schools with – if possible – public funding. Whether Baroness Blatch's concessions to the proposers of the amendments were because the Government saw the wisdom of the argument or because time was running out before the dissolution of Parliament that preceded the 1992 election we will probably never know.

It is unlikely that the 'diversity' that John Patten was fond of referring to during his two years as Secretary of State for Education was intended to include diversity of *values*. Certainly, the 1993 discussion paper that the National Curriculum Council produced talks of absolute values, with limited concessions to different ways of thinking about beliefs and ethics. More recent pronouncements on Religious Education and Collective Worship, including Circular 1/94 (Department for Education, 1994b), seem to reflect a desire for uniformity under a 'broadly Christian' position.

Mission Statements: Origins and Ideas

This broadly Christian uniformity can, of course, be traced back to the 1944 Act (Great Britain, Statutes, 1944), which gave both an official value base for all schools and a recognition that denominational schools would have a distinctive ethos. This distinctiveness has meant that the Church schools, in particular, were in the business of pronouncing on their values well before 1992. Even if it emerged only as an aspect of the school's admission policy, the prospectus of a typical Aided (i.e. state-funded denominational) school would point towards a commitment to certain beliefs and attitudes.

One can trace, too, another, more recent development that has played its part in the current demand for statements of values. During the 1980s, mission statements and vision statements emerged as key features in the world of business and industry, drawing particularly on the work of Deming, the mind behind the Japanese quality revolution (see, for example, Covey, 1989). Total Quality Management (TQM) had become an over-riding concept in industry well before local management of schools became the norm in educational provision. It was inevitable that educational management would learn from the Quality Movement in industry, following the Deming principles that any organization needed a very clear statement of purpose and that poor management processes rather than people prevented good quality. Covey argues for the concept of principle-centred leadership, showing that the designers of processes incorporate their values or principles into them, making it essential to understand the values as well as the mission of an organization in order to improve each aspect of it.

The Quality Movement has been international, and surveys suggest that its ideas have been adopted by most of the world's successful companies. National quality awards have sprung up on both sides of the Atlantic; Government departments in Britain have vied with each other in promoting awards and standards, a process accelerated by John Major's Citizen's Charter. In Britain, as originally in the USA, it is being claimed that quality principles can be made to work in schools. Avon Training and Enterprise Council (TEC), for example, was involved in this well before 1992, helping schools and colleges to undertake an examination of their principles. The typical process begins with a strategic review in which all the stake-holders brainstorm vision, mission and values. They use the resultant information to guide them to the activities and processes which are critical to their success – avoiding mere rhetoric.

There is evidence that both the Department for Education and OFSTED have been aware of these approaches. I mention it here because it is crucial in any understanding of the nature of official values in schools to trace the genesis of the current quest for values statements. The fact that clear statements about schools' values and ethos are now required by law is by no means the whole story.

It is not insignificant, however, that schools were being offered help with the process of drawing up such statements well before they were legally obliged to have them. In some cases, as we have seen, the local TEC may have been involved, and help has been offered by religious groups, who have been used to thinking about vision, mission and values for quite some time.

The Revalues Project Four Five, directed by Veronica Williams (1991), is an example of this, although the production of mission statements was not one of the original aims. The project began in April 1988 with the task of exploring and developing the teaching of beliefs and values in secondary education. One of the original aims was 'to help teachers . . . to articulate the content of the INSET they require' (p. 1), and the findings showed some interesting ways in which this could be done. Reflection, analysis and commitment were required from teachers, resulting in INSET that helped them 'to go through the process of examining their own values and beliefs in relation to specific issues . . . by a series of group exercises involving the value-mapping technique' and 'to work out a Charter of Values' (p. 13).

Paper Two of the resource pack that was subsequently published was about how to produce a Charter of Values. This is defined as 'a document expressing those things which a school considers of greatest worth', containing 'agreed statements which have been reached through a process comprising of dialogue, evaluation and the disclosure of hidden assumptions.' Everybody involved with the school should be involved in the process of developing it, from the Chair of Governors to the youngest child (Williams, 1990:2–3).

Although the report on the project reiterates that 'an education in values and beliefs is not provided by one or two isolated areas of the curriculum but by the total ethos and style of the school' and states that 'the project has encouraged schools to go through the process of examining their value systems and to develop a charter' (Williams, 1991:10), it concedes that the take-up might not have been very great even amongst the schools involved in the project. The report concedes that the whole project 'was easier to develop in schools where Religious Education was not recognised as being a low status subject', but 'unfortunately in many schools this was not the case' (p. 4). Even the whole school INSET that might have led to the process of drawing up a charter was only possible 'in some schools', mainly smaller schools. In many schools, it seems, 'staff were reluctant to work with colleagues from other departments and found it difficult to reach agreement over a Charter of Values' (p. 7).

Who knows whether these schools, with others, will have had more inclination to look at their values since the 1993 Regulations appeared? The materials produced by the Revalues Project deserved wider use, though it was predictable that they would be more likely to be used in schools where the Head was enthusiastic about them. The Christian Education Movement (CEM) which managed the Revalues Project is in touch mainly with RE teachers, and not all of them; RE teachers are often lone voices in their schools.

Catholic Schools

However, a very different picture can be seen in the case of schools where the importance of values has been stressed at the highest levels. In the Roman Catholic schools in England and Wales, clear statements of values have proliferated in the past two or three years, following an important document from their Bishops' Conference in 1987, reissued in 1990 in a revised form. In its introduction, the document argues for 'the need to produce Mission Statements, to clarify aims and objectives, and . . . for policy statements of all kinds' (Bishops' Conference of England and Wales, 1990:1).

The need for distinctiveness has no doubt galvanized both the Catholic hierarchy and their Aided schools into action, leaving other schools on the starting blocks. The Bishops' Conference followed up their philosophical statements with a series of very practical materials. The first pack, *Developing a Mission Statement* (1990), set the pattern. As well as notes on *why* a mission statement is essential, there were carefully developed materials to help individual schools set up the process. This pattern was followed in the subsequent packs of materials that emerged: *Developing Objectives and Tasks using Key Result Areas and Performance Indicators* (1990), *Evaluation, Staff Development and Review* (1991) and *The Mission Statement into Action* (1993). The materials go on to help schools organize a process for auditing what they are doing, as well as having clear aims and objectives; they are both extremely practical and unreservedly Christian.

Unlike the CEM materials, the Catholic development materials have been used extensively, being regarded as an obligatory part of INSET from their inception, and leading to mission statements that demonstrate the level of their commitment to Christian values. A typical example comes from one particular Catholic High School: after a brief summary statement, five areas of commitment are listed, each being followed by up to nine action points. The summary statement sets the tone: the school 'seeks to be a living Christian community in which effective learning takes place. By recognising Jesus Christ in each one of us we aim to develop fully the unique talents of each pupil.'

Other Catholic schools have produced similar documents, but it is important to note that although they have had access to the same INSET materials, they have not been given off-the-peg mission statements. Individual ownership is essential for each school; as the various stakeholders – staff, parents and pupils as well as headteacher and governors – all have their input into the statement of official values, they are drawing together as a community as well as drawing up a document.

While noting the kind of variations that reflect local circumstances, one is obliged, however, to admit that the mission statements of Catholic schools do not vary significantly, and perhaps this is to be expected. Within a typical RC Aided school, one would expect to find broadly similar values held by staff who are appointed because they are sympathetic with the school's ethos, by pupils from at least nominally Christian families, and by governors whose very motivation for serving is their commitment to the faith.

Church of England Schools

Anglican schools have been a year or two behind their Catholic counterparts, but they too are probably well ahead of the non-church schools in drawing up mission statements. It is generally recognized that the ethos of a rural Aided school, which is often *de facto* the neighbourhood school, will differ from that of an Aided school in a town where real choice can be exercised. Even where the rural church school has staff who are totally committed Christians, they tend to be aware that the families they serve come from a variety of backgrounds, and respect that diversity. On the other hand, rural schools are rarely multi-ethnic; it is a paradox that there are Aided schools in inner cities with a strong ethnic mix, and even majorities of children from, say, Muslim homes, in some cases. The implications of this are noted in Gay *et al.,* (1991:33). It is probably fair to to say that, in general, Anglican schools exhibit much more religious diversity than do Catholic schools. To set up a process for the introduction of mission statements has, therefore, been a more complex issue.

Nevertheless, by early 1992, dioceses had access to materials to help them in this task, thanks to a working group drawn from the National Society, the Culham Institute and the Southwark diocese. The materials were trialed in five dioceses in different parts of England. In the introduction to the Anglican pack, the authors argue that church schools must 'justify their existence and support from local parishes and communities' by showing 'that their day-to-day life reflects their Christian foundation and purposes' (Louden and Urwin, 1992). Hence the need for a mission statement. Interestingly, it is acknowledged that some schools might want to use a different term to describe a statement of their values and purposes – although the term is 'widely used in business and in public and voluntary services', it could be 'open to misrepresentation', for instance implying 'that a school is setting out to evangelise its pupils' (*ibid.*). The Catholics have no such qualms: in *Evaluating the Distinctive Nature of a Catholic School*, it is stated that although the primary role of the school is to educate, 'evangelisation and/or catechesis' will be taking place as each member of the school community, teacher and pupil, 'is ready for it'. It will depend on 'the school's faithfulness to the Catholic vision as a community, not in terms of thrusting it upon one another, but rather in the sensitive appropriateness of interrelations between school member and school member' (Bishops' Conference of England and Wales, 1990:A-2).

Schools are invited to work through the Anglican pack on their own, though outside help is recommended – indeed Diocesan Education Officers have been kept busy servicing church schools in this way. Governors as well as staff are to be drawn in; shared ownership is stressed. After considering the general purpose of church schools, each school, whether aided, controlled or special agreement, is then invited 'to set out its own purposes in its own unique situation'. Situations are bound to vary, so 'no single mission statement could ever apply to all the Church's schools.' The introduction to the pack emphasizes the need to focus on school purposes 'in relation to Christian beliefs and principles and links with local churches and parishes'. The programme is also intended to move from 'general emphases' to 'practical areas of school life' (Louden and Urwin, 1992). Data collected in the Diocese of St Edmundsbury and Ipswich show a strong preference for references to Christian values, RE and worship, but no enthusiasm for rigid discipline or other features designed to attract parents.

County Schools

Church schools, it would appear, have had ample help in drawing up official statements of their values. County (i.e. non-denominational) schools have been left to their own devices, by and large, though one must acknowledge the role that individual Heads, senior management teams and governors have played in particular schools. In some local authorities, advisers have prompted activity in this area, and not only where OFSTED inspections loom on the horizon. There are courses available, often run by independent consultants, on producing mission statements. Some county schools, however, have worked out statements of their values from scratch, with little input from outside.

My own research into school values (see Marfleet, 1995), which has been based on case studies, has involved significant discussion with Heads, senior managers, governors, parents and pupils on their perceptions of the schools with which they are involved. However, it may be too early yet to measure how far parental choice of schools is being influenced by official statements of values. More research is needed in this area, though Knight (1992) has made a start.

Nevertheless, schools are taking the production of their prospectus, including a mission statement, much more seriously. The example of one county primary school that I have studied illustrates a growing trend. It recently produced a glossy brochure and a separate flyer as part of its marketing strategy. A few years ago, the school was content with a traditional prospectus, typed and duplicated in-house. The advent of local management, however, seems to have focused the minds of senior staff and governors. The school saw itself losing out financially if children were sent to other local schools either because of the supposed superiority of the other schools or because of ignorance of the existence or location of this school. A working group of governors was set up to produce the new prospectus, a process that involved interviewing possible designers and publishers as well as collating material from different members of the school community. A central feature is the statement of values – a series of bullet points ('what we believe in') in the flyer, and a more narrative approach, in the form of a letter by the Headteacher, in the main prospectus. The initiative for this came from discussions between the Head and the Chair of Governors, leading to a meeting between all staff and governors to discuss values. Lists were drawn up and refined, though the process was not without friction. *Tolerance* was rejected as a value (who wants to be merely *tolerated?*) in favour of *respect* and *kindness.* The role of the community was acknowledged – an aspect of which the governors were more aware than the staff. But all involved appear to have been happy with the product, which might not seem very original, as listed below, but involved some very useful thinking by staff and governors.

- Our school recognises the partnership between home and school. We want to work together with you, as parents, to ensure that your child is happy and successful.
- We value your child as an individual and we recognise their abilities and qualities. We do our best to develop these, and provide for all children's needs.
- We value fairness, kindness and a harmonious atmosphere in our school community.
- We encourage your child to celebrate their own achievements and those of others.
- We expect your child to develop pride in themselves, their school and a respect for those around them. This includes self-discipline coupled with a growing sense of responsibility.
- We set high standards in all that we attempt and expect your child to work towards these.

These points are followed by a statement about the importance of links with the community, industry and the business world. 'We are especially interested in our role in the local community and continue to use opportunities to develop this.' References to links with local churches are not included, though a curate (a co-opted governor) and several other Christians in the community now go into the school to help with the occasional assembly. Under Curricular Aims, it is stated that 'the Christian faith forms the basis of our Religious Education, exploring the teaching of Jesus Christ and the effects this has on our own lives', and that sex education 'is taught within the context of a moral framework reflecting family values in our society'.

Parental Choice

It is noteworthy that a county school should stress aspects like these, when many parents would mention them as reasons for choosing a church school. For many parents, the evidence they want in choosing a school for their children will not be derived from a prospectus alone: they will find out by other means, too, what a school actually does. This has emerged in my interviews with parents who have chosen denominational schools.

A parent who had chosen a Catholic High School told me her story. She and her family attended a large Baptist Church in the town, and had chosen the Catholic High School for their daughter after she had left a Church of England Aided Primary. Their sons, ten or twelve years earlier, had had no choice and had gone to the neighbourhood County High. The fact that the Catholic High School had changed its policy, to admit children from non-Catholic families, where a real commitment to another church could be demonstrated, had encouraged them to apply there for their daughter, as in fact others at their church had done. They had looked into how far the Roman church was instigated or impressed upon the children, but in fact it seemed to take a very low profile: the school seemed to be Christian, with Christian values, rather than just Catholic. The only obvious signs of the latter were the crucifixes around the school. Pupils were expected to attend mass, but non-Catholics could go up for a blessing. In almost every respect, the school was, for their family too, an extension of the work of home and church. Their home had a strongly evangelical ethos, but this was echoed at the school, she felt, where a significant minority of the staff were evangelical Protestants, who met with their Catholic colleagues for prayer and took a full part in school life. This was confirmed by my own visits to the school, where I saw Anglican staff leading worship and was told by several people about the varied Christian input. The Head and senior staff admitted, too, that the change in admissions policy had meant that the large group of non-Catholic pupils there tended to come from very committed Christian families, as they needed to demonstrate strong church allegiance to get a place: the school was heavily over-subscribed. Paradoxically, the Catholic children could be fairly nominal in their commitment. The impact of this on the school ethos was fairly noticeable.

Reasons given to me for choosing Roman Catholic or Church of England Aided schools do not seem to differ much from each other. A father who had chosen a Church of England Aided school, rather than the nearest County Primary school, told me why he had wanted this school for his son – 'so that he would grow up in an environment where Christian values, beliefs were the norm, presented by people who believed them rather than being part of Government policy ("you will teach this")'. He wanted teachers who were committed to what they taught, and a Christian influence for his son 'from day one'. This particular school had impressed him; it had a family atmosphere, with older children taking special care of the younger ones. The school had close links with the parish church, though ministers from various local churches came in to help with assemblies. More than the other two Church of England schools in the town, it drew its pupils from the immediate neighbourhood, so there was considerable continuity between church life and school life. The other two schools were in less residential parts of the town, and families brought their children in; their geographical centrality kept them on a pedestal, and they were popular, too, for slightly different reasons.

It is difficult to generalize from individual case studies, but the stories I have been told are illuminating. Most of the parents I have spoken to have chosen the nearest primary school for their children, especially where denominational schools are not available. Some express concerns about the schools they have chosen – about the need for more discipline, or reading schemes, or (in the case of some Christian families) more appropriate RE teaching. But only a small minority would appear to choose a more distant school, apart from those with the resources to buy private education. Most parents are not prepared for the inconvenience of taking their children further afield. I have detected a greater willingness to move in urban areas, where a number of secondary schools lie within a reasonable distance – sometimes cohorts of primary school leavers split into several groups.

What does this have to say about parental choice? 'You can say which school you would prefer your child to go to,' says the Parent's Charter. 'Your choice is wider as a result of recent changes' (Department for Education, 1994a:9). But how is parental choice actually exercised? West considers much of the evidence from recent research, though she acknowledges that the findings (especially at the secondary stage) vary somewhat. 'This is not surprising', she states, 'as the studies differed considerably in both their approach and methods' (West, 1994:119). What consensus there is confirms that 'the proximity of the school or its location and performance issues (examination results or academic record)' are important factors. Good discipline still matters for some parents. How much the child wants to go to the school influences many: if the child's friends are going there, alternatives could well be ruled out. West notes 'some marked and interesting differences between parents with different social, ethnic and religious backgrounds' at the secondary stage, but suggests too that 'it is possible that parents are now focusing more on performance issues – school examination results – and performance-related issues – a pleasant atmosphere or ethos – than they were in the past' (1994:119).

Parents do not only have prospectuses to go on. Policy documents now appear in schools on a host of value-related topics: on behaviour and discipline, on multicultural education and on equality of opportunity, for example. Inspectors take particular note of such documents, it might be added. It is interesting to observe that the policy documents are beginning to be informed by the explicitly stated values of the school; the head of a primary school recently told me that the teacher redrafting the behaviour policy had gone back to the school's mission statement for guidance. It is possible to be unduly cynical about statements of official school values, seeing them as bearing no resemblance to actual practice. They are, of course, a reflection of ideals, but if the ideals are those agreed by all the stakeholders in a community, they stand more chance of being followed than if imposed from the top. OFSTED inspections will no doubt draw attention to disparities between what they read, what they are told and what they observe.

Before leaving the topic, we must consider families from minority groups and what they expect from schools. This is a vast area, that cannot be dealt with adequately here, though it would not be unfair to say that some minority groups are less than happy with the choice of schools available. Criticisms by the Islamic Academy (1993:2) are perhaps typical.

> The Muslim community with its wide diversity and different life experiences has, on the whole, not found the British educational and political establishment very receptive to its aspiration and ideals.

Many Muslims are pressing for their own voluntary aided schools, though it is also interesting that many prefer the ethos of Christian-Aided schools to that of the more secular common schools. Gay *et al.* (1991:3) cite six Church of England schools in London where over half the pupils come from Muslim families, but it must be acknowledged that most of these schools are in Tower Hamlets, where there is a dearth of school places and therefore little real choice. What is clear, however, is that both Muslims and other faith groups are uneasy about liberal attitudes to issues like sex education in the common schools (cf. Thomson, 1993). Many Christians would probably agree with them, which is a factor in the continuing demand for denominational schools in most areas.

Where is it All Leading?

I have tried to show in this chapter why and how official statements of school values have had a higher profile in recent years, and have tried to relate this to parental expectations of schools. The desire for greater parental choice might feature in the minds of some politicians, but the present Government cannot claim credit for inventing the mission statement. Indeed, the movement towards the production of such statements was already underway in the church schools at the start of the present decade; it can hardly have been driven by market forces, as many of the schools that were first in the field seemed to be already over-subscribed. Subsequent legislation may have quickened the pace and spread the process to other schools, but who is to say that this would not have happened anyway in due course? It would be interesting to investigate whether schools have found the process of drawing up a statement is of value to them as a community, whatever the value of the product in terms of 'selling the school'. For me, questions will remain. Is the finished statement a fair reflection of the school's ethos, summarizing what the school stands for, or is it intended to be an aspiration, an ideal towards which the school is moving? Do parents, to the extent that they are concerned about school values, base their thinking on what they know about a school? Or are they, on the whole, satisfied that most schools are probably doing a good job? The minority who want more evidence may well look at school policy documents and mission statements, but they will cast their nets wider, one hopes, than on what they read in a school prospectus.

References

BISHOPS' CONFERENCE OF ENGLAND AND WALES (1990) *Evaluating the Distinctive Nature of a Catholic School* (2nd Edition), London, Catholic Education Service.

BISHOPS' CONFERENCE OF ENGLAND AND WALES (1990–93) *Development Materials for Catholic Schools*, packs 1–4, London, Catholic Education Service.

COVEY, S. (1989) *The Seven Habits of Highly Effective People*, New York, Simon and Schuster.

DEPARTMENT FOR EDUCATION (1993a) *The Parent's Charter: Publication of Information about the Performance of Colleges in the Further Education Sector in 1993*, Circular 3/93, London, DFE.

DEPARTMENT FOR EDUCATION (1993b) *The Parent's Charter: Publication of Information about Secondary School Performance in 1993*, Circular 4/93, London, DFE.

DEPARTMENT FOR EDUCATION (1993c) *The Parent's Charter: Publication of Information about Primary School Performance in 1993*, Circular 5/93, London, DFE.

DEPARTMENT FOR EDUCATION (1994a) *Our Children's Education: The Updated Parent's Charter*, London, HMSO.

DEPARTMENT FOR EDUCATION (1994b) *Religious Education and Collective Worship*, Circular 1/94, London, DFE.

GAY, J., KAY, B., NEWDICK, H., and PERRY, G. (1991) *A Role for the Future: Anglican Primary Schools in the London Diocese.* Abingdon, Culham College Institute.

GREAT BRITAIN, REGULATIONS (1993) *Education (Schools Information) (England) Regulations 1993*, London, HMSO.

GREAT BRITAIN, STATUTES (1944) *Education Act 1944, Ch. 31*, London, HMSO.

GREAT BRITAIN, STATUTES (1992) *Education Act 1992*, London, HMSO.

ISLAMIC ACADEMY (1993) *The Annual Report, 1992–93*, Cambridge, Islamic Academy.

KNIGHT, P. (1992) 'Secondary schools in their own words: The image in school prospectuses', *Cambridge Journal of Education*, **22**, 1, pp. 55–67.

LOUDEN, L.M.R. and URWIN, P.S. (1992) *Mission, Management, Appraisal – a guide for schools of the Church of England and the Church in Wales*, London, National Society.

MARFLEET, A.G.R. (1995) 'Investigating school values: A case-study approach', *Spectrum*, **27**, 1, pp. 35–46.

NATIONAL CURRICULUM COUNCIL (1993) *Spiritual and Moral Development, A Discussion Paper*, York, NCC.

THOMSON, R. (Ed) (1993) *Religion, Ethnicity and Sex Education: Exploring the Issues*, London, National Children's Bureau.

WEST, A. (1994) 'Choosing schools – the consumers' perspective', in HALSTEAD, J.M. (Ed) (1994) *Parental Choice and Education: Principles, Policy and Practice*. London, Kogan Page.

WILLIAMS, V. (1990) 'Developing a charter of values for a School', *Revalues Project Four Five*, Paper 2, Derby, Christian Education Movement.

WILLIAMS, V. (1991) *Revalues Project Four Five, A Report on the Project*, Derby, Christian Education Movement.

Chapter 13

Planning for Values Education in the School Curriculum

Janet Edwards

ABSTRACT: *Drawing upon the author's experience as a second-ary school teacher and manager, this chapter first considers some of the whole school issues concerned with values and goes on to discuss the ways in which values education comes into the cur-riculum. Modes of delivering values education in the curriculum through PSE and RE are considered and examples are offered of ways in which values find their place in the statutory subjects. Finally, there are sections on teaching and learning styles and on professional development and resources.*

'Values lie at the heart of the school's vision of itself as a community' (National Curriculum Council, 1992).

'Values permeate all educational activity' (Scottish Curriculum Council, 1991).

In the years of my teaching career in comprehensive schools during the 1970s and 80s there was a groundswell of commitment to ideas of pastoral care, counselling, active learning methods and the importance of the values dimen-sion in education. Personal and Social Education (PSE) was in its infancy. Courses, often not examined, in Social Education, Personal Relationships, Child Development, Health Education and Community Service emerged to fill a per-ceived gap in the education of teenagers, and optional courses as well as core modules for all students became established in a significant proportion of schools. PSE may have been something of a rag-bag of curricular areas but the methods used and aims for it we felt were central to the purpose of schooling. There was very little support from outside the school and few resources were available. We innovated and shared our ideas with other teachers. Academics writing on these aspects of education helped some of us to develop our think-ing constructively.

Significant in my thinking was the publication, in 1984, of Hargreaves' report for ILEA, *Improving Secondary Schools*. Included in the aspects of achievement was a category (Achievement Aspect IV) which included 'motivation and commitment; the willingness to accept failure without destructive consequences; the readiness to persevere; the self-confidence to learn in spite of the difficulty of the task'. The report stressed the importance given to PSE in many schools and noted the diversity of practice as a result of the bottom-up way in which the innovation had taken place. Pring (1984) encouraged us to think hard about the aims and content of PSE courses and to be rigorous in evaluation and planning. Documents from HMI such as those in the *Curriculum Matters* series gave support. They provided descriptions of good practice and policy guidelines in a practical format.

In the 1990s the National Curriculum Council (NCC), albeit in an uncoordinated and bolt-on manner, spoke of the importance of breadth and balance in the whole curriculum, reminded schools that the whole curriculum is broader than the core and foundation subjects and RE, named cross-curricular themes, and gave the responsibility to schools to decide how the timetable should be planned and what resources and teaching methods should be used.

In a section entitled Attitudes and Values in a NCC working document which was not widely circulated (NCC, 1992), there was formal recognition of the intention that the themes should

> provide opportunities to promote the following attitudes and values:
> - respect for evidence and rational argument;
> - respect for different ways of life, beliefs, opinion and the legitimate interests of others;
> - regard for equal opportunities including the challenging of stereotypes and an active concern for human rights;
> - respect for non-violent ways of resolving conflict;
> - concern for quality and excellence;
> - valuing oneself and others;
> - constructive interest in community affairs;
> - independence of thought;
> - tolerance and openmindedness;
> - consideration for others;
> - flexibility and adaptability to change;
> - enterprising, persistent approach to tasks and challenges;
> - determination to succeed;
> - self-respect, self-confidence and self-discipline;
> - sense of responsibility for personal and collective action.

But the emphasis in recent years on back to basics, league tables, vocational qualifications and information technology has meant that the non-statutory parts of the National Curriculum have been neglected in many institutions. The cross-curricular themes are in danger of being seen as an additional burden for the hard-pressed busy teacher.

Whole School Planning for Values Education

Many dilemmas still exist in whole school planning. Some of these are explored by West:

> The fact is there is no moral consensus and convention based on a publicly recognised religion which can be unproblematically invoked for all children: it is like trying to put a cork back in a bottle which for a significant number of people is now devoid of its content. It is not a lack of concern to instil a sense of values and meaning that is at question, it is finding the appropriate forms to do it . . . It is, in fact, the school's whole approach in the overt and hidden curriculum which conveys the real message of values and the 'how' of what is taught and done is as important as the 'what' (1993:123).

As we have already seen in Chapter 12 of this volume, a statement of values is often used as a way of attempting to find common ground in a school community. It may provide a realistic starting point from which timetabled courses and permeation of values across all subjects in the curriculum might follow. Williams explains that 'a Charter of Values should state in clear, simple terms those things which the school considers to be of greatest worth and importance to its function as a community of persons engaged in the process of education' (1990, Paper 2:3).

A statement of values is quoted overleaf as an example of what might be produced. This school is an 11–16 comprehensive serving a large housing estate in a midlands city. All users of the school were involved in working towards this agreed statement. It was debated in tutor groups, staff meetings, youth club discussions, parent and governors' meetings. Many drafts were produced before this version was adopted. The statement appears as a foreword to most school documents and aims to set an appropriate common context.

A values statement acts as a check-list against which practice can be measured. It is a trigger for evaluative action. OFSTED inspectors will want to know what is being done to put brochure and values statement claims into practice.

From Values Statement to Practice

Putting values statements into practice is not without its difficulties for school management. I recently witnessed an interesting contrast in stance taken by three headteachers from comprehensive schools in the same county as they discussed how they were managing the issue of compulsory daily worship. **A** explained that he had no problem conducting such a daily act and encouraging many of his colleagues to do likewise as he believed that education is like

---

Values Statement

In this School
- we care for all our members, past and present
- we believe that none of us have ever finished learning. Some of the most important things we learn are about ourselves and other people.
- each member is encouraged to make the most of their ability and to achieve a sense of personal worth.
- we try to prepare our members for life in a fast changing world. This means that we must try to become capable of
  - coping with change in our lives
  - becoming independent
  - accepting others for what they are
  - solving problems in our lives
- we try to offer a learning programme which covers our all round needs and our different abilities.
- we recognise that we are part of a wider community. We must take care to work closely with the people and organisations around us.
- we must be proud of our successes and capable of learning from our failures.
- we accept that good learning only takes place if our students' basic human needs are met first.
- we must try to make the way we teach fit the learner's needs.
- we will keep a record of each student's achievement. There will be regular opportunities for parents to talk with teachers about their children's progress.
- we expect our members to do the best they can all of the time.
- we are always pleased to see and to help our ex-students.

ABOVE ALL, EACH MEMBER MUST, EACH DAY, ACHIEVE A LITTLE BIT OF SUCCESS.

---

a triangle with God on one apex and teachers and students on the other two. The nearer individual teachers and students come to God the closer they will become to each other. **B** told how his school had submitted a statement that it could not and would not conform with the requirement to hold daily worship with a predominantly Christian content. This had been the result of deliberation by parents, teachers and governors prior to an OFSTED inspection. **C**, on the other hand, had appealed to her staff to assist her in finding ways, consonant with the aims and objectives of the school and the wishes of the community, to uphold the legal requirement for communal daily worship. Most staff had appreciated her dilemma and were working collaboratively to find acceptable ways forward. These differing approaches reflect different management styles, stages of institutional development and school catchment areas. **A**'s school, a Catholic foundation, recruits pupils from homes where religious belief is important. **B**'s is a small town centre school drawing a high percentage of its pupils from professional families. The school where **C** is headteacher is a large suburban community college on the outskirts of a city. Consensus had been achieved in different ways in different contexts.

West (1993:123–4) describes the aims and objectives of the Personal, Social, Vocational and Moral Education programme in the school of which she is head. These look very much like the aims of the whole school. If the aims of PSE and those of the school generally are so similar, is there a case for separately timetabled courses? Or should there be a permeation of all that a school does, whether in formal lessons or through the ethos and hidden curriculum, by the ideals that promote the personal and social development of young people? Should there be a special course where moral education is to be explored, or should moral implications be picked up and addressed as they arise?

Pring points out that

> in many people's minds personal, social and moral development should be a major concern of schools. But it is mistaken to conclude that the way of translating this concern into curriculum terms is to put another subject, namely, personal and social education, into the timetable (1984:92).

He argues that young people learn more from the behaviour and attitudes of those around them than they do from formal instruction. 'No amount of in-struction in personal, social and moral development can compensate for the destruction of dignity that the constant experience of failure brings to so many pupils' (Pring, 1984:92). Does this mean that the best way forward is to con-centrate on whole school ways of working for consensus and to look towards all teachers taking responsibility for the personal, social and moral develop-ment of their pupils? Does this mean that separately timetabled courses are not essential?

In *Developing Citizenship Across the Curriculum* (Edwards and Fogelman, 1993) subject specialists describe the relationship between their academic dis-cipline and education for citizenship. In the introduction the editors write:

> If the cross-curricular elements are to permeate the curriculum an essential pre-requisite seems to us to be that those responsible for the implementation of the core and foundation subjects should consider the relationship between their own subjects and the themes . . . Our ambition is that no teacher will want to claim that education for citi-zenship is someone else's responsibility (Edwards and Fogelman, 1993:4–5).

But the organization of the curriculum and the permeation of values education across it is a complex and demanding task.

Curriculum Planning

The issue of a specialist team delivering RE and/or PSE or every teacher being given responsibility for tutorial time and values in the subject-based curricu-lum still exists. Williams comments that 'every area of the school curriculum is value-laden to some extent' and points out that within the classroom, the choice of lesson content reflects underlying judgments about what is thought to be worthwhile, effective, relevant and essential in the educational process. The content of courses in values and beliefs may be drawn from many areas of the curriculum and is not specifically subject related. Science, Humanities, Arts, Business Studies, Home Management, Personal and Social Education and Religious Education all have much to offer (1990, Paper 4:2).

If permeation through subjects is the preferred route then there are issues to be faced. Will every topic that needs to be addressed fit into one of the core or foundation subjects? How can there be assurance that the coverage will be certain – every year, if the prime enthusiast leaves, for all teaching groups – with a value base rather than a narrower subject focus? Will every teacher be committed to the depth of exploration that is needed if value issues are to be thoroughly and adequately explored? The best solution will not be identical in every school community. It is more possible that in a school which starts from a particular value position, and which recruits staff committed to this position and pupils from families that have chosen this particular type of school because of its stance on moral issues, permeation of these values will be achieved in all curricular areas. But in addition a course such as PSE or RE which has a particular focus upon values education is probably a good way forward in most situations.

Personal and Social Education

PSE courses have a contribution that is important in many schools. Typical PSE course content includes many heavily value-laden issues some of which are of a controversial nature and may touch on deeply personal, religious and cultural belief and value systems. As there is no nationally prescribed content for PSE it offers an opportunity to cover areas that may be neglected in the core and foundation subjects. Examples of such areas might be: crime and punishment; the understanding of legal systems; rights and responsibilities; international relations; current affairs; education for parenthood; community study and service. PSE courses often emphasize the use of active learning techniques and discussion. Visitors from community partners can enrich the experience of pupils and teachers and offer a rich resource. There is the opportunity to make a bridge between the impersonal treatment of content and knowledge and the personal experience and understanding of the implications for the individual of such knowledge. Of course this opportunity is not the special preserve of PSE, but in PSE lessons it may be an overt aim whereas in other places in the timetable it may seem to be of secondary importance. Certainly in literature lessons there are many opportunities for such connections to be made but the pupil may not be explicitly encouraged to make them (McCulloch, 1993). Similarly, of course, in a poorly structured PSE lesson pupils may not, for a variety of reasons, make these connections (Pring, 1984). Indications from

OFSTED inspections suggest that some of the worst lessons observed are PSE lessons. Pupil behaviour and motivation are often found to be poor and learning significantly below the standard observed in other areas of the curriculum. What does this imply for curriculum planning and delivery?

The opportunity exists in PSE to bring together cross-curricular issues which if well-planned and sensitively delivered can provide insights and coherence to the curriculum and an opportunity to reflect on key questions. Buck and Inman summarize this thus:

> We must ensure that any provision includes a body of knowledge: young people's understanding of themselves cannot take place in a vacuum but must be set within the context of knowledge of their family, community, national and wider world in which they live. It is through an understanding of the social, political and environmental aspects of the world that they come to develop and understand their own personal qualities, attitudes and values. It is through this form of understanding that young people are empowered to act in an informed and purposeful manner. This form of understanding also requires a particular teaching style – one which is participatory and experiential (1993:11).

Religious Education

Religious Education (RE) clearly has a contribution to make. Since RE is a statutory requirement in the curriculum there are obvious reasons for RE taking some responsibility for values education.

> RE facilitates an understanding of the beliefs structures which underlie value systems. It provides evidence and examples of ways in which beliefs and values have directly affected people's lives through the making of choices and selection of priorities. It provides a critical frame of reference which transcends personal, group, ethnic, political and national interests and enables pupils to use it. It takes account of faith as an important motivating factor in people's lives. It offers a wealth of heavily value-laden content rather than process. It offers an alternative approach to life than either secularism or materialism. It offers opportunity for controversial issues to be examined sensitively, avoiding possible indoctrination by default. It offers cross-cultural insights (Williams, 1990, Paper 4:2).

Other Academic Subjects

All academic subjects have potential for contributing to the permeation of values across the curriculum. By way of illustration, quotations from *Developing*

Citizenship in the Curriculum (Edwards and Fogelman, 1993) follow. Subject tutors in the School of Education at Leicester University were asked to write about the contribution their specialist subject might make to education for citizenship. Encouragingly no tutor declined our request; on the contrary they found a wide range of links.

English

I would argue that it is in the English classroom that the variety of human experience can be explored, and the parameters of moral actions discussed, more effectively than in any other subject . . . The skilful English teacher . . . will encourage children to engage with, but also to preserve a sense of detachment from, the characters in a story, and will do this through the characteristic activities of the English classroom – Did you feel X was right to do this? How did you feel when Y said that? Can you think of reasons why Z reacted as she did? What would you have done in situation S? All these questions urge pupils to make the story their own, by developing their personal response to the actions, values and attitudes that the story has presented to them. But in doing that they probe their own moral values – what is fair, what is appropriate, how people should be treated, what people's responsibilities are, what they are entitled to. These questions, crucially concerned with the development of a personal code of values, are surely at the heart of citizenship (McCulloch, 1993:52–3).

Science

By confronting issues of a controversial nature we enable pupils to form opinions and beliefs, and to have existing ones challenged and reformed. They can debate 'respect for life' versus the advantages of animal dissection, and the implications for personal choice and freedom of mass screening of immigrants using genetic fingerprinting techniques. The challenge for teachers is to create a climate in which they can listen to what the pupils say, allow pupils to express an opinion, and provide the time for such reflection.

There are opportunities too for emphasizing ethnic and cultural diversity in our society by careful choice of different social contexts for topics such as diet and nutrition, energy, or examples of ecosystems. The white, eurocentric images of science have been all too common in many classroom activities in the past. Similarly, much has been written on ways of encouraging girls to take up the physical

sciences (Kelly, 1987). The focus of many studies has been on changing classroom practices and teacher attitudes, emphasizing the development of an atmosphere of mutual respect, trust, community, of
shared leadership, and looking for ways of integrating feelings and
ideas in science. It is known that girls become more involved if their
own perspectives on problems, issues and ideas can be articulated in
the lessons. It is clear that a lack of personal scientific knowledge
results in a sense of powerlessness and inaction but if, as well as
knowledge, a sense of self esteem, and of belonging to the classroom
culture can be encouraged, 'citizen science' will go some way to re-
moving the cold and clinical image of science, by presenting it in the
context of a caring and responsible society (Harrison, 1993:48–9)

Physical Education

Opportunities to consider *fairness, justice* and *moral responsibility*
occur frequently within lessons, in competitive situations outside lessons and in the world of sport. Although a controversial area there is
a consensus of opinion as expressed by Parry (1986) that games can
provide the opportunities for the presentation of values. More recent
discussion in this area (Kirk and Tinning, 1990) suggests that Physical
Education provides a key area in which cultural mores, values and
symbols can be both produced and legitimated (Wortley, 1993:76).

Further evidence of the potential for values education through academic subjects
is provided elsewhere in the present volume, especially in Chapters 3 to 8.

Teaching Methods

However the teaching of values is organized in the timetable, it must, to be
effective, be based upon good teacher/pupil relationships, the encouragement
of reflection, an experiential mode and pupil responsibility for the learning
process. Methods particularly appropriate to values education include:

- *circle time*, where young children are encouraged to share experiences and views in a supportive group discussion;
- *peer tutoring*, where pupils are encouraged and trained to share interests and expertise in situations such as mediation to combat bullying,
  paired reading schemes, campaigns designed to help smokers give up
  the habit;
- *service learning*, where pupils study the needs in the community, take
  action and review and reflect upon the experience;
- *discussions*, where structured activities ranging from informal discourse

following a particular agenda, to formal debate, form part of the learning process;

- *problem-solving exercises*, where participants seek possible solutions and are encouraged to develop objectivity and impartiality;
- *games*, where players conform to a set of defined rules;
- *simulations*, where participants adopt roles and work through a scenario;
- *role-plays* and *drama*, which, unlike simulations are open-ended and where real life is portrayed in a fictional way. Drama is not a national curriculum subject in its own right. Rather it may be seen as a method applicable to many areas of the curriculum.

As Kitson points out,

> The majority of drama work is based upon the notions of moral dilemmas, values and beliefs. By encouraging the children to work in this way they are being offered the opportunity to:
> - compare values and beliefs held by themselves and others and identify common ground;
> - examine evidence and opinions and form conclusions;
> - discuss differences and resolve conflict;
> - discuss and consider solutions to moral dilemmas, personal and social;
> - appreciate that distinguishing between right and wrong is not always straightforward;
> - appreciate that the individual's values, beliefs and moral codes change over time (1993:104–5).

In its broadsheet *Citizenship and Values Education* (1993), the Centre for Citizenship Studies in Education suggests some activities for use with pupils as can be seen overleaf:

Each of these suggestions begins with an active verb. School is not a philosophy seminar – action is required. We cannot wait for things to change in the external influences before taking action. We need to get on and do something and keep it under review so that we can react to external pressures with confidence and speak from experience. An example of relevance here might be a school's approach to drug education. The place and nature of education about substance abuse has long been contested. Funding of training and resources for drug education has been subject to many fluctuations in recent years. A school cannot put such education on the back burner while government sorts out changed priorities or issues new guide-lines. There is a need to pursue a chosen route while constantly keeping such activity under review in readiness for developments which may come both from the desire to respond to the needs of the young people and local circumstances as well as to national initiatives. Not yet having all the answers is no reason to refrain from action.

- working towards a list of classroom values accepted by all and seen as influencing acceptable relationships and behaviour;
- taking cuttings from newspapers of recent incidents and asking pupils what these show about the values of those involved, the impact of behaviour on others, their own views of right and wrong in these contexts;
- inviting local religious leaders to school to discuss the values embedded in their beliefs and traditions. (Why have they lasted so long? Are they breaking down now? What may be taking the place of traditional values?);
- debating who gives a good moral lead today. Royalty, MPs, religious leaders, business leaders, media, teachers, parents?
- using a current problem in the school (dishonesty, racial attack, teasing, bullying, sexism, truancy, fighting) discuss various attitudes to a situation and the actions which should logically follow these attitudes. What could have been done differently? Who is to blame? Could anything have been done to avoid the problem? What are the consequences of the incident?
- taking one agreed value from the school values statement each week. Focus assembly time, PSE, RE, tutorial time, assembly presentations upon this. Ask pupils to name heroes/heroines who give good examples in this value area – study biographies and other literary examples of for example courage, commitment, friendship, thrift, selflessness.
- establishing and maintaining School or Year Councils. They are models of the value that is invested in student views. They are not usually trouble free and demand a great deal of commitment if they are to fulfil their potential. The processes of democracy can be practised at school.

What happens in classrooms is very influential and will vary with the teacher, the class, the topic and the particular circumstances of the time and the location. How much consistency matters is a question for debate. However long it is debated, consistency will not be absolute. Guidance and a broad sense of direction will be valuable in assisting teachers in helping pupils to develop their own personal sense of values. Pupils are very adaptable and perceptive. They learn from a range of adults, making their own judgments and seeing variety as an advantage not a disadvantage. All teachers communicate their values whether consciously or unconsciously. 'Values are inherent in teaching. Teachers are by the nature of their profession "moral agents" who imply values by the way they address pupils and each other, the way they dress, the language they use and the effort they put into their work' (National Curriculum Council, 1992). Ideally a school community will give authority to teachers to handle the value-laden and often controversial aspects of their work with professional standards and personal confidence. This is not automatic or simple and can best be achieved by teams of teachers working together giving each other support and guidance (Morrison, 1994).

Professional Development and Resources

As these aspects of school life are among the most difficult teachers face there needs to be a policy to ensure adequate provision for professional development. Pring (1984) emphasizes the need for 'in-service training of teachers in the skills and strategies which shift the approach from instruction to facilitating active and experiential learning'.

Similar findings result from work done by Carr and Landon. In conclusion of a research project in which they worked with teachers in six secondary schools in Scotland examining practice and understanding of moral and ethical issues, they write:

> It is high time that greater attention was given to the education of teachers concerning basic ethical and moral questions of education at the various stages of that training. For far too long have courses of professional preparation been allowed to focus predominantly on the managerial and technical aspects of the general business of teaching to the deplorable neglect of wider concerns of values education and educational values (1993:66).

If values education is important then investment of time (in team or whole staff meetings or training days, governors meetings) and money (for posts of responsibility, curriculum resources, expenses of visitors to classroom) prove it has importance in relation to the demands of the statutory parts of the curriculum. If it underpins everything a school is and does then investment in nurturing it will be well spent. In initial teacher training such pressure exists on the timetable that philosophy of education and discussion of values in education is in danger of disappearing completely. New teachers may well enter the profession lacking confidence in this fundamental dimension of their work.

Conclusion

There are no right answers or universally applicable methods or structures for values education. School ethos, relationships between members of the school community, separate courses in ethics or in personal and social education, community service and tutorial programmes may all have a part to play, as will the permeation of values issues and participative teaching and learning styles through all curriculum subjects, in developing morally aware and socially responsible people as parents of the next generation and citizens of the future. In the current educational climate, the curriculum debate focuses on time, assessment, league tables, funding, core and foundation subjects, but it needs also to be about values, processes, relationships, community, coherence and cohesion of the whole curriculum. Confidence in teachers to handle value-laden issues to the best of their professional ability is a requisite of sound development. Whatever is planned in the formal curriculum it is the quality of exchange that is crucial and this is in the hands of all classroom teachers. They play a critical role in helping their pupils to make the connection between the impersonal and the personal and so to grow as morally aware people able to make sense of their lives, develop a value base and contribute to the well-being of society.

References

BUCK, M. and INMAN, S. (1993) 'Making values central: The role of the cross-curricular themes', *Careers Education and Guidance*, February.

CARR, D. and LANDON, J. (1993) *Values in and for Education at 14+*, Edinburgh, Moray House Institute of Education, Heriot-Watt University.

CENTRE FOR CITIZENSHIP STUDIES IN EDUCATION (1993) *Citizenship and Values Education* (Broadsheet No 38), Northampton, Centre for the Study of Comprehensive Schools.

EDWARDS, J. and FOGELMAN, K. (Eds) (1993) *Developing Citizenship in the Curriculum*, London, David Fulton Publishers.

HARGREAVES, D. (1984) *Improving Secondary Schools*, London, Inner London Education Authority.

HARRISON, J. (1993) 'Science', in EDWARDS, J. and FOGELMAN, K. (Eds) *Developing Citizenship in the Curriculum*, London, David Fulton Publishers.

KELLY, A. (1987) *Science for Girls*, Milton Keynes, Open University Press.

KIRK, D. and TINNING, R. (1990) *Physical Education, Curriculum and Culture: Critical Issues in the Contemporary Crisis*, London, Falmer Press.

KITSON, N. (1993) 'Drama', in EDWARDS, J. and FOGELMAN, K. (Eds) *Developing Citizenship in the Curriculum*, London, David Fulton Publishers.

McCULLOCH, R. (1993) 'English', in EDWARDS, J. and FOGELMAN, K. (Eds) *Developing Citizenship in the Curriculum*, London, David Fulton Publishers.

MORRISON, K. (1994) *Implementing Cross-curricular Themes*, London, David Fulton Publishers.

NATIONAL CURRICULUM COUNCIL (1992) *Overview of the Cross-curricular Themes: A working paper*, York, NCC.

PARRY, J. (1986) 'Values in physical education', in TOMLINSON, P. and QUINTON, M. (Eds) *Values Across the Curriculum*, Basingstoke, Falmer Press.

PRING, R. (1984) *Personal and Social Education in the Curriculum*, London, Hodder and Stoughton.

SCOTTISH CURRICULUM COUNCIL (1991) *Values in Education*, Dundee, SCC.

WEST, S. (1993) *Educational Values for School Leadership*, London, Kogan Page.

WILLIAMS, V. (1990) *RE Values Project: Papers 1–4*, Derby, Christian Education Movement.

WORTLEY, A. (1993) 'Physical education', in EDWARDS, J. and FOGELMAN, K. (Eds) *Developing Citizenship in the Curriculum*, London, David Fulton Publishers.

Chapter 14

An Inner-city Perspective on Values Education

Elaine Foster-Allen

ABSTRACT: *This chapter provides a case study of Handsworth Wood Girls' School, Birmingham, written from the perspective of the former headteacher. Grounded firmly in the realities of inner-city life, it tells the story of the development of policies relating to values education, with particular reference to the school's ethos and structures. The chapter examines the different contexts from which the pupils come, and considers how these might have affected the ways in which their values and standards of behaviour have been influenced and shaped. Other influences on young people at the school, such as the media, peer group and the local community, are also briefly discussed. The major part of the chapter concentrates upon the steps the school has taken to ensure that there are clearly agreed parameters, policies and procedures within which values and standards can be laid down, maintained and reviewed.*

'What's Wrong with Stealing a Pair of Knickers?'

One Friday afternoon as I was leaving school during my first year as headteacher of Handsworth Wood Girls' School, I came face-to-face with one of the local police officers. He was holding and pointing to a security video while in deep, animated conversation with a member of staff, behind whom, some little distance away, stood two pupils. It transpired that a major criminal investigation was going on in the school. A multiethnic, multifaith group of about six young people had decided to truant over a period of weeks and to steal from various shops within a three-mile radius of the school. Some of them had been caught red-handed in one of the local stores and there was ample evidence to substantiate the criminal activities.

Faced with a major problem of truancy and organized theft, l had to act quickly. I decided to a) retrieve the articles the pupils had stolen and return them to the store; b) get to know who the culprits were; and c) mete out some punishment. My initial concern was to bring the children to understand that it is wrong to steal, for several reasons: stealing can have a devastating effect on the individual from whom things are taken, but even more so on the person (and her family) who steals, especially when this becomes a pattern. The child or young person learns not to trust herself, loses her sense of integrity and self-confidence and ends up behaving in ways contrary to those expected of her by the majority. Who wants to spend her life looking over her shoulder? But the incident was a learning experience for me as well as for the pupils, as I found myself questioning my own taken-for-granted values and asking how influential these values are on the lives of young people.

During the course of the six-hour investigation, I found out something about the nature of peer group allegiance, which at the time superseded that of allegiance to parents and family, and about the flexibility with which values could be applied and disapplied to similar situations. I also came away with a simple but profound question, posed by one of the young people: 'What's wrong with stealing a pair of knickers?' This question has stayed with me. In my most liberal of moments, my answer, with qualifiers of course, would be, 'Nothing'. In other moments, my Christian beliefs and moral values push me to take an uncompromising stand: 'Thou shalt not steal.'

But 'what *is* wrong with stealing a pair of knickers?' is a reflection of the uncertainty and the lack of clarity about right and wrong; it is an opportunity for questioning, challenging and arriving at an appropriate position. The question also pushes us to ask further questions about our responsibility as adults who make laws, set standards and have values which are at times lived out with duplicity.

The value lying behind the question is not at all one which is the monopoly of working-class black children. On the contrary, it resonates across the class and ethnicity divides, although some would have us believe that only inner-city black children are lacking in 'cultural baggage'. Some of the pupils in the school come from families and communities where there is much poverty, adults are unemployed, their housing situation is bleak and their families are fractured. In these situations, people are forced to 'hustle'. This does not mean that hustling is inherent to the poor and the dispossessed. What it means is that there are creative responses to situations of desperation which might sometimes lead to a breakdown of acceptable standards and norms. But even in these situations, I have found kindness, tenderness, love and thoughtfulness, often surpassing that which I have experienced in situations of plenty.

Furthermore, the pressure on these, and every community, to have, and to have more than your neighbour, must not be underestimated. It might be necessary to look at 'the plank' rather than the 'speck of dust' – the causes rather than effects – which beset the local and wider communities to find the answer we need.

Although I would not wish to join the anti-media lobby with regard to the portrayal of values and standards, I do believe that the emphasis placed on crime, the shifting parameters of right and wrong, the power of the gun or violence to solve crimes and resolve differences and the high financial stakes put on crime stories in the written media, amongst others, all serve to encourage a dereliction of standards and values which could promote acceptable, life-enhancing behaviour and attitudes.

It is also worth noting that people, young and old, who have to withstand the perennial bombardment of racist and sexist (in the school's case) abuse and assault on themselves, their families and friends receive a series of messages which say, 'You are not important, nothing about you is.' In the face of the assault of your mother, the murder of your brother, the burning down of your home, how pained the oppressed must feel, and how ironic to have to stand by values and standards which require you to turn the other cheek. In this respect, the victims of such abuse must surely be seen as monopolizing certain virtues and values.

Influence of Cultural Background on Pupil's Values

Handsworth Wood Girls' School is a multiethnic, multifaith school with pupils from a range of socio-economic backgrounds. The majority of the pupils have heritages in the Indian sub-continent, while a significant minority hail from the Caribbean. At the time of writing, the children and their families have religious affiliations, in descending order, to Sikhism, Islam, Hinduism and Christianity. There is also a small group of children who are members of the Rastafarian cult and there are others who do not identify with any faith community.

The religious affiliations set an invaluable base line from which certain values arise and are sustained. This is regardless of the apparent exclusivity of each faith. For example, there is agreement within the various religious traditions over lying, murder, greed, honouring parents, stealing, helping others and so on. I have known many teachers who have invoked or alluded to what is taught in the Guru Granth Sahib, the Qur'an or the Bible when trying to instil discipline or make a point about children's behaviour. I have also listened to children using Scripture when scolding their friends from the same faith as well as from other faiths. Parents too have reminded their children, in my hearing, about their faith and the sorts of values which they are expected to have. Indeed, many children are persistent and conscientious in trying to live out the values set by their faith. Of course, the faith is not always fully understood or followed with total commitment by all members of the faith community. So it is not uncommon to find that there are a number of inconsistencies between what scriptures say and how Dalvinder, Amina, Maya or Corina live out their lives.

Some children and young people, as they become more sophisticated and questioning, find that the closed nature of faith does not permit them the space to interrogate, challenge and ask why. Because 'it says so' in the Qur'an or the Guru Granth Sahib, is not enough to satisfy an enquiring mind, or a mind faced with comparisons and choices. Not even family and faith community pressure can cause such minds to relent from their critical questioning. On the other hand, there are young people who are just as sophisticated who have arrived at a committed faith position because they have questioned their faith, non-religious stances and other faiths, and are satisfied with the faith they have found. Others have drifted unquestioningly with the crowds.

In all schools, there is also the need to ask questions about values and standards which might have come out of, or are emphasized through non-religious, humanistic models. Indeed, some would say that these models or parameters give young people even more scope to challenge standards of behaviour and values and to arrive at a more committed stand. I believe this to be important because for many teachers, pupils and parents, the set of values to which we adhere and the ensuing actions which we take are more important than the reference points from which these values and standards come.

So pupils come to Handsworth Wood Girls' School with standards and values derived from a variety of cultures, faith and non-faith backgrounds, and influenced by traditions from across the world. The omnipresence of pop music and the film worlds, whether it be from Kingston, Bombay or New York, as well as the new technologies, with their various messages and values, all give our children much to contend with, much more than their parents and forebears had to deal with as young people. Perhaps we should give them credit simply for surviving their youth!

Values Within the School

How does the school respond to the question of values and standards, given the social, economic and cultural background of its pupils? I would wish first to make a few general points on the national educational context within which schools have been asked to develop standards of behaviour and values in terms of priorities and what is valued.

It is important to note that the National Curriculum orders and the preferred curriculum content are not value-free. Each of the subjects of the curriculum has generated heated discussion, and people have taken positions based on what they see as the values and standards which subjects should be transmitting. In many cases, the values are implied rather than being overt. Some teachers, subject working groups or individuals have been keen to point out that many values which imply or overtly support oppression, exploitation, aggression, among others, have remained unchallenged in some areas of the curriculum. For example, *Mathematics in the National Curriculum* (Department for Education, 1995), like its pre-Dearing predecessor, is totally silent on race equality and gender issues. This silence doubtless has its roots in the argument set out in the preliminary National Curriculum report which stated that

> a 'multi-cultural' approach to mathematics with children being intro-
> duced to different numeral systems, foreign currencies and non-
> European measuring and counting devices . . . could confuse young
> children (Department of Education and Science, 1988: para 10.22).

Another issue worth noting is the fact that over the past fifteen or more
years there has been an emphasis on the work-related curriculum, in which
values such as competitiveness, profit making, entrepreneurship and the acquisition of property have been given pre-eminence, and the Education Reform Act has placed education in the market-place with its attendant values
(see Chapters 2 and 9 in this volume). We certainly need to recognize the
various parties and forces with which we are working when we try to establish
values and standards of behaviour in our schools. We need to recognize the
contradictions and help young people to develop the tools with which to deal
with these.

The aims of Handsworth Wood Girls' School, which are listed below,
were derived mainly out of discussion with staff, governors and parents.

A   To provide equal access to a broad and balanced curriculum to all
pupils regardless of race, ability or class.

B   To encourage pupils to acquire knowledge, skills and attitudes that
are relevant to their present and future adult life.

C   To develop young people as learners who have lively enquiring minds
and the ability to question and challenge statements and assumptions
as well as apply themselves to set tasks.

D   To enable pupils to acquire and use reading, writing, speaking, listening, mathematical, technological and scientific skills across the curriculum and in a variety of contexts.

E   To develop in pupils self-discipline, self-respect, and pride in themselves as learners and young women.

F   To celebrate our religious, cultural and social diversity while ensuring
that those values which the school population agrees are oppressive
and patriarchal are challenged.

G   To give pupils the opportunity to experience a balanced arts education curriculum.

H   To work in partnership with pupils/students, parents, staff and the
wider community to develop the School as a caring centre of educational excellence.

I   To give pupils the opportunities to exercise responsibilities.

While three of these (E, F and I) are explicitly about values and standards
of behaviour, it is clear that the other six aims all have implicit values and
could only be successfully practised if certain standards of behaviour were in
place. The remainder of this chapter consists of a more detailed examination
of the school's attempts to implement the more explicitly value-orientated
aims.

Developing Children's Values through School Structures and Ethos

Promoting Self-Discipline and Self-Respect

In my first term at Handsworth Wood Girls' School, I took the opportunity to look at a range of things, including pupils' behaviour in classrooms and around the school. There were not many surprises, but there were important reminders related to classroom management, including how pupils entered, how they were grouped, the pace of the work, the opportunities given to children to be responsible for their learning, the relationship between staff and pupils and between pupil and pupil.

Certain teachers, because of their planning, the execution of their work and their rapport with pupils, gave young people the opportunity to exercise self-discipline with regard to keeping on task, not interrupting others, listening attentively, organizing their time and work, working co-operatively with others and working on their own; some of the same pupils with other staff were disruptive, refused to work with others, or to do any work at all and were totally disorganized.

Around the school, the prefects fought a losing battle with some children to keep some control during break and many children reported bullying. Parts of the playgrounds were a tip and shouting and screaming appeared to be the norm in some areas of the school. It was felt by some of us that if our children were going to become responsible citizens, then they needed opportunities to exercise responsibility and to be held accountable for their behaviour in and around the school. Giving pupils guidelines and parameters within which to operate seemed to be a sensible way forward. Although some staff were not with me all the way on this, I took the decision with the support of the Senior Management Team to do two things.

The first was to establish who was responsible for the management of classrooms and to get from staff some common features of what they thought was good and effective classroom management. Surprisingly, there was common agreement among staff as to what constituted effective classroom management. This included rules and guidelines for both staff and pupils and further agreement on how they could through their teaching help to develop and support pupils' self-discipline. I was, and still am, of the opinion that it is one of the functions of the teacher to have structures and parameters within which young people can develop acceptable and appropriate standards of behaviour. It seems to be the case that when we have some of these parameters and structures in place in our schools and classrooms, young inner-city black children become responsible for their learning and excited about learning. In the event, both behaviour and academic results improved. It was a real joy to see young people who had been labelled ineducable and boisterous responding positively and taking pride in their work and in themselves, in many classrooms, around the school and when we had school functions. The fact that the school could boast a significant increase in the percentage of pupils gaining five or more GCSEs at Grades A–C over the four years I was headteacher is testimony to the possibilities. In 1991, 13 per cent of candidates obtained A–C grades; in 1992, 11 per cent; in 1993, 22 per cent; and in 1994, 24 per cent.

The second thing I undertook was to give pupils access to their classrooms before, during and after school. After nearly four years, this still causes consternation and dissent among some staff. Basically, pupils had not been allowed into their classroom unless a member of staff was present. Under such a system, many young people did not get the opportunity to take the responsibility for their environment, for individual and collective property and space, for the noise level and to negotiate what was acceptable or unacceptable behaviour when there were no adults to supervise them. Regardless of the attendant problems (such as the lack of private study and quiet rooms, because of the general shortage of space in the school), pupils have generally risen to the challenges of responsible and orderly behaviour around the school.

In order to support pupils and to quell the dissenting voice among the staff, an Open School Policy was drafted and circulated to every member of staff and to pupils. Simply to save time, it was drafted by the Senior Management Team. The policy outlined the rights and responsibilities pupils had and the rules they were expected to follow. Pupils' rights included the following:

- All pupils have a right to have admission to the school premises prior to school and during breaks and lunchtimes.
- All pupils have a right to a clean environment.
- All pupils are entitled to be treated with respect by staff supervising them and by other pupils.

Pupils' responsibilities included punctuality, maintaining a quiet and clean environment, respecting areas that are out-of-bounds and treating each other and staff with respect. Other rules covered such diverse issues as the chewing of gum, the use of equipment, and the consequences of racist and sexist abuse and fighting. After some whole school discussion, the document was agreed on and accepted as policy.

It was during this period of debate and discussion around the Open School Policy that a group of pupils took it upon themselves to become grafitti artists, writing very abusive terms around the school. I was incensed by this open defiance and in a letter to all pupils which I read and delivered to each class myself, I explained, using their term, 'fuck you', that this was not appropriate, neither was it acceptable for such language to be used around the school. I also called assemblies and reminded pupils of what was and was not acceptable in the school. During the assemblies, I told the pupils that I wanted to know who was responsible for the grafitti and I also wanted it removed. Moments after arriving back at my desk, a small group of young people came to confess, apologise and to clean up.

This very small, internal school matter was to make national headlines, when one or more anonymous parents sent copies of the letter to the press, claiming that a headteacher should never use such language as they never did themselves and their children were not exposed to such language at home.

Without dwelling too much on the publicity, the incident triggered off a debate about standards of behaviour in schools, who sets what standards and how these are maintained. For me, the key points were related to how headteachers and Senior Management teams lead on issues of standards of behaviour in their schools and how we set parameters in which young people work. The incident also helped me to question how school can negotiate with young people the basis and terms on which those standards are set and adhered to.

Out of the two things mentioned above came a much more comprehensive policy document, entitled Rewards and Sanctions Policy. The Policy was drafted by a cross-section of staff on a working group which was chaired by a member of the Senior Management Team (SMT). The implementation, including staff training and review, was also led by the SMT member. In the Policy, the emphasis is placed on rewarding good and acceptable behaviour, academic effort and achievement via a merit system. It seeks to approach discipline from a very positive position starting with the teacher setting the tone in his/her own approach to work and relationships in the classroom. There are rights, responsibilities and rules covering work, belongings, environment, how pupils are to be treated including being listened to, and, interestingly, the right to well planned and stimulating lessons. Auxiliary, technical and administrative staff are also expected to reward pupils via the merit system.

Achievements and attainments are celebrated half-termly during asssemblies and annually during the Year Awards Ceremonies. Teachers are encouraged to put pupils forward for letters and citations from prominent people. Pupils have so far received these from a High Commissioner, a well known poet, BBC producers and others. The school has a series of commendation certificates which are given to pupils around the school and in their classroom.

School rules cover listening, working, belongings, politeness, safe and clean environment and school uniform. I am of the opinion that we all live by rules, arrived at through one route or another, and further, there is a need for institutions to regulate themselves. However, it is important that rules are not oppressive, fossilized and pointless, but responsive to the needs of the institutions and the people in them.

Challenging Oppressive and Patriarchal Values

While the major part of the responsibility for helping pupils to understand and challenge oppressive and patriarchal values rests with subject teachers, issues such as bullying, exploitation, racist and sexist abusive are aired informally and formally by pupils (and staff) via the School Council.

The School Council is a body of approximately fifty-five pupils who meet fortnightly to discuss issues of concern or to be proactive in suggesting and seeing through certain activities. Pupils are elected by their forms and they have a draft job description of what is expected of Council members. This includes attending meetings regularly and reporting back to form members as well as speaking up on the issues which form members have asked them to bring to Council. Council members, especially the presidents and vice-presidents of the Key Stages are vigilant in ensuring that decisions are carried through.

There are a number of incidents where pupils have articulated their concern and raised issues about the sexist behaviour of men working on the school building which led to their immediate removal. Equally, young people have complained to staff about their perception of staff and pupils who they consider to be displaying oppressive sexist and or racist behaviour. These too, have led to verbal warnings to staff and warnings or exclusions where pupils are concerned.

The school is not exempt from its share of conflicts, which pupils may try to resolve through fighting. The Personal and Social Education programme and the Year Tutor system are there to do several things, one of which is to help pupils to resolve their differences without resorting to fights. However, from time-to-time children do fight, and on such occasions, both the perpetrator and the victim are excluded. This is on the assumption that the victim should, where possible, have reported the problem, or at least tried to back away from it. Pupils accept this, but have argued for leniency where the victim is concerned. They wanted clear differentials between the two parties. The perpetrator must have more time out of school than the victim.

The School's Draft Policy on Equal Opportunities and Multicultural Education also seeks to encourage teachers to teach from a values position which eschews oppression and exploitation in whichever form it occurs. So, for example, the aims of the Policy include:

- To teach a curriculum which creates an understanding and respects different cultures.
- To develop positive images within the school community in order to promote pride in one's own heritage.
- To build on the diverse linguistic experiences of the pupils.
- To oppose racism, inequality and stereotyping.

The most important job which the school needs to undertake is putting into practice this policy in a consistent manner.

Encouraging Pupils to Exercise Responsibility

There is a wide range of activities which give pupils the opportunity to exercise responsibilities around the school, and with more teachers becoming aware of the value of independent learning, the possibilities are becoming apparent in many classrooms.

Apart from the School Council mentioned above, which gives a significant minority of children the opportunity to develop democratic skills and cooperative ways of working as well as taking initiative and leading on issues, pupils from Year 7 to the 6th Form can become librarians, monitors and prefects.

One of the systems which I put in place when I arrived at the school means that if a student wishes to become a prefect, she has to apply for the post via a letter of application and go through an interview. She is expected to undertake responsibilities and tasks as outlined in a job description. Many pupils have commented upon how proud they are to have been selected as a school prefect and all have worn their badges with pride. In fact, the greatest insult and punishment is to have one's prefect badge/status removed.

Some of the most conscientious prefects can be seen or overheard engaged in peer counselling. A recent example I came across related to two pupils reported as smoking. The prefects' arguments were not condemnatory, rather they tried to help the pupils concerned to realize that their behaviour was harmful to themselves, and set a bad example for younger pupils. They invoked the school rules and questioned the pupils' commitment to these. Indeed the young people in this example showed real care and concern about the health of their peers.

Students who become librarians or Resource Area Students are expected to demonstrate a number of skills and competences. These include taking responsibility for fiction, non-fiction and information resources, organizing and managing book fairs, demonstrating reliability, assertiveness and maturity in dealing with other students and staff. Young people engaged in the Careers Education work are expected to show skills and undertake duties similar to those above.

School fund raising events are undertaken almost monthly by different groups of young people. The pupils have raised funds for causes near and far. In their activities, they demonstrate youthful vitality and creativity, but also show how to work cooperatively and display an empathy and a level of compassion with the ill, those hit by disasters, and those less fortunate than themselves. Again, many young people in the school who are themselves quite poor, still find it possible to give.

Conclusion

Schools are no doubt engaged in passing on values which society feels are worthwhile. However, while society is marked by cultural and social diversity and inequality, it is perhaps a little unfair to criticize schools for not displaying a certainty about values and standards of behaviour. It is even more unjust to level major criticisms at inner-city schools for failing to instil these yet undefined standards and values in children. It is unhelpful for politicians to insist that traditional values are those to which schools should aspire. Some of these standards and values are clearly out of touch with contemporary reality and do not help children to respond to an ever more sophisticated and highly technological world full of dilemmas.

Schools like Handsworth Wood Girls' School should continue to struggle with the question of values and standards. They should be engaged in a continual process of fine-tuning those values and standards which are said to have withstood the test of time, while being open to values and standards which are developed in response to the rigours of our new circumstances. The curriculum, both formal and informal, must be planned in such a way as to help pupils to think, make judgments and act in ways which are not exploitative nor detrimental to themselves or others and to develop values built on equality, justice, non-violence, cooperation and community.

References

DEPARTMENT FOR EDUCATION AND WELSH OFFICE (1995) *Mathematics in the National Curriculum*, London, HMSO.
DEPARTMENT OF EDUCATION AND SCIENCE AND WELSH OFFICE (1988) *Mathematics for Ages 5 to 16*, London, HMSO.

Chapter 15

Assessing Children's Personal Development: The Ethical Implications

Ruth Merttens

ABSTRACT: *Over the last few years there has been a move to a) widen the scope of assessments to include matters other than the purely cognitive – including the moral and spiritual dimensions; and b) extend involvement in the production of these records beyond teachers to parents, community workers, youth workers and pupils themselves. These moves arise out of an 'empowerment/ liberal' philosophy. However, in this chapter I argue that the effects of these wider and more comprehensive records is likely to be diametrically opposed to the stated intentions of their proponents. The argument utilizes the work of two thinkers: Lacan, whose notions about the constitution of identity and its concomitant alienation illuminate the formative and constructive aspects of language, and Levinas, who suggests that we are born into 're-sponsibility for others'. In conclusion, I suggest that it is seeking a chimaera to attempt more accurate profiles, and that these records have a life of their own. In their production, we construct a significant entity whose effectivity we cannot, even theoretically, control. Thus we should attempt to preserve the moral and the spiritual as a dimension which remains unassessed.*

The last ten years have witnessed a remarkable growth in the numbers and scope of written records produced by and through schools in the UK about their pupils. The demand for such summative assessments of children has arisen as a result of pressure from two sources:

- the demands of the National Curriculum and the 1988 Education Reform Act.
- the democratically-inspired view that it is necessary to involve parents – and pupils – in the production of school records and summative assessments.

The first of these has resulted in a plethora of assessment and records and an obsessive interest in *results* in an effort to satisfy what may, I believe, be accurately described as a government's obsession with visible competence. The final assessments produced are now part of a complex system by which pupils, teachers, schools and, ultimately parenting practices, are evaluated and come to be ordered hierarchically. The second has resulted in a substantial broadening of the scope of these assessments in order to include aspects of *the whole pupil* rather than persist with a traditional and narrow focus upon purely cognitive attainment. Many such assessments now include a section explicitly labelled 'moral and spiritual development or experience', and even those that do not may be said to incorporate such dimensions implicitly.

Broadening the Scope of School Records

These two forces then, have shaped the development of records and the ideologies underpinning them are remarkably different. The first is framed within a largely authoritarian and traditionalist set of beliefs in which the rhetoric of a market economy is mapped onto a notion of the parent – or the pupil – as a consumer and schools – or teachers – as providers of a service which can best be improved through consumer choice exercised in the light of relevant information such as league tables, appraisal reports and aggregated assessment outcomes. By contrast, the second relies upon a liberal/radical argument concerning the empowerment of those who are at the receiving end of the professional activity within education. Thus pupils and parents, the laity, are seen as relatively disempowered by a profession of teachers and educationalists. The attempt to involve this laity in the production of school-based assessments and records, hitherto an entirely professional domain, has been linked with an expressed commitment to a more libertarian and democratic education system.

The desire to widen the scope of school records, particularly at the beginning and end of the schooling process (i.e. on entry into primary school with baseline assessments, and on leaving secondary school with records of achievement), also has its origins in an appreciation that the restricted view of real attainment as strictly cognitive ignores important areas of skill acquisition, knowledge and development, especially the moral and spiritual aspects. In an attempt to value the non-cognitive, these are increasingly included in school-based records of both types referred to earlier. And since a competence in skills falling under these headings may not be manifested at school but rather may be evident in pupils' out-of-school activities, whether at home or elsewhere, these records perforce encroach into domains previously invisible to the professional educational gaze.

The contrasting motivations behind the increase in scope and quantity of assessments is reflected in the confusion in the views and justifications provided by teachers. Summative assessments, associated as they are with evaluation and appraisal procedures, are generally regarded as educationally undesirable *per se*. However, records of achievement, no less summative in effect, and baseline assessments, arguably the same, are usually considered to be educationally progressive in both conception and effect. The radical and critical notion of empowerment, as developed by Paulo Freire (1972), is utilized in much of the discussion surrounding the development of parental and pupil involvement in assessment records. Indeed, so strong is the general feeling that the boundaries between professional and non-professional are blurred through the introduction of these practices that it is not unusual to hear them described in the context of a move towards 'deschooling society' (Illich, 1973). Such descriptions derive further strength from the fact that these records commonly incorporate skills perceived as being a part of normal life rather than strictly cognitive or academic.

Reasons for Limiting the Scope of Records

However, in the face of all this I shall argue that, despite our best intentions, such records act to increase the likelihood of certain children, and their parents, being further marginalized and, arguably, disempowered in what may turn out to be material ways. Further, in a consideration of their ethical and spiritual dimensions, I claim that the inevitable results of the introduction of such mechanisms are likely to be completely contrary to the stated intentions of their proponents. My claim is that we should act to minimize the number and restrict the scope of educational records for fear of the damage that is the automatic outcome of their insertion into current schooling practices. *We should, I believe, attempt to keep the spiritual and moral dimension as much out of the whole assessment process as possible.*

First, it is necessary to consider the context into which these records are being read. Schools, teachers and children are all being assessed to produce a hierarchy of competence and effectiveness. We thus have *effective schools* with *competent teachers*, and *less than effective schools* (to use the terminology of the new OFSTED inspection arrangements) with, presumably, less competent teachers. We have children who are competent at different 'levels', and by aggregating their numbers we can produce league tables of the schools and teachers.

We work with an idea of ability as a quality – more or less constant over time – located in the individual. This is powerfully evinced in the rhetoric of individual educational progress as growth, as exemplified by the Giraffe height chart which appears on the front of the government leaflet for parents about National Assessments (Central Office of Information, 1991). Children progress through the levels of the National Curriculum very much as they grow – it is a natural process, some grow faster than others, some do not grow much, some are destined to be taller, some are just plain short, and whatever we do, individuals grow in their own way and at their own rate. The notions of individual development, of more and less able/intelligent children and of the inherent or 'natural' character of these qualities, are those which underpin the discourse of education at all levels from the overtly political pronouncements of the policymakers to the conversations of parents waiting at the school gates.

In this context, then, a number of crucially important questions suggest themselves:

- How can these records of achievement and baseline assessments be construed? What readings are possible – or probable – in the situation described above?
- Are we to include children's moral and spiritual development in these processes, in our attempt to deal with the whole child?
- Do children have naturally spiritual or moral natures, in the same way that they are naturally quick or gifted at maths? Are some children on a higher level of spirituality than others?

By way of answer, a number of salient points need to be made.

- Baseline assessments rely upon information about children's behaviour supplied by parents – for example, at what age the children took their first step or ate their first mouthful of solid food, or whether they have attended a religious service or can empathize with the feelings of others. Two questions arise. Who is being assessed, the parents or the child? And what is the connection between the experiences mentioned and cognitive or any other named skills? If there is no established relation, then the relevance of the age at which a child first learns to walk or the fact that he or she has attended a religious service becomes a means by which the child's background is characterized. In other words, we have a suspicion that these records are a way of producing a taxonomy of experiences and child-rearing strategies, ranging from the *good* on the one hand, to the *poor* or *deprived* on the other.
- Records of achievement depend upon information about non-academic activities supplied mainly by the pupil themselves. This has two immediate repercussions. First, the pupils may with reason feel that this encroaches on aspects of their lives hitherto regarded as private, i.e. outside the scope of the teacher's eye. 'What do you do in your spare time, Fred?' may appear as a question which invades a closely guarded space. There is a social class aspect to this; the pupil who does piano lessons, belongs to a drama group and is a member of the Boy Scouts, may not read the question in the same way as the youth whose spare time is spent smoking, talking to his mates and listening to rock music. Indeed, it is difficult to imagine that these records will not act to widen social differences and further marginalize particular sub-cultures. Second, the demand that pupils write part of their own assessments

transfers the responsibility for the place which the final assessment occupies in some (notional) hierarchy of good and bad records from the school to the home. So, it is because Fred has nothing he can or wants to write about that his record of achievement is lacking in comparison to Annie's. This situation is made more complex by the way in which particular activities may be re-described in such a way as to present them as 'high value' in educational terms. So parents and children from particular backgrounds may be familiar with the necessity of re-casting what is done in words which may carry more kudos in the context of a Record of Achievement. Thus, in one example we came across, 'lying on your bed and reading comics' had been transformed by the parent into 'displaying a sustained interest in alternative forms of contemporary literature'!

Although the pedagogical gaze of the Victorians did focus on the moral and spiritual development of children, this moved consistently toward an appreciation that the role of schools, and certainly that of assessment and testing, was firmly located within the domain of the cognitive. Currently, there is a real sense in which these records are a manifestation of the ways in which this has now been extended from children's academic and cognitive skills to their moral and spiritual development. It is, I argue, dangerous enough to subscribe to the myth that we may assess children's cognitive or intellectual abilities, without seeking to encompass also the domain of the spiritual or the moral. This argument, which draws upon a theory of signifying practices drawn from recent thinking in linguistics and philosophy, presupposes nothing about the intentions, stated or otherwise, of the participants. That is to say, it does not depend for its validity on the assertion that the teachers, or anyone else involved, want to make judgments concerning the relative value of children's spiritual experiences or moral developments. Once these records become part of educational discourse, I shall argue that they may truly be said to possess a life all their own.

How these Records have an Effectivity Beyond our Control

The following argument incorporates three stages. First, I shall emphasize the formative and productive role of language in the construction of identities. This contrasts with the traditional view of language as providing a series of representations and descriptions of some pre-existing reality, in particular of pre-discursive *selves*. In a Lacanian mode, I suggest that language is the medium through which identity is structured. This leads to the assertion that identity and alienation are correlate. Second, I shall draw upon an idea suggested by the writings of Emanuel Levinas. His theory of the primacy of the ethical over the ontological suggests that we are inevitably born into a 'responsibility for others'. As well as being in some sense constituted by language, our identity is that of a being 'summoned'. This philosophy entails that language is, concomitantly, responsibility. Finally, I shall indicate what I believe to be the practical consequences of this argument in terms of the production of school records.

Lacan: Language as Signification

We know that words, once they are spoken – or written – have, not only an existence, but an effectivity which is entirely independent of the speaker. The French psychoanalyst and thinker Jacques Lacan spent a great deal of his life insisting on the primacy of language, attempting to underscore the very real domination in modern culture of the symbolic. He describes how humanity is 'fallen' into language or knowledge, into *symbolism*. The word is certainly 'the murderer of the thing' (Hegel, 1977, quoted by Lacan, 1977), but this is not the worst of it. The symbolic, although it remains unquestionably definitive of humanity, dominates all forms of social and personal intercourse. 'As the symbolic order, civilisation (in its modern version at least) is a vast unconscious' (Lacan, in Flower MacCannell, 1986:125) and, for Lacan, there is no escape from the Symbolic which is essentially the process of alienation.

Lacan describes how identity and alienation are correlate – a person's very identity comes to be constituted simultaneously as he or she is alienated from interhuman contiguity. Lacan describes the constitution of the ego in the mirror stage, a theory to some extent anticipated by Marx, as Zizek (1989) points out:

> Since he comes into the world neither with a looking glass in his hand nor as a Fichtian philosopher to whom 'I am' is sufficient, man sees himself in other men. Peter only establishes his identity as a man by first comparing himself with Paul, as being of like kind.

However, Lacan is concerned to emphasize the central importance of the symbolic in the construction of an ego-identity.

The infant, entirely dependent and existing in a symbiotic relationship with the mother, comes to see itself as an image, an *identity*. Through a process of further individuation, subjectivity comes to be structured symbolically, not only through the visual image (in the mirror), but also through the verbal code. It is because the child can take the point of view of *le regard*, the 'gaze', of the other seeing it, that the Other (what Lacan calls the Symbolic Order) enters the scene immediately to disrupt the contiguity of self and (m)other. The self becomes a *self* as against the (m)other and the original relation of contiguity or mutuality becomes the '*lack*', the kernel around which desire is structured. It is this third dimension of 'seeing ourselves being seen and seeing' (Lacan, 1959–60) which ensures that alienation which is constitutive of subjectivity.

Lacan describes three constitutive orders of subjectivity – the Real, the Imaginary and the Symbolic. The Real is that kernel or hollow around which subjectivity is constituted, it is that which the imaginary posits as real, and the symbolic attempts to symbolize. The Imaginary is that which the subject believes will make good the lack, the repetoire of images which the Other invokes to fill the gap. The Symbolic Order is what Lacan terms the Other – the rules, laws, constraints, codes to which, through the Oedipus complex, subjectivity is structured as social. Lacan clearly believed that the supremacy of the symbolic over the other two registers (the real and the imaginary) is co-extensive with the human condition. This is part of what he is getting at in his remarks that 'man is fallen into language' (Lacan, 1972–3) and that 'only within a symbolic world does a beating heart make sense' (Lacan, 1959–60).

Thus, for Lacan, when we start with language, it is always back to language that we return – 'signification always relates back to another signification' (Lacan, 1959–60). This is so because *all* uses of the word are metaphorical. 'Metaphor is irreducible in language. It accompanies the originary violence of language' (Derrida, 1967:108–9). Following Jacobson, Lacan believed that the metaphoric mode of selection and substitution, hence of classification, dominates language and thus culture, repressing the metonymic, combinatory mode. Not only does language 'multiply distance', producing divisions, catagorizations and, inevitably, hierarchies and value systems, where what we seek is mutuality, contiguity and closeness, but language *is* form, a cardinal concept in reading Lacan. The minute that language comes into play, communication has already ceded to something else, to *significance*.

There is a powerful warning here. Language is not so much to be seen as our means of expression but as the medium through which and in which our very identity is structured. 'I am a poem, not a poet.' (Lacan, 1977). Language can no longer be characterized as the transparent medium through which realities are represented or described, or emotions expressed. Language creates us, as it creates the world around us. This is not to suggest that 'things' do not exist, but rather that it is only through language that materiality becomes meaningful.

The Myth of 'Accurate' Records

Where then does this reading take us? Our identity is bound to our alienation in becoming, as Steiner puts it, 'language animals' (Steiner, 1972). 'The first alienation of the human fixes upon itself an image which alienates him from himself . . .' (Lacan, 1977). We can, perhaps, begin to glimpse how the production of records becomes immediately something outside of our control, beyond what we mean it to be. There can be no question of producing *accurate* records – a hope which assumes precisely the representational, descriptive view of language I have been concerned to displace. It is chasing a chimaera to envisage profiles which are closer to some supposed reality.

These *profiles* – an illuminating word illustrating the sense in which a record of achievement is projected as an image, a self – once written, become formative both in the production of an educational self and also in the constitution of the reality within which these come to be read. There is no way of widening the scope to include *more* of the person, as if by increasing the length of the symbolic chain we can somehow encompass the whole. Every signifying chain can serve only as the metaphor for the subject. 'In it, the subject is always (mis)represented, simultaneously disclosed and concealed, given and withdrawn, indicated, hinted at between the lines' (Zizek, 1991). Records of achievement and baseline assessments signify and are signified within the complex field of discursive practices which comprise school and schooling in our culture. They assume their part within educational discourse.

It is in an attempt to plot a way forward here, that I turn to the work of Emmanuel Levinas. He insists throughout his writing on the possibility of encounter between self and other where *self can be nothing else than for-the-other*. That there is meaning, that there can be understanding, that language is not a blind-man's-buff, are convictions central to his, and our, purpose. Bridging the distance imposed by the (inevitable) intrusion of the symbolic order, we have here a notion of concord, in which what George Steiner (1991) terms 'the archaic and confident distance between self and other' is contracted by this notion of the for-itself (Sartre's term for conscious being) as a for-the-other, a being whose ontological posture is that of one summoned.

Responsibility For-the-other

Levinas moves, in a powerful and radical turn, toward a discourse in terms of 'otherwise than being', based on a relationship of the for-itself not with the in-itself (materiality), nor with death, but with the other. Subjectivity is continuously the condition of being hostage to the other: 'the self is through and through a hostage, older than the ego, prior to principles . . .' (Levinas, 1968). We are come not into the world but into question, where the 'for-itself' is the 'for-the-other', where my responsibility *for* the other is the 'for' of the relationship. 'The subjectivity of a subject is the responsibility of being-in-question . . . in the form of the total exposure to offence in the cheek offered to the smiter.' Since, for Levinas, the ethical predominates, 'subjectivity must become subjection' (Levinas, 1968). Responsibility, the 'impassive burden of the weight of the other', is the condition for all subjectivity, for intentionality itself, and *our identity, then, is precisely the uniqueness of someone summoned.* And, crucially, '*language,*' he writes, '*is born in responsibility* . . . Responsibility is prior to dialogue, to the knowledge of questions and answers' (Levinas, 1984, my emphasis).

It is the primacy of the ethical over the ontological and the notion of responsibility which is pivotal here. 'We are all responsible for everyone else – but I am more responsible than all the others,' a remark made by Aloysha

Karamazov (Dostoyevsky, 1880) and fondly quoted by Levinas on several occasions. It is, he tells us, in the face-to-face with the other, in the 'nape of his neck' that we may seek confirmation of our being (Levinas, 1968).

We can see here grounds for a belief that *what* we decide to include in our repertoires of speech and action may make a great deal of difference. Language is constitutive of identity, but identity and responsibility are also correlate. As we produce these profiles, we construct a signifying chain whose effectivity we cannot, even theoretically, control and which can never – however long or comprehensive – successfully represent the subject. However these statements (*mis*-representations), once articulated, quite literally have a life of their own. They have effects, produce narratives and construct identities which no-one, not even their producers, can anticipate, predict or prevent. We should, I suggest, cultivate a healthy caution about the production of such statements – particularly in a written form, as are these Records of Achievement. The written fixes the past and therefore endures for the future.

Records fix 'Identities', Inevitably within Hierarchies

The more general point here is that we are trying to preserve the spiritual and moral dimension as a sphere which remains outside the pedagogical relation, and therefore as a realm which we leave, as far as is possible, unarticulated, in all senses of the word. The inherent dangers of records in this domain here are increased by the context into which these articulations must necessarily pitch. However, we are compelled to address the demand that these aspects of children's lives be valued and developed by schools and teachers. If they are left out of baseline assessments and records of achievement, goes the argument, then they will inevitably be ignored, and once again, only the cognitive aspects will be seen to be of importance.

This produces somewhat of a dilemma. Since including the moral and spiritual dimensions within the records can only produce hierarchies in this domain as well as the cognitive, how can we safely acknowledge them? It is here that the notion that we are called to responsibility, that our relation with the other is first and foremost ethical, is crucial. It is surely in our daily practices, in the day-to-day rituals and observances of our lives together, that we demonstrate the moral and spiritual dimensions of our single and joint experiences. Rather than attempting to include children's moral and spiritual development in their records, we can appreciate them in our interactions. This becomes then, not an assessment or a record, but rather a daily acknowledgment, a recognition of both our responsibility for them and theirs to us.

Conclusion

It is true that the judgments that we make about children, about their moral or spiritual standing, are as likely to be flawed as the judgments we make about each other. Even more than with academic or intellectual skills, it is foolish or presumptious to talk of levels of development or hierarchies of experience. Once statements about these dimensions are recorded they become part of the world of taxonomies and categorizations. This thought should engender caution. But my argument here is that *any written records at all, however 'justified' or 'accurate' become part of what we cannot control.* What they come to signify, their significance within the world of competencies and appraisals, is beyond our ability to predict. But too often such statements will be returned to us, whether we recognize them or not, in another guise.

As an example, perhaps a warning, of the difficulties faced by the readers of such records, I include part of a record of achievement written by a pupil. This boy had left two previous schools, where he had been accused of disruptive behaviour, and had joined another school at the start of Year 10. Eighteen months later, in his personal statement, he describes the ways he is seen. This excerpt is not presented as typical. Nor is it easily categorized in terms of reference either to his cognitive skills or to the spiritual/moral dimensions of his character.

> It was late March. The day was bright, but cold. It was unusually early for me, even for a school day, but considering it was my third new experience of secondary school life; I thought I'd better make the effort.
>
> One year later I look back at my time at X school. On reflection it appears that at times, some of my earlier 'effort' was lost. Or at least, it dwindled in places. To tell the truth, my first month here went surprisingly well on the academic side of things. Not knowing many people was certainly a plus in this area. My school-days were spent doing homework and my weekends were spent with old friends. However, one cannot remain a social hermit for long. Even without trying, life on the outside of school soon kicked up. Some may say, looking at my original academic motivation, I got in with the wrong crowd. I, on the other hand, like to think I don't look out with such a narrow mind in this area. I may be wrong.
>
> Out of my friends; three have stuck by me with outstanding bravery and conviction through thick and thin. I personally don't consider my intelligence to have lessened any due to my friends. If anything it has increased greatly owing to them and the experiences they and I have gone through. I would like to believe that when intelligence is measured, it is done so not purely on an academic ruler.
>
> Lying would be to say that so far, my time at X school has gone smoothly and without fault. But I do believe in some areas I have grown and even blossomed. Aside from other people's views, I would say that in two lessons I have greatened both my understanding and my ability. The first of these is art. I have always liked art, and have studied it at both my previous schools. However, unlike my other

schools, the work conducted at X school has largely influenced that which is done off my own back; and vice versa. I think that my work in art has improved both creatively and in technique.

The second phase of my self improvement has been in English. My time in Y school taught me to despise menial tasks and to write essays. My time at Z school taught me to despise teachers and to stick up for your friends above anything else. Neither taught me to appreciate anything remotely to do with English. It was the start of my eleventh year and the coming of a new teacher that saw the fruits of my English labour. The only teacher I have ever got on with truly. In or out of the lesson. It is my contention that due to her, an area of myself yet undiscovered, was touched upon and cared for. I am pleased greatly by my own progress in English and deeply saddened if I ever miss a lesson.

I can't say that in other lessons I have matured so noticeably. In fact, with some frustration I would have to admit that I have conducted my time with the same robotic defence that so many students adopt while at school. Perhaps this frustration would account for the numerous outbursts I appear to have. I don't think my heated conflicts with figures of authority have achieved quite what I originally planned. The unwanted and tiresome reputation I hold with most teachers and pupils alike. Some look up to me, some look down. But none, save my English teacher, look straight at me.

In conclusion I would say to sum up my time at X school would be extremely difficult. The nearest analogy to it is a long dark trek over an icy terrain through thick snow and a gale. The action I have served both in and out of school has put me on very thin ice and through very thick snow. Sometimes I feel good to know how hard I'm working at pushing on. Sometimes I feel bad at my seemingly too slow progress. At other times, I just feel.

The purpose of a record of achievement must inevitably be to enable or facilitate an assessment of the quality of the student by the potential employer, college/university tutor or youth worker. This particular record was variously marked as 'not acceptable' and as 'superb' by different teachers in his school, and their difference of opinion reflects the complexity of reading such documents. Once we recorded *only* the cognitive skills. If I failed on these, I could nevertheless still be 'nice', 'kind', 'caring', 'lively', 'good fun', 'sociable' and so on. These qualities are now included, and the quality of my whole identity is up for grabs. That identity, now fixed, is a part of a hierarchy. In the words of the above teenager, 'Some [people] then look up to me, some look down.' But do any look straight at me?

Acknowledgments

I would like to acknowledge the help of Dr Terry McLaughlin in presenting this paper for discussion at Cambridge, and in obtaining valuable feedback. I also derive much enjoyment and stimulation from our on-going discussions.

References

CENTRAL OFFICE OF INFORMATION (1991) *How is Your Child Doing at School? A Parents' Guide to Testing.* London, HMSO.

DERRIDA, J. (1967) *Of Grammatology* (trans. SPIVAK, G. (1976) Baltimore, MD, John Hopkins University Press.

DOSTOYEVSKY, F. (1880) *The Brothers Karamazov* (trans. MAGARSHACK, D. (1964) London, Folio Society.

FLOWER MacCANNELL, J. (1986) *Figuring Lacan: Criticism and the Cultural Unconscious*, London, Croom Helm.

FREIRE, P. (1972) *The Pedagogy of the Oppressed*, Harmondsworth, Penguin.

HEGEL, G.W.F. (1977) *Phenomenology of Spirit*, Oxford, Oxford University Press.

ILLICH, I. (1973) *Deschooling Society*, Harmondsworth, Penguin.

LACAN, J. (1959–60) *Le Séminaire, Livre xix*, Paris, Éditions du Seuil.

LACAN, J. (1972–3) *Le Seminaire 20: Encore,* Paris, Éditions du Seuil.

LACAN, J. (1977) *Écrits: A selection* (trans. SHERIDAN, A.) London, Tavistock Publications.

LEVINAS, E. (1968). 'Substitution', in HAND, S. (Ed) (1989) *The Levinas Reader* , Oxford, Blackwell.

LEVINAS, E. (1984). 'Ethics as First Philosophy', in HAND, S. (Ed) (1989) *The Levinas Reader*, Oxford, Blackwell.

STEINER, G. (1972) *Extraterritorial*, London, Faber and Faber.

STEINER, G. (1991) 'Levinas', *Cross Currents: Religion and Intellectual Life*, **41**, 2 (summer), New York, New Rochelle.

ZIZEK, SLAVOJ, (1989) *The Sublime Object of Ideology*, London, Verso.

ZIZEK, SLAVOJ, (1991) *For They Know not What They Do*, London, Verso.

Notes on Contributors

David Best is Professor in the Department of Philosophy, University of Wales, Swansea; Visiting Professor, School of Theatre, Manchester Metropolitan University; Senior Academic Fellow and Honorary Professor, De Montfort University; and Visiting Professor, International Centre for the Study of Drama in Education. Until recently, he was Professor of Philosophy at Birmingham Institute of Art and Design. He is the author of four books, and numerous articles. His latest book, *The Rationality of Feeling* (Falmer Press, 1993), won the main prize as the best book of 1993, given by the Standing Conference for Studies on Education. He is an Appointed Member of the Midlands Arts Centre, and was formerly a member of the Arts Council of Wales.

Francis Dunlop is an Honorary Research Fellow at the University of East Anglia. His recent publications include *Scheler* in the series *Thinkers of our Time* (Claridge Press, 1991). He is the editor of Kolnai, A. *The Utopian Mind and Other Essays* (Athlone, 1995). Among recent articles are 'The importance of Jackanory: Reading aloud and teaching emotion', in Beveridge, M.C. and Reddiford, G. (Eds) *Language, Culture and Education* (Multilingual Matters Ltd, 1993); 'Gehlen, motivation and human nature', in Klages, H. and Quaritsch, H. (Eds) *Zur seisteswissenschaftliche Bedeutung Arnold Gehlens,* (Duncker and Humblot, 1994); and a critical review article in *Cambridge Journal of Education,* **24**, 1 (1994).

Janet Edwards taught Geography for twenty years in independent, grammar and comprehensive schools. Her recent school posts were as Head of the Sixth Form at Impington Village College and Deputy Head at Bottisham Village College, both in Cambridgeshire. She currently works as Deputy Director of the Centre for Citizenship Studies in Education at Leicester University. She is co-editor with Professor Ken Fogelman of *Developing Citizenship in the Curriculum* (David Fulton Publishers, 1993).

Elaine Foster-Allen was Headteacher at Handsworth Wood Girls' School and Sixth Form Centre in Birmingham from 1991 to 1994, having previously spent two years on secondment to HMI. She chaired the Special Interest Group on Disability for the Birmingham Training and Enterprise Council, and also chaired the Dance Education and Outreach Committee of the Dance Panel of the Arts Council of Great Britain. She is the author of 'Women and the inverted pyramid of the black churches in England', in Sahgal, G. and Yuval-Davis, N. (Eds) *Refusing Holy Orders: Women and Fundamentalism in Britain* (Virago, 1992) and of two chapters in Duncan, C., *Pastoral Care: An Antiracist/multicultural Perspective* (Blackwell, 1988). She now lives in her native Jamaica.

J. Mark Halstead is Principal Lecturer in the Faculty of Arts and Education at the University of Plymouth and Director of the Centre for Research Into Moral, Spiritual and Cultural Understanding and Education (RIMSCUE Centre). Prior to this, he was a journalist in Lebanon, a lecturer in Saudi Arabia and a schoolteacher in Bradford and Cambridge. He is the author of *Education, Justice and Cultural Diversity* (Falmer Press, 1988), editor of *Parental Choice and Education* (Kogan Page, 1994) and author of numerous articles on the education of Muslim children in the West.

John M. Hull is Professor of Religious Education in the University of Birmingham and a former Dean of the Faculty of Education and Continuing Studies. He has been Editor of the *British Journal of Religious Education* since 1971, and is the General Secretary of the International Seminar on Religious Education and Values. His autobiographical study *Touching the Rock, An Experience of Blindness* (Random House Vintage Books, 1990) is available in many foreign translations. In 1992 he was presented with the William Rainey Harper award of the Religious Education Association of USA and Canada for his services to religious education, and in 1995 he was granted the DTheol Degree (*Honoris Causa*) of the University of Frankfurt for his contributions to practical theology.

Andrew Marfleet taught in secondary schools for over twenty years before becoming a Senior Research Associate at the Centre for Applied Research in Education, in the School of Education at the University of East Anglia. He is currently researching school values through a series of case studies. He has written articles for various publications, including *Spectrum*, the journal of the Association of Christian Teachers, which he edited for seven years. He is a member of the Suffolk SACRE, a governor of two LEA schools and an OFSTED team inspector.

Ruth Merttens is Professor in the School of Teaching Studies at the University of North London. She is also the initiator and Director of the IMPACT project, an educational intervention and research initiative currently running in an estimated 8000 primary schools. She is the author with J. Vass of *Sharing Maths Cultures* (Falmer Press, 1992) and *Partnerships in Maths: Parents and Schools* (Falmer Press, 1993) and of *Ruling the Margins: Problematising Parental Involvement*, an edited collection of papers published by UNL Press, 1993.

Richard Pring is Professor of Educational Studies in the University of Oxford, where he is a Fellow of Green College. He has also taught at the Universities of London and Exeter. Among his many publications are *Knowledge and Schooling* (Open Books, 1976), *Personal and Social Values in the Curriculum* (Hodder and Stoughton, 1984) and *The New Curriculum* (1989). Since 1986 he has been editor of the *British Journal of Educational Studies*.

Michael J. Reiss is Senior Lecturer in Biology at Homerton College, Cambridge. He is also a Priest in the Church of England, a psychodynamic counsellor and a Vice-President of the Institute of Biology. He was a member of the Health Education Authority/Family Planning Association group whose work resulted in the publication of *Sex Education, Values and Morality* (Health Education Authority, 1994). He has written extensively on sex education, and is the author of *Science Education for a Pluralist Society* (Open University Press, 1993).

John C. Smyth, OBE, is Emeritus Professor of Biology in the University of Paisley. He is President of the Scottish Environmental Education Council, and chaired the group set up by the Scottish Office to prepare proposals for a national strategy for environmental education in Scotland. He has been active for many years with the World Conservation Union (IUCN), has been a consultant for the UNESCO/UNEP programme and was rapporteur to the working group which advised the UNCED secretariat on the content of Agenda 21, Chapter 36, on education, public awareness and training.

Monica J. Taylor is a Senior Research Officer at the National Foundation for Educational Research, and has been editor of the *Journal of Moral Education* since 1976. During the early 1980s she was commissioned by the Rampton and Swann Committees to undertake a series of critical reviews of research on the education of ethnic minority pupils (published in four volumes by NFER-Nelson). She has undertaken research for many major sponsors and specializes in personal and social education, religious education and multicultural antiracist education, particularly in secondary education and with a pupil focus. She has recently completed a comparative overview and an annotated bibliography of Values Education in 27 European countries for UNESCO and CIDREE. She has also recently been instrumental in the formation of the Values Education Council. She is a governor of an LEA primary school.

Jasper Ungoed-Thomas is an OFSTED Registered Inspector and Educational Consultant and was previously a member of Her Majesty's Inspectorate. He was for several years a member of the Schools Council Project on Moral Education and is the author of various books and articles on religious, moral, and personal and social education, including *Our School* (Longman, 1972) and *The Moral Situation of Children* (Macmillan Education, 1978). His most recent publication is 'Inspecting spiritual, moral, social and cultural development', *Pastoral Care in Education*, **12**, 4 (1994).

Mary Warnock (Baroness Warnock of Weeke in the City of Winchester) is an Honorary Fellow of Lady Margaret Hall and of St Hugh's College, Oxford. She was formerly Mistress of Girton College, Cambridge, and previously Headmistress of Oxford High School. Her many publications include *Ethics Since 1900* (Oxford University Press, 1960), *The Philosophy of Sartre* (Hutchinson, 1965), *Existentialist Ethics* (Macmillan, 1967), Existentialism (Oxford University Press, 1970), *Imagination* (Faber, 1976), *Schools of Thought* (Faber, 1977), *Memory* (Faber and Faber, 1987), *A Common Policy for Education* (Oxford University Press, 1988), *Universities: Knowing Our Minds* (Chatto and Windus, 1989) and *The Uses of Philosophy* (Blackwells, 1992).

Index

Abrams, M. *et al.* 5
academic values *see* intellectual values
accountability 4
Ackerman, B.A. 18, 19, 22
Adorno, Theodore 35, 36
aesthetic values 80–1
Allen, I. 102
Althusser, L. 41
Alves, R. 35
Anglican schools 159–60, 163, 164
anorexia nervosa 95–6
Aronowitz, S. and Giroux, H.A. 28
Arthur, J. 28
artistic values 79–80
  distinguished from aesthetic values
    80–1
  objectivity 82–4
  opening horizons 88–90
  significance for life 86–8
  social comment 87, 88
  subjectivity 80, 81, 82, 83
    associations 84–5
    attributing meaning 84
    individuality 85–6 (*see also*
      individualism)
  trivialisation 80–1, 83–4, 88, 110
ASH (Action on Smoking and Health) 98
Ashraf, S.A., Mabud, S.A. and Mitchell,
    P.J. 100
assessment
  records *see* pupil records
autonomy 24–5, 100–1, 113
Avon Training and Enterprise Council
    (TEC) 157

Bailey, C. 24, 28
Baker, C. and Davies, B. 101
Baker, Kenneth 105

Bambrough, J.R. 85–6
Barker, D. *et al.* 5
Baudrillard, Jean 40
Beardsley, M.C. 87
Beauchamp, T.L. and Childress, J.F.
    93
Beck, C. 5, 6, 9, 25
Benditt, T.M. 19
Benn, S.I. and Peters, R.S. 21
Bentham, J. 19
Berlin, Isaiah 18, 148, 149
Berry, R.J. 56, 58
Best, David 79, 88
Bettelheim, B. 146
biodiversity 60, 62
Bishops' Conference of England and
    Wales 160
Black Papers 104
Blatch, Baroness 156
Blatt, M.M. and Kohlberg, L. 10
Bloch, E. 35, 36
Bondi, H. 83
Booth, D.A. 96
Botkin, J.W., Elmandjro, M. and
    Malitza, M. 64
Breiting, S. 63
Brennan, A. 55
Bridges, D. 28
Bronowski, J. 83
Brundtland Report 62
Buck, M. and Inman, S. 173
Buckroyd, J. 96
bulimia 95, 96
bullying 175, 185, 187
Burns, G. 28

Caduto, Michael 63
Callaghan, James, Baron 105

capitalism 34
  base and superstructure 35–6
  consumerism 38–9, 192
  Fordism 37–8
  market principles 7–8, 22, 27–8, 38–9,
    144–5, 184, 192
  money 40–1, 42
  post-Fordism 38
Carpenter, R.A. 62
Carr, D. and Landon, J. 11, 178
Carr, W. 28
Cartledge-Hayes, M. 35
Castoriadis, Cornelius 36–7
Catholic schools 101, 158–9, 162–3
Catholicism 28
Cha, Y.-K., Wong, S.-Y. and Meyer, J.W.
  9
Chamberlin, R. 26
character education 9–10
choice 155–6
Christianity 156, 162 (*see also* church
  schools)
church schools 156
  Catholic 101, 158–9, 162–3
  Church of England 159–60, 163, 164
  parental choice 162–3
cigarette smoking 96–100
citizenship 26, 75, 151, 152, 176
Clarke, Kenneth 148
class, social 7, 96, 99, 194
classroom management 18
Coleridge, Samuel 143
collective worship 127, 169–70
Combes, Gill 96, 99
communitarian values 10, 27, 73–4, 151,
  152
Confederation of British Industry 105
conflicting values 50–1, 54–6, 58–9, 72,
  105
Conservation and Development
  Programme 60
constitutionalism 72, 77
consumerism 38–9, 192
Cooper, D.E. 58
coronary heart disease 95, 100
Covey, S. 156
Cox, C.B. and Dyson, A.E. 104
critical enquiry 23–4, 73, 106, 107,
  108

cultural diversity 4, 25, 26, 182–3
  (*see also* multicultural education)
  shared values 7, 46, 48–9, 148
cultural relativism 47–8
Cupitt, Don 47
curriculum 151
  English 174
  mathematics 183–4
  physical education 175
  religious education *see* religious
    education
  science 83, 174–5
cynicism 52

Dawson, Dee 96
Dearden, R.F. 23, 24
Defoe, Daniel 34
democracy 21–2
  education for 26 (*see also* political
    education)
democratic values 9
  citizenship 75
  community 10, 27, 73–4, 151, 152
  constitutionalism 72, 77
  definition 70
  equality 18, 20, 25, 74, 104, 106, 188
    (*see also* fairness; respect)
  individualism 35, 38, 72, 73
  liberty 18, 19–20, 74
  political traditions 72–3
  predominance in political education
    71–3
  tolerance 74–5, 139–40, 161
  utopianism 71
Derrida, J. 197
Devlin, P. 21
Dewey, J. 108
Dickens, Charles 34
diet 93–6
discipline 163, 187
distributive justice 19
diversity 4, 25, 26, 147
  biodiversity 60, 62
  school provision 156
Dostoyevsky, F. 199
Douglas, M. 35
drama 176
drug education 176
Duncan, G. 21

Dunlop, Francis N. 26, 27, 74, 76
Dunning, William 47
Dworkin, R. 18, 22, 24

eating disorders 95–6
eating habits 93–6
economic liberalism 22
education (*see also* values education)
  aims 111–17
  liberal *see* liberal education
  vocational 105, 108, 109–11
Education Reform Act 1988 97, 104
educational standards 104–5
Edwards, J. and Fogelman, K. 174
Eliot, T.S. 143
elitism 108–9
Elliott, J. 7, 62
employers 104–5, 110
empowerment 193
English 174
enterprise culture 27, 28, 184
Environment and School Initiative 63
environmental education 56–8, 63–4
environmental values
  biodiversity 60, 62
  conflict 54–6, 58–9
  definition 59–61
  'green living' 62
  new visions 64–5
  social justice 63
  sustainability and renewal 60, 61,
    62–3
equality 18, 20, 25, 74, 104, 106, 188
  (*see also* fairness; respect)
ethnic diversity *see* cultural diversity
examination results 164, 186
existentialism 35

failure 171
fairness 129–31, 152
feminism 28, 47
Findlay, J.N. 68
Fishkin, J.S. 22
Fitzgerald, F. Scott 34
Flower MacCannell, J. 196
food
  cultural significance 96
  education about 93–6
Ford, Henry 37

FOREST (Freedom Organization for the
    Right to Enjoy Smoking Tobacco)
    98–9
Fox, W. 61
Fraenkel, J.R. 5
free markets 22, 27–8, 144–5
Freeden, M. 18, 22
Freire, Paulo 193
Friedman, M. 22
friendships 137–8
fund raising 189

games 176
Gaus, G. 18, 20, 22
Gay, J. *et al.* 159, 164
Gewirth, A. 20
Gilligan, C. 10
Goggin, P. 9
Gouldner, A.W. 39
governmental control 4, 108, 112
grafitti 186
Graham, G. 28
Graham, H. 99
Gramsci, A. 36
Grimmitt, M. *et al.* 41
Grove-White, Robin 62, 65
Gutierrez, G. 35
Gutmann, A. 18, 24, 26

Habgood, John 148, 149
Hall, S. and Jacques, M. 38
Halstead, J. Mark 4, 7, 8, 25, 26, 28, 93
Hammond, J. *et al.* 41
Hampshire, S. 21
Hare, W. 23
Hare, W. and McLaughlin, T.H. 23
Hargreaves, D. 8, 167
Harmin, M. 11
Harris, A. 100
Harris, K. 28
Harrison, J. 175
Hart, H.L.A. 18, 22
Hartsock, N. 35, 38
Haug, W.F. 39
Haworth, L. 101
Hay, D. and Hammond, J. 41
Hay, David 41
Haydon, G. 7
Hayek, F.A. 18, 22

health education
  aims 92–3, 95, 97–8, 102
  class bias 96, 99
  drug education 176
  food 93–6
  sex education 100–2, 162, 164
  smoking 96–100
Health Education Authority 97, 98
heart disease 95, 100
hedonic values 69
Hegel, G.W.F. 196
Hemingway, Ernest 34
Her Majesty's Inspectorate (HMI) 117,
  148
hermeneutics 35, 36, 41
Hildebrand, D. von 69
Hirst, P.H. 23, 24, 27
Holligan, C. 11
Hollis, M. and Lukes, S. 19
hope 146
Horkheimer, M. 36
Hull, John M. 41, 42
Humanities Curriculum Project 10
Hume, D. 45, 51

identity 132–3, 196
Illich, Ivan 144, 193
individualism 35, 38, 72, 73
  artistic appreciation 85–6
industrial production 37–8
inspections 11–12, 123–4, 141, 156, 160,
  164, 169, 173, 193
intellectual values 69, 104, 105, 114
intuitionism 19
Islam 28
Islamic Academy 164

Jackson, P.W., Boostrom, R.E. and
  Hansen, D.T. 4
Jarrett, J.L. 8
Jenkins, I. 21
Jickling, B. 62
Jones, R. 100
just community 10

Kant, I. 19
Kelley-Laine, K. 63
Kelly, A. 175
Kilpatrick, W. 10

Kimball, B.A. 23
Kirk, D. and Tinning, R. 175
Kirschenbaum, H. 11
Kitson, N. 176
Kleinig, J. 24, 25
Knight, P. 161
Koerner, K.F. 22
Kohlberg, L. 10
Kohlberg, L. and Higgins, A. 10
Kolnai, Aurel 72

Lacan, Jacques 196–7
language 196–7
Larrain, J. 34, 36
Lawrence, D.H. 88–9
league tables 192, 193
Lee, J.-H. and Wringe, C. 25
Lefort, C. 36
Leopold, Aldo 60
Levinas, Emanuel 195, 198–9
Lewis, C.S. 37
liberal education 23, 106–7
  challenges to 27–8, 77, 106, 107–9
  education for citizenship and
    democracy 26, 151, 152, 176
  elitism 108–9
  equality of respect 25
  multicultural education 25–6
  personal autonomy 24–5
  rationality 23–4
  vocational preparation 109–11, 114,
    115
liberal values 17–18
  citizenship 75
  community 10, 27, 73–4, 151, 152
  conflict 18
  constitutionalism 72, 77
  democracy 21–2 (*see also* democratic
    values)
  distributive justice 19
  economic liberalism 22
  equality 18, 20, 74, 104, 106, 188
    (*see also* fairness; respect)
  individualism 35, 38, 72, 73
  intuitionism 19
  liberty 18, 19–20, 74
  political traditions 72–3
  predominance in political education
    71–3

private and public 21
rationality 18, 20, 72, 75, 77
rights 20–1
tolerance 74–5, 139–40, 161
utilitarianism 19, 27, 107
utopianism 71
liberty 18, 19, 74
Lickona, T. 9
local education authorities 117
Lorenz, K. 59
Louden, L.M.R. and Urwin, P.S. 160
Lovelock, J.E. 61
loyalty 137–8
Lucas, J.R. 22
Lukacs, G. 36

MacIntyre, A. 23, 27, 150
management principles 156–7
Marcuse, H. 35, 36
Marfleet, Andrew 122, 155, 160
market principles 7–8, 22, 27–8, 38–9,
    144–5, 184, 192
Marxism 19, 28, 36
mass production 37–8
mathematics 183
Matthews, M. 28
McCloskey, H.J. 20
McCulloch, R. 172, 174
McLaughlin, B. and Rorty, A.O. 35
McLaughlin, T.H. 4, 8, 26, 101
McMurtry, J. 27
Meadows, D.H. 60
media 134–5, 181–2
Mill, John Stuart 19, 21, 46
Miller, D. 21, 22
minority groups 8
mission statements 156–8, 184
    catholic schools 158–9
    Church of England schools 159–60
    county schools 160–2
    effect on parents 164–5
    putting value statements into practice
        169–71
money 40–1, 42
moral reasoning 10
moral rights 20, 121–2
moral values
    controversies 50–1
    importance in the curriculum 122–3

perceived decline 4, 122, 181–2
political education 72, 76
relativism 47–8
shared values 48–9, 148
societal expectations 45, 49, 51–3, 149
teacher neutrality 50–1
transmission 46–7, 51–3, 189–90
virtues 150–3
Morrell, D. 116
Morrison, K. 177
Mulhall, S. and Swift, A. 27
multicultural education 25–6, 184, 188
    (*see also* cultural diversity)
Murdoch, Iris 146
Muslims 28, 164

National Curriculum 110, 183, 191, 193
National Curriculum Council 8, 9, 122–3,
    126, 168, 177
Nauser, M. 56
neutrality 50–1
Noddings, N. 10
noise levels 185, 186
Norman, R. 18

Oakeshott, M. 107
objectivity 82–4
OFSTED (Office for Standards in
    Education) 8, 11, 123, 127, 141,
    156, 160, 164, 169, 173, 193
O'Hear, A. 24, 27
oppression 187–8
O'Riordan, T. 59
Osborne, J., Wadsworth, P. and Black,
    P. 94
overeating 95, 96

Parekh, B. 26
parents 122, 131–2
    choice of school 155, 162–4
    contribution to pupil records 194, 195
Parry, J. 175
Pascall, D. 149
Pateman, C. 22
patriarchal values 187–8
patriotism 75
Patten, B.C. 66
Patten, John 156
Pearson, M. 101

peer counselling 175, 189
peer group allegiance 181
performance indicators 163–4, 192
personal and social education (PSE)
172–3
Peters, Richard S. 20, 23, 72–3, 77, 93,
111
phenomenology 68
physical education 175
Picasso, Pablo 87
pluralism 6–8, 26
relativism 47–8
political education
constitutionalism 72, 77
education for democracy 20
emotional commitment 76–7
importance of tradition 72–3
liberal democratic ideological takeover
71–3
moral values 72, 76
participation 76
Popper, K.R. 21
Porter, A.N. 34
Posch, P. 57, 63
post-modernism 28, 47
practical intelligence 108, 109, 114–15
prefects 185, 189
Pring, Richard 25, 27, 28, 168, 171, 172,
178
problem-solving exercises 176
professional development 177–8
professionalism 136
prospectuses *see* mission statements
PSE (personal and social education)
172–3
pupil records
broad scope 192–3
reasons for limiting 193–5
class bias 194–5
ethical responsibility for consequences
198–9
inaccuracy 197–8
self-assessment 200–1
pupils
experience of values 125–6
community traditions 132–4, 182–3
cultural and social conflicts 133
curriculum contribution and
collective worship 127

fairness 129–31
friends' loyalty and trust 137–8
media 134–5
parental influence 131–2
racism 132
residential courses 139
respect 128–9
responsibility 138
school ethos 126–7, 185–9
teachers' personal qualities 135–7
tolerance 139–40
expressed values 140–1
interviews with 123–5
rights 121–2, 186

quality assurance 156–7
quality of life 95, 113
Quinton, A. 106, 108

racism 132, 136–7, 187, 188
Raphael, D.D. 19
Raths, L.E., Harmin, M. and Simon, S.B.
5, 10
rationality 18, 20, 23–4, 72, 75, 77
Rawls, John 20, 22, 152
Ray, C. 102
Raz, J. 18, 28
records of achievement *see* pupil
records
Reiss, M. 101
relativism 47–8, 70 (*see also* subjectivity)
religious education 127, 158, 173
church schools *see* church schools
collective worship 127, 169–70
religious minorities 8, 104
religious values 9, 28, 69, 182–3
(*see also* spiritual values)
cultural bias against 41
expressions of identity 132–3
influence on the concept of the
school 144
sex education 100, 101, 164
residential courses 139
resources 177–8
respect 128–9, 152
responsibility 138, 152, 185–6, 188–9
rewards 187
Rich, J.M. 7
Ricoeur, P. 36, 41

rights 20–1, 134–5, 186
Rodger, A.R. 60
role-plays 176
Roman Catholic schools 101, 158–9, 162–3
Roman Catholicism 28, 101
Royal Society of Arts (RSA) 108
rules 187

sanctions 187
Sandel, M. 27
Scheffler, I. 23
Scheler, Max 69
school councils 187–8, 189
school records *see* pupil records
schools
  curriculum *see* curriculum
  definition of purposes 143–5
  denominational *see* church schools
  education for citizenship 26, 151, 152
  ethos 126–7, 185–9
  expressed values 3–4, 122, 125–6, 148–50, 183–4
    mission statements *see* mission statements
  influence on values 43, 46–7, 51–3, 189–90
    curriculum contributions and collective worship 127
  relationships
    fairness 129–31
    respect 128–9
  vision
    absence of 146–7
    definition 145–6
    diversity 147
    experienced by individuals 147
Schools Council 116, 117
Schuster, V. and Osborne, A. 102
science 83, 174–5
Scottish Office Environment Department (SOEnd) 56, 64
Scruton, R. 18, 25
self-assessment 200–1
self-discipline 185–7
self-knowledge 112–13, 115
self-respect 185–7
sex education 100–2, 162, 164
sexism 137, 188

Shaver, J.P. and Strong, W. 6
Siedentop, L. 18
Siegel, H. 23
Sikhs 127
Simon, S.B., Howe, L.W. and Kirshenbaum, H. 10
Smart, J.C.C. and Williams, B. 19
smoking 96–100
Smyth, J.C. and Stapp, W.B. 59
Smyth, John C. 57, 58, 59, 62
Snook, I. 23
Sobrino, J. 35
social class 7, 96, 99, 194
social rights 21
social values 3, 51–3, 104, 106, 113, 149
Sohn-Rethel, Alfred 38–9, 40
spiritual values (*see also* religious values)
  base and superstructure 35–6
  consumerism 38–9
  definition 33–4
  education and 41–2
  human solidarity 42, 43
  individualism 35, 38, 72
    artistic appreciation 85–6
  money 40–1, 42
  social imaginary 36–7, 41
  sociological appraisal of 34–5
  symbols 37, 39
St Paul 42
standards 104–5
Starkey, H. 26
Starkings, D. 8
stealing 180–1
Steinbeck, John 34
Steiner, G. 197, 198
Sterling, S. 63
Stone, C.M. 25
Strike, K.A. 21, 22, 23
subjectivity 80, 81, 82, 83, 196–7, 198
  (*see also* relativism)
  associations 84–5
  attributing meaning 84
  individuality 85–6 (*see also* individualism)
summative assessment
  records *see* pupil records
sustainable development 60, 61, 62–3
symbols 37, 39, 196, 197

Tamir, Y. 22
Taylor, C. 19, 27
Taylor, Mark Kline 35, 40
Taylor, Monica J. 4, 8, 9, 11, 125
Taylor, R. and Andrews, G. 80
teachers
    cultural mediators 116
    dissatisfaction with market values 28
    expressed values 3–4, 48–9, 52–3,
        177
    intimidation of pupils 134–5
    moral and political values 50–1, 76–7
    qualities valued by pupils 135–7
teaching methods 175–7
Thatcher, A. 41
theft 180–1
Thiessen, E.J. 23, 24
Thompson, J.B. 35
Thomson, R. 164
tolerance 74–5, 139–40, 161
Tones, K. 97
Total Quality Management (TQM) 156–7
truancy 180
trust 137–8
truth 152
TVEI (Technical and Vocational
    Education Initiative) 115

Unesco/UNEP 56
Ungoed-Thomas, Jasper 11
United Nations Conference on
    Environmental Development
    (UNCED) 62, 63
universities 107, 108
utilitarianism 19, 27, 107
utopianism 71

values
    aesthetic 80–1
    artistic *see* artistic values
    communitarian 10, 27, 73–4, 151, 152
    conflict 50–1, 54–6, 58–9, 72, 105
    definition 5–6, 46, 68–70
    democratic *see* democratic values
    educational 111–17
    environmental *see* environmental
        values
    experience of pupils *see* pupils
    government's 4, 108, 112

health education *see* health education
hedonic 69
incommensurability 70, 72
intellectual 69, 104, 105, 114
liberal *see* liberal values
market principles 7–8, 22, 27–8, 38–9,
    144–5, 184
moral *see* moral values
patriarchal 187–8
pluralism 6–8, 26
    relativism 47–8, 70
priorities 3, 75
religious *see* religious values
schools' expression of 3–4, 122,
    148–50
    mission statements *see* mission
        statements
schools' influence on 3, 51–3
    curriculum contribution and
        collective worship 127
scientific disciplines 83
shared 7, 46, 48–9, 148
social 3, 51–3, 104, 106, 113, 149
spiritual *see* spiritual values
virtues 150–3
vision *see* vision
vital 69
values clarification 10
values education 8–9, 167–8, 178–9
    America and Britain 9
    character education 9–10
    cross-curricular themes 168, 171
    English 174
    inspection 11–12, 123–4, 141, 156,
        160, 164, 169, 173, 193
    just community 10
    moral reasoning 10
    physical education 175
    planning 169, 171–2
    professional development 177–8
    resources 177–8
    science 83, 174–5
    status 11
    teaching methods 175–7
    timetabled courses 170–1
        personal and social education (PSE)
            172–3
    values clarification 10
Values Education Council 8

virtues 150–3
vision
   absence of 146–7
   definition 145–6
   diversity 147
   experienced by individuals 147
vital values 69
vocational preparation 105, 108, 109–11,
   114, 115

Walsh, D. 19
Weare, Katherine 102
Weber, Max 36
Weil, Simone 75, 89
Welschon, R. 35
West, A. 163
West, S. 169, 170
White, John 7, 9, 20, 24, 25, 26

White, P. 20, 26, 71, 73
White, R. 23
Whitty, G., Rowe, G. and Aggleton, P.
   95
Williams, T., Roberts, J. and Hyde, H.
   95
Williams, Veronica 157, 158, 169, 171–2,
   173
Wilson, J. 93
Wolf, E.R. 34
World Conservation Strategy 60
worship 127, 169–70
Wortley, A. 175

Young, M.F.D. 77
Young, S. 96

Zizek, Slavoj 196, 198